Survivin

ISBN 1-58898-621-7
Published by BookSurge, LLC
North Charleston, South Carolina
Library of Congress Control Number: 2004109991

Surviving Broken Promises

Cornelia Gibson

greatunpublished.com
Title No. 621
2002

Surviving Broken Promises

I would like so very much to thank the following people: Nathan Goodlow for giving me that extra little push. Beverly Hardwick for being more than a boss. Terri Goss for always being there. Antoinette Price for lending me your ear. Stormy Lee for letting me practice my psychology on you. Lawrence Dillahunty for designing and drawing the cover of this book for free. Kimberly Pitcher for encouraging me to follow my dreams while reminding me that most successful people only get four to five hours of sleep per night so I was never alone.

SURVIVING BROKEN PROMISES

Here I am a thirty-three year old black woman and very proud of who I am and what I have accomplished. Although this book took a long time coming, it's finally here. So what is it like to have your life drastically altered while surviving broken promises? Well, thanks to the five stupid jerks that have been in and out of my life for the past sixteen years, I've had to survive quite a bit. But because of my experiences, I'm finally going to get what's coming to me and so will they. And now that I have finally gotten rid of them, I am able to speak out and tell my story, and what a story it is. Sometimes I can't believe that I've been through so much and was able to get through it all. Life sure hasn't been easy, but overcoming obstacles has made me what I am today. You go girl!

When I was twelve, my parents got divorced and were forced to sell the house. My mom packed us up and moved us to a new city. My brother was going out of state, off to college, where he received a full basketball scholarship and majored in music. So he missed out on all of the fun. Yeah, right. Although Mom and Dad kept the divorce pretty low-key, there still was nothing funny or amusing about it.

Dad retired many years ago from a back injury. During the divorce he moved into an apartment, but he came to pick us up faithfully every other weekend and any other time we picked up the phone and wanted him, he was there. Mom was awarded fifty dollars a month child support for each of us four girls until we turned eighteen. On her primary job, Mom worked nights as a nurse's aide. Though she had an hour commute each way, she weathered the storm like a champ. She would say a prayer and through the rain, hail, sleet and fog, five nights a week, off she went. When she wasn't working at the hospital she did private duty work and housecleaning. She would do anything to keep us just above being poor.

By the time I was sixteen, my oldest sister Gwen had moved out on her own and had a baby. My next oldest sister, Sharon, had moved in with Dad, which left just me and my younger sister, Monica, at home with Mom. With Mom working so much trying to give us some of the things other children would have, we hardly spent any time with her. In fact, I began to feel more like Monica's mother than her sister but I didn't mind at all.

That summer I got a job to help Mom out. I bought my first car, an old used one, of course, and I helped Mom buy school clothes for Monica while I offered any other help that I could. I took Monica everywhere I went. Well not quite everywhere, you'll see.

That summer was also when three stupid boys entered my life and later turned out to be three of the stupid men in my life. Will I ever learn? Yes, because although I used to be young and naïve and believed just about every promise that was made to me, I don't any more. In fact, by the time I'm finished writing this story, I will have heard every promise in the book and will have changed from that young little girl into an all grown up woman. And not just any woman, but a black woman with an attitude.

That summer was when I had my first crush on a boy. Well, actually my first three crushes. No, I wasn't fast. I was really a quiet person; I just had male friends. Most of the girls at my school thought of me as being cute and stuck up, or probably just plain stuck up. But did that bother me? No. I never really cared what others thought of me unless they had something positive to say, and for the life of me I can't understand why other people's negative opinions would bother anyone.

RUMOR HIGH

Well, the first boy in my life was Marcus. We went to the same high school but we were just the opposite of each other. He was loud and popular while I was quiet and shy. I was always into my schoolwork while he was always into other girls and hardly ever into his books. He wasn't afraid of anyone or anything and it showed.

During the times I spent with Marcus, he seemed really caring and I felt really secure. He would come over to my house and we would watch television or we would go to his house and listen to music. He would always try to get me to dance with him but I wouldn't. The fact is I didn't know how to dance; actually I still don't, but oh well. But why did Marcus like *me*? He was on the baseball team, football team and basketball team. I really wanted to be around him, but why did he want to be around *me*?

I used to go to all of his games. I felt so proud when he would come and talk to me at half time. But I still couldn't help but wonder, why *me*? I was a nobody. I was an unknown. I was this quiet stuck up girl from school that no one had even heard of, let alone spoke to. Then it happened. He asked me for sex.

Sex? What was that? Sex was the last thing on my mind. I had never even kissed a boy before. I still played with dolls at home with Monica. Sex? He's got to be kidding! So now I get it. That's why he's been my friend. So that's why he didn't mind ruining his reputation by speaking to me in public. Maybe he had a bet going on that he could get me in his bed. Maybe this was some kind of game to see if he could get the least popular girl to sleep with him. But I was still in shock. Sex? I just wasn't ready for that. Besides, there were rumors going around that he had been having sex with other girls. After all, he could probably get just about any girl he wanted. I knew that and he knew that.

I told him I wasn't ready but I kept promising it would happen soon. I told him to just be patient and that I still liked him. In fact, we had told each other on several occasions that we loved each other. I'm not sure if it was love, maybe puppy love, because I just couldn't get enough of being around him. I wanted to be with him all the time, just not in the bed with him. We had a lot of fun together, going to the fair, or to the mall or just hanging out at home.

But ever since he asked me to sleep with him, I felt pressure whenever we were together. We used to hug a lot and I must admit that it felt really good being in his muscular arms. I would just melt being in those big broad shoulders. Then the hugs progressed into us touching each other. I felt comfortable with the touches too, but I still wasn't ready for sex. But I must admit it did make me start thinking about it.

I started thinking that if I were going to lose my virginity, I certainly didn't want it to be with someone who had been with everyone else. My body was much more precious to me than that. I wanted my first time to be special. I wanted to spend the rest of my life with whoever this special person would be.

One time I spent the night at Marcus' house on the invitation of his sister who is two years younger than I am. That night I couldn't believe what Marcus did. He came into his sister's room, got into the twin bed that I was in and got on top of me. The only thing he had on was a pair of boxer shorts, while I had on a long flannel nightgown. Talk about scared. If he thinks I'm going to have sex with him right here in his parents' house, while his parents are right in the next room, he has got to be crazy. I was scared to death. But was he scared? No. I don't think anything scares him. His sister was either asleep or pretending to be asleep in the other twin bed. I kept telling him in a very low voice to get off of me and that his parents would catch us. He thought the whole thing was funny, but I was scared enough for the both of us. When he finally left the room I was relieved. But once he left, I'll admit it did feel kind of nice just having him lay there on top of me. Of course, I got no sleep the rest of the night.

I continued going to Marcus' games, but after a while he wouldn't be with me, not even a "hello" at half time. In fact, after the games he started being with other girls right in front of my face. I was really hurt. I would have done anything for him, anything but sleep with him. I found myself begging for his time and affection. I had even loaned him money; money he never seemed to pay back. Then I knew the rumors weren't just rumors. They were all true. Like I really didn't know that before.

We were spending less and less time together. Periodically we would talk on the phone, although it seems as if I did all of the calling. Even though it took me a while, I finally figured it out. If I weren't going to sleep with him, he didn't want to waste his time on me. So I guess we officially broke up, but we were both mature about it. We were both decent to each other at school, even though every time I saw him he was with other girls, but mainly with Rochelle. Sometimes when I saw them together I would get upset, but I figured she was giving him what he wanted. Actually, I heard Rochelle was giving all the guys what they wanted. I didn't know it at the time, but I was really the lucky one.

The next boy in my life was Aaron. Aaron and I are the same age also, but he attended the other high school in town. Besides Aaron being an only child, we were so much alike. I didn't think there were any boys out there as quiet as I was until I met him. I enjoyed doing things with Aaron such as playing tennis, riding bikes or watching television, and I felt completely comfortable because he would never try to come on to me. But how far could two quiet and shy kids get without any help?

Help, I thought, was what we needed. Since Marcus had really put sex on my mind, I thought that's what all teen-age boys wanted. I used to think about having sex with Aaron but wondered why wasn't he pressuring me. I would go over to his house when his mother wasn't home and ask him if we could watch television in his room. Once I was in his bedroom, I would prance around on his waterbed trying to tease him, but he would never get the hint.

Even though I don't think I was ready for sex, I wondered why Aaron wasn't pressuring me. I thought that maybe he just didn't like me. Unlike Marcus, I knew Aaron didn't have another girlfriend. Maybe Aaron thought I was ugly or something. And I was too shy to bring up the sex issue and ask him how he felt about it. However, I did know he was a virgin. I still enjoyed spending time with him doing the things we both were comfortable with; going skating and doing the things teenagers should have been doing. That is, until my best friend Beverly asked me if Aaron and I were having sex.

I told Beverly that no, we were not, and she seemed shocked. I told her Aaron was still a virgin and I was too scared to talk to him about it. Then she told me she would do me a favor and break him out of his shyness. So I said okay. I knew Beverly had been having sex for years but I didn't know how she could help Aaron and me. Talk about naïve.

Well, several weeks passed and I didn't hear too much from Aaron or Beverly but I started hearing rumors at school that they were sleeping together. I couldn't believe it. I thought Aaron was the boy for me. And even worse, I thought Beverly was my friend. If the rumors were true, it looks like I was wrong about both of them.

While the rumors were spreading, Aaron kept calling me and I kept avoiding him. Beverly was no longer my friend. Actually, I guess she never was my friend. I was so hurt. I had to find a way to pay him back.

That summer I also met Robert. He was a year older than I was and he lived about thirty miles away. Robert told me all about himself. He had a job. Actually, he had two jobs. He told me he did construction work with his father on the weekends and during the week he had another job doing maintenance work. He really had it going on. He also told me he had a son a year old but he and his son's mother broke up shortly after their baby was born. He went on to tell me how he watched his son being born and how it was an experience he would never forget.

I thought, what a way to pay both Aaron and Marcus back. If I got involved with a boy from out of town, that should do it. Actually, Aaron is the one I really wanted to pay back because I knew Marcus and I would never be more than friends. So, after several more unanswered phone calls from Aaron, I finally told him I was seeing someone from out of town. I told him that Robert was going to be my husband some day so not to call back again.

Since Robert lived out of town and had two jobs, we didn't see each other too often but we talked on the phone quite a bit. We really learned a lot about each other. Then one weekend we found some time and Robert came to get Monica and me and took us to meet his parents and his sisters. He had three teenage sisters at home and, would you believe, two of them already had children of their own. I was shocked but I didn't say anything. After all, he had a baby too. In fact, his son's mother was only fourteen when she got pregnant.

For about eight months, Robert and I would see each other on the weekends and during this time he never mentioned sex to me and I was glad. Robert knew I was a virgin. I never teased him like I teased Aaron because I knew he had already done it. He was experienced. But I knew the day would come. Then it did.

Robert asked me for sex. By then, I felt comfortable talking to him about it and expressing my true feelings and concerns. I told Robert I would have sex with him if he had protection. He told me we didn't need any protection, because when his son was born, there was a problem. The doctors told Robert he would never be able to have any more children. I asked him why he didn't tell me that a long time ago but he said he didn't want to lose me so he didn't mention it.

I explained to Robert that wouldn't have broken us up. Actually, I felt relieved because having children had never crossed my mind. I wasn't even sure I would ever want children.

I told Robert my first priority was my schoolwork because I definitely wanted to attend law school immediately after I graduated. If I couldn't get a scholarship, I would work part-time and go to a junior college. So I told Robert I was really sorry he couldn't have any more children but I was honest and told him that I was also quite relieved.

So Robert asked again. When could we have sex? I told him I still didn't think I was ready and he said that if I didn't believe him I could ask his mother. I told him I believed him because I had no reason not to. I was just scared because this would be my first time. I told him to be patient and that it would happen sooner or later. So we continued going together and talking on the phone.

Meanwhile, I ran into Beverly one day at school and Little Miss Innocent acted as if she had not done a thing. I pretended I had not heard the rumor that she was sleeping with Aaron, and I told her I was going with this boy from out of town but to keep it a secret. A few days later, just as I thought, my secret was out. When Marcus got the word that I was seeing someone else he wanted to spend more time with me. I guess he thought I was ready to sleep with him, or just ready to sleep around, but he was wrong.

One day Rochelle saw Marcus and me walking together and she looked very upset. I guess she thought Marcus and I were getting back together. From that day on, I started hearing rumors that Rochelle was going to beat me up so I started avoiding her. I didn't want to fight her and I certainly wasn't going to be fighting over Marcus. He was history and, besides, Marcus and I were only friends, but I'm sure she thought I was sleeping with him too. If she had only known that I was still a virgin.

TONIGHT IS THE NIGHT

One of Robert's sisters was having a slumber party and I asked my mom if I could go. At first she couldn't believe I had asked her that. I never went to any parties and this would have been just my second time spending the night away from Monica. Mom called Robert's mother to make sure it was okay. At first my mother was very hesitant, but she ultimately let me go because she trusted me. So Robert came over that evening to pick me up.

On the way to his house we must have heard Betty Wright's, "Tonight is the Night," on at least three different radio stations. When it first came on, I didn't want Robert to be reminded of sex, so I changed the station and sure enough it was on that station too. So I changed it again. Okay now I'm safe, I thought. Well, at least I was for about fifteen minutes, and then there it was again. Was the record trying to tell me something?

We finally got to Robert's house and what was actually a thirty-minute ride seemed more like several hours. As we walked up to the front door I felt awkward. I didn't know his sisters very well and I felt out of place. Robert told me if I felt uncomfortable I could just watch television in his room. So I went in and spoke to his parents, then I asked his mother if I could watch television in his room and she said it was okay.

Robert came in his room and we watched television together. As we sat there, one of his sister's sons kept coming in the room in his baby walker. He kept bumping into everything and running over our feet. I thought it was so cute but Robert was annoyed and so he put his nephew out and closed his door. Then I got scared. Not scared of Robert, but scared of what his parents might think we were doing. I told him how I felt but he told me not to worry about it. He said his parents wouldn't say anything but I still could not relax. I told Robert it was getting late and that I was ready to go to sleep. So when he left his room I put on my pajamas and got in his bed.

Robert later knocked on his door. When he opened it, he said he just wanted to say good night, but he came in and closed the door behind him and this time he locked it. I told him to unlock the door before we got in trouble. He told me not to worry because his parents were asleep.

It was dark in his room but the television was still on. He sat next to me on his bed and put his arms around me but I did not respond. Actually I didn't know how to respond. Not only was I afraid of what his parents would think, I was also afraid of what I thought was about to happen. Then he put my arms around him and we began to kiss. He slowly guided me, laying me down on his bed. Then he gently raised my gown up above my waist and he completely undressed himself. This certainly wasn't the way I pictured my first time having sex would be, and yet he was completely comfortable.

What am I going to do? I think I'm ready for sex now, and I don't have any hesitations about Robert being my first, and at least I know I can't get pregnant. So what's the problem? His parents are the problem. This atmosphere's the problem. This room's the problem. My mother's trust in me is the problem. But why wasn't I stopping him? What am I doing? Then he pulled my panties down and I helped him take them off by bending my knees. I guess this is going to be it.

He lay there on top of me and we started kissing. He stuck the tip of his tongue slowly in my mouth. What was I doing? He was moving around on top of me, slowly spreading my legs apart. There was no way I could relax and enjoy what was about to happen because I was still nervous about his parents catching us. I kept telling him that we were going to get caught but he wasn't worried about it.

So I just lay there while he was moving around, up and down, panting like he was a dog or something and sweating like crazy. I guess he thought it was in but it wasn't and I didn't tell him any different. After a while he kissed me on my forehead and went into the living room. Even after he left the room, I was still nervous but I was glad it was over. Well actually nothing ever got started. And now that I think about it, it's kind of funny. Robert really thought we did something and I didn't tell him any different. After all, he's the pro, not me. The next morning I got up, took a shower and nobody suspected a thing.

On the way home Robert asked me how I felt. I thought to myself, "How am I supposed to feel? Nothing happened."

"I feel fine, Robert. Why?"

"Just fine?" he said.

"Yes. How am I supposed to feel? Nothing happened," I told him.

"You mean it wasn't in last night?" he said shocked.

"No."

"Why didn't you tell me?"

"Because I was scared and I don't want to talk about it anymore."

We got to my house and my mom asked how the party was. I got so nervous, I didn't know what to say, so I told her it was okay and, lucky for me, she didn't have any more questions. After that Robert stayed at my house for about an hour. We watched television a while and then he went home.

We continued to talk on the phone almost every day. I really missed being with him and he said he missed being with me too, and asked me to spend the night again. I asked him how were we going to get our parents to agree on that happening again. His sisters certainly couldn't have a slumber party every weekend. Robert said it wouldn't be a problem with his mother. So I decided that I would just ask my mother. Yeah, right. That's much easier said than done.

I must have walked by her bedroom door ten times in an hour trying to build up my nerves. I guess I didn't have any nerves because I just couldn't make myself do it. So, on my eleventh time walking past her door, I said to myself, "This is it. I'm going to ask her this next time." So I got a little closer by going into her room and lying on her bed. She asked me what I wanted and I told her, "Nothing." But, if she only knew. I lay there for a few more minutes, counting to ten. On ten I'm going to ask. But a few more minutes went by. I must have counted to ten at least a dozen times by now. "Think" I said to myself. "Okay, one more time on ten."

"Mom, can I spend the night at Robert's house tonight?"

There! I said it. Even though I got all of that out in less than a second, I still said it. Now it's up to her. What can she say? All she can say is yes or no.

She replied, "What did you ask me?"

Hey, that wasn't one of the choices. Now what do I say?

"Um, nothing Mom," I said.

I immediately got off of her bed and went into my room and closed the door, hoping she wouldn't come in behind me. I wasn't sure if she heard me and was just shocked that I had asked her that, or if she really didn't hear me. I was so scared; I really hoped she didn't hear me.

I called Robert and told him I just couldn't do it. Maybe next weekend, I told him. That would at least give me more time to build up my nerves again. Robert and I continued to talk on the phone. It seems like all we did was talk about having sex even though I was still nervous about the whole thing. But Robert kept promising me there was nothing to be afraid of.

Meanwhile, back at Rumor High, I heard that the next time Rochelle saw me she was going to beat me up. I really didn't want to fight her because Marcus and I were just friends. Another reason I didn't want to fight was because I was sure everyone would side with her because I was so quiet in school and no one really knew me. Or maybe I was just plain scared. I had never been in a fight before, at least not one that didn't involve an older sibling, but I wasn't going to spend everyday at school trying to avoid her.

Just then I saw Rochelle looking out of the window of one of her classes. Now was her chance. All of a sudden I got this burst of courage and went to her classroom door and asked her about the rumors.

"Here I am, Rochelle. I heard you wanted to beat me up."

She started shaking. I think I really shocked her by confronting her. Shoot, I even shocked myself. When I saw that she was more nervous than I was, I got bad.

"From now on, keep my name out of your mouth," I said loudly.

"I didn't say I was going to beat you up. I just wanted to know if you and Marcus was getting back together, that's all."

"No, I'm going with a boy from out of town."

"Oh, I just wanted to know."

Then I rolled my eyes, turned my head, and walked away. Whew! I didn't know I had it in me.

That evening I called Robert to tell him all about my day at school. He listened but then he wanted to know when was I going to spend the night over his house again. I told him I would ask my mom again this weekend but that weekend came and went and so did the next one and the next one and the one after that.

Robert and I continued talking on the phone and he came over every weekend. I really enjoyed being with him, but I knew the more time I spent with him the more chances he had to pressure me about sex. One day I finally built up my nerves to try and ask Mom if I could spend the night again. This time was going to be a little bit different because I wasn't going to give her an excuse this time. I planned on just asking her plain and simple, "Can I spend the night at Robert's?"

Since Monica usually comes with me wherever I go, I made sure that before I asked Mom, it would be her weekend off. That way she wouldn't have that excuse to use to say no. So here we go again, you know the routine. I counted to ten a few times and then I finally said it, and it didn't hurt at all.

Mom responded by saying, "Are you crazy? What makes you think you can go and spend the night at some boy's house? Have you lost your mind?"

"But Mom, his parents will be there and they already said it was okay with them."

I really wanted to share with Mom the fact that Robert

couldn't have any more children but I didn't because I didn't want her to think that sex and or babies were on my mind. And I purposely didn't share with Mom the fact that two of Robert's teen-age sisters were already mothers themselves. One of them actually had one child with another one on the way. But Mom finally said okay because she trusted me. I went in my room to pack my overnight bag.

That evening at Robert's was very much a repeat of my first evening there. We watched television for a while and then I asked him to leave his room so I could go to sleep. He left but only to return about twenty minutes later. He closed his bedroom door, sat on his bed next to me and we started kissing. Somehow, I knew this would be the night; however, I was still uncomfortable. Why did I tell him nothing happened last time? Now he'll make sure "it's in" this time. But why am I so scared?

Robert undressed himself and then slowly undressed me. He could tell I was very nervous.

"Why are you so jumpy? It's not like I can get you pregnant," he said.

"I know but I'm scared it's going to hurt."

"I promise I won't hurt you," he said.

Then I told him I still wasn't ready and that this was not the right time. But Robert told me to just relax as he lay me down on his bed and climbed on top of me. He tried at least ten times to put it in. Actually, I don't know where he was trying to put it because it was nowhere near where he wanted it to be. Then he asked me to put it in for him and I said, "uh uh" before he could even finish asking me. If he thinks I'm going to touch him down there he's crazy. Not only was I a virgin, but I couldn't even say the word 'penis'. So what am I doing here?

I really liked Robert and, in fact, he had just told me that he loved me. I really had strong feelings for him and I really enjoyed being with him and talking to him on the phone. I only wish he wouldn't ask me for sex. I would have loved being his steady girlfriend, at least for the next four or five years while I finished high school and went on to U. C. Berkeley.

"Ouch," I said.

"I'm sorry. Am I hurtin' you?" Robert asked.

"Um no," and we both realized it was finally in. At first, I actually couldn't tell whether it hurt or if it felt good. It was kind of like hitting my funny bone, except it wasn't my funny bone that Robert was hitting. He kept telling me over and over that he loved me and he kept pausing as if he was waiting on me to say the same thing. By this time it was feeling good to me so I told him I loved him too. I was still scared though, because after all, his parents and sisters were here, just a room away. I wondered if they heard us. Robert started sweating like crazy so he got up and opened his bedroom window. I told him I was glad he opened it because not only was it burning up but it was also stinking in here. I told Robert I hoped that smell was gone before anyone came in here tomorrow.

I explained to Robert that I was still nervous and, like I said before, this was not how I pictured my first time to be. Even though it felt good, I'm glad it was over and I still think it could have waited another four years. I don't mean to sound like it wasn't good. It's just that I had other priorities and goals that I really wanted to stick to. Robert finally left his room and returned to the couch in the living room until morning. Of course I could not get any sleep that night.

As soon as the sun started rising, I hurried and jumped in the shower before anyone saw or smelled me. Trying to avoid Robert's parents and sisters, I told Robert I was ready to go home. But too late, there came his mother. She stopped at his bedroom door and asked me how last night was. As my heart jumped out of my chest and all of my vocal cords seemed to have jumped with it, I was wondering what she was really asking me. Talk about paranoid.

Did she know? Did she care? Was it okay with her since she already knew all of her children had sex already?

"It was okay," I said in a low and cracking voice.

"You mean you weren't scared spending the night at a boy's house?" she said.

So I lied and told her no. Then she wanted to chat and tell me about a conversation she had with my mother.

"I told your mother she had nothing to worry about, her." Robert's family was from New Orleans and I guess that's the way they talked there. "I told your mom we would all be at home and I told her that Robert would be sleeping on the couch. So when you go home you make sure you tell her that he slept on the couch just like I promised her."

"Uh huh," I said. But I was really thinking, "will you just leave from in front of the door now?"

Then she walked away and little Mr. Innocent Robert came in his room and whispered, "I told you, you had nothin' to worry about. She don't know nothin', her." Then she came back to his door and asked me what I wanted for breakfast.

"Nothing. I'm going home in a few minutes. But thank you anyway."

Then I told Robert I was ready to go, and I said Goodbye to his mom and we left. But as soon as we got in the car, I told Robert I was starving and so we stopped at McDonald's for breakfast. He kept staring at me as if he had something to say.

"What is it? What's wrong?" I asked him.

"Nothin', I just think you're so pretty," he said. So of course I started blushing. Then he took my hand and said, "Will you marry me?"

I looked at him in shock and said, "Will I do what?"

"Will you marry me?" he repeated.

"You're joking. I know you're joking."

"There's no joke about it. I'm dead serious. I want you to be my wife."

I guess I should have been speechless but I wasn't. If I didn't speak up then, I may not have gotten another chance. I told Robert I really liked him and I wanted to be with him but I tried to explain that we were too young for marriage.

"I'm still in high school and I want to go to U. C. Berkeley next year. I'm not ready for marriage," I told him.

Robert looked really upset and asked me if the sex wasn't good enough last night to marry him. I tried to be as honest as possible when I told him that marriage was the last thing on my mind and especially the last thing on my mind last night.

"I really want to finish high school and then go to law school and if I get married right now I know I will never go on to college. Robert, I really need to stay focused."

Then he gave me this look that was almost frightening. I told him again that I really cared about him and that I didn't plan on seeing anyone else, but it was just that seventeen and eighteen were just too young of ages to get married.

"Okay, I'm not gonna pressure you. Whenever you're ready just let me know," he said.

"Okay," I said. Then I picked up my sausage biscuit but put it back down because all of a sudden I wasn't very hungry any more. On the ride home Robert asked me if I loved him. I told him yes and he said he loved me too.

When I got home, Mom had just gotten off the phone talking with Robert's mother. Mom told me how proud she was of me and how Robert's mom had told her that I was a really nice young lady. Mom said she really wanted to talk to me about something though. I said, "Sure Mom. Can I just tell Robert Goodbye and unpack my bag first?"

When I finished unpacking, I went in Mom's room and sat on her bed. Mom got straight to the point and asked me if Robert and I were having sex but I lied and told her no.

"You mean to tell me that boy hasn't asked you to have sex with him?"

I told Mom Robert had asked but I promised her I wasn't ready yet and confirmed my plans to go to law school. Then she hugged me and told me again how proud she was of me and said that I was turning out to be quite a young lady.

I really hated lying to Mom about having sex with Robert so I called him and told him I could not do it any more. I explained to him that my relationship with my mom was too precious to let something make me start lying to her. Mom trusted me so much that she even started letting me drive to Robert's house, which was the first time I had driven on the freeway.

So for the next few months, on the weekends, I would either take Monica with me to hang out at Robert's or he would come over to my house and we would take Monica with us wherever we went. We took her to the park, movies, shopping, just about everywhere. I really wanted Monica to be with us because I wanted to set a good example for her. I wanted to show her that teenagers didn't have to have a relationship based on sex. However, whenever Robert could sneak a moment alone with me, he would still ask me to have sex with him but each time I told him no and I meant it.

Meanwhile back at school, the newest rumor going around was one about Rochelle being pregnant. And not only was she pregnant, but I heard she didn't know who the father was. It was either Marcus or some other boy. What a tramp. I immediately went to Marcus and asked him if she were pregnant. He said not that he knew of, so I told him what I had heard. Marcus said that wouldn't surprise him because Rochelle had sex with one of his best friends. He called Rochelle a "fuckin' tramp". He said he never wanted to go steady with her, but he just had sex with her because, unlike me, she was giving it up. Then he looked at me and laughed and said he was just joking, but I knew he was really speaking the truth.

The next day at lunchtime Rochelle and I happened to be walking towards each other. I hoped she didn't try to start anything because I was really not in the mood. In fact, I was on my way to the office to get a pass to be excused from school for the rest of the day because I thought I was coming down with the flu. Then, here she came with two of her friends and she started pointing her finger in my face and asking me why I told Marcus that she was pregnant and that she didn't know who the father of her baby was.

"Yes, bitch, I'm pregnant and, yes, Marcus is the father. You're just jealous he ain't fuckin' your ugly ass."

Then she slapped me. It was *on* then. She was swinging wildly at me, and at first I closed my eyes as I was swinging at, I guess the air, because I wasn't hitting anything else. Then she pulled my hair.

My hair was my pride and joy. I knew my hair looked just as good as everyone else's at school. Girls would come up to me all the time and ask me how I got my hair so curly on some days and so straight on other days. They wondered if I had a perm but I didn't. Mom couldn't afford to get Monica's and my hair permed all the time. I washed my hair every other weekend and Mom would press it. Then I would use those sponge rollers and wet the ends of my hair. That's what made it so curly, but I kept that little secret all to myself.

So when Rochelle pulled my hair, I snapped back into reality and opened my eyes. I swung at her using both of my fists and started hitting her dead in the face. Then her nose starting bleeding and someone broke us up and we had to go to the office. I was really scared because I had never been to the office before, at least not because of anything bad.

We both went into the main office and the principal asked us if we could both come into his office and tell him what was going on without starting World War II all over again. Being scared, I immediately said, "She started it by slapping me." Then he asked the question again.

"Do you think you both can come into my office and tell me what's going on without starting World War II all over again?"

"Yes Mr. Browne," I said as I looked at Rochelle and saw that she was holding some wet paper towel over her nose trying to stop the bleeding.

We sat in his office in two chairs, side by side, with about five feet separating us. Then Mr. Browne asked us how this got started. Rochelle replied by saying that I had told Marcus a bunch of rumors about her and she was tired of me lying about her. Then I got smart and said, "It's not my fault if she doesn't know who the father of her baby is." Then Rochelle called me a bitch and said that was her business. Then I said, "See I told you she doesn't know."

"Is this whole thing about Marcus Ward?" Mr. Browne asked.

"Yeah it is," Rochelle said.

"No it isn't. I didn't fight her because of some boy. Marcus and I are just friends. I hit her because she slapped me first."

Then he asked Rochelle if it were true that she had started the fight and she admitted that she did. He told us that Marcus was not worth us fighting over and that he was probably somewhere laughing at both of us right now. Then he made us both promise not to spread any more rumors about each other and also in a very threatening voice he said, "I don't want to see either one of you in my office again, especially you Rochelle." Then he told Rochelle she was suspended from school for the next three days for starting the fight and he excused me from his office. When Rochelle walked out I asked if I could be excused for the rest of the day because I wasn't feeling well. He said that it was okay as long as I brought in a note when I returned tomorrow.

I went home to lie down for a couple of hours and then I called Robert and told him what had happened. He said he was lying down too because he didn't feel well either. However, the next morning I felt fine so I went on to school. I guess I just had a twenty-four hour flu.

All day long people were talking about the fight. I guess that was the fight of the century. Either people were coming up to me saying, "I heard you beat Rochelle up yesterday," or people were just pointing me out saying, "she's the one that beat Rochelle up." Not too many people knew me until then. I guess that fight made me somewhat popular. Even though Rochelle knew a lot of people, I found out that most of them didn't like her. Most girls who knew her really didn't like her because she had slept with their boyfriends and most boys knew her for that same reason. To my surprise, it didn't seem as if anyone was disappointed that she had been beaten up.

When Rochelle came back to school a few days later she and I saw each other several times but acted as if we didn't. I had really thought about what the principal said. Marcus was not worth us fighting over and I certainly didn't want to be suspended. Those that knew me knew I was an honor student and that I wanted to go to law school. I certainly wasn't going to let Rochelle or Marcus spoil the reputation I had built up with my teachers and my counselor. So, I ignored Rochelle every chance I got. I even went out of my way sometimes just to avoid her.

NO APRIL FOOL'S

Robert and I continued to talk on the phone and we made plans for the weekend to pack a lunch and take Monica with us to Dan Foley Park. I knew she would really enjoy that. The park was really nice. It had hiking trails, peacocks, swing sets, and lots of tetherball courts, which Monica loved to play. Monica was really excited and Mom was glad we were going out somewhere so everyone was disappointed when Robert and I both came down with the flu again that weekend. First it was him. He called me on Friday and said he had the flu and I woke up Saturday morning feeling nauseated too. I thought, "Why me?" This was the second time that month that I had a cold or the flu.

Although I dragged myself to school the following week, I really felt awful. But there was something different about the flu this time; it was lingering too long. Since Mom worked at a hospital, she knew of a really bad flu that was going around and so she suggested I go to the doctor and have it checked out to make sure it hadn't turned into pneumonia. So I did.

While at the doctor's office, the nurse took my temperature and blood pressure and asked me if I were pregnant. I immediately said, "No. Robert can't have any more children." She looked at me really funny and then she asked me when my last period was. I told her I didn't know because it really wasn't that regular. Actually, I had only started my period about four months prior. I knew I was a late bloomer. All of my friends, all two of them, had started their periods around thirteen years old but here I was, seventeen, when mine started. The nurse then asked me if I were sexually active and I told her I had sex

one time. Then she confirmed that yes there was a really bad
flu going around but she wanted to make sure I wasn't pregnant
before she treated me for the flu. I said, "Sure. Where do I go
for that?" She told me it was easy. I just had to take a urine test
and they would have the results back in twenty minutes.

While I was waiting for the results, I went to the pay
phone and called Robert. I told him where I was and, in a
laughing voice, I told him what they were doing. He told me
he had just come from the doctors himself and he was given
some medicine. Then he asked me what I would do if I were
pregnant. I said, "Yeah right. Don't even start playing." I told
him I felt awful at school so I decided to come down and get
some medicine myself. Then I heard the nurse call my name and
so I told Robert I would call him as soon as I got home.

I went back into the doctor's office and this time the
doctor came in with the nurse. He asked me my age again and
I told him I was seventeen. He said, "Did you know you were
pregnant?"

My chest nearly jumped out of my shirt. I know he didn't
say I was pregnant. It must have been a mistake because Robert
couldn't have any more children. I looked at the doctor and
laughed, "You're joking, right?" But he didn't have a smile on
his face and neither did the nurse. They both looked at me as
if they wanted me to say something. But I was waiting on them
to say something. Hey, I get it! Today just happens to be April
Fools Day. But I'm still waiting and there is still no smile on
their faces. So I broke the silence and explained, "I only had sex
one time and Robert can't have any more children." Then in my
calm little voice I said, "You must have my test mixed up with
someone else's, so I'll take another one."

Then the doctor wanted to give me a sex education lesson
as he explained that it's very possible to get pregnant on the first
time just like you can get pregnant on the second, third, fourth
and fifth time and so on; but I already knew this. He must have
thought I was stupid or something. Then the nurse advised me
of my options. I said, "Okay thank you," and I walked out of the
office. I know they are wrong. I will just have another doctor do
another test so they can go ahead and give me some medicine

for this flu.

But now I was feeling worse. I was about to throw up. So I leaned up against the wall next to the pay phone and I called Robert again. The first words out of his mouth were, "So are you pregnant?"

"What do you mean, am I pregnant? They think I am but I told them you couldn't have any more children. Why would you ask me that anyway?" I said.

Then Robert told me to stay at the hospital because he was on his way. I told him not to bother. I had caught the bus so I didn't have to worry about feeling bad and driving at the same time. But he said he was on his way anyway and for me to wait for him. I told him that was fine and that while I was waiting for him I would go and make another appointment to be seen for the flu.

When I hung up the phone I stood in this really long line waiting to get to the appointment clerk. I finally made it to the front of the line and told the receptionist I wanted to make an appointment, preferably for today, because I wasn't feeling good. When she looked up my medical number she said she would make me an appointment in OB/GYN.

"What's that?" I asked her. She said from now on, or at least for the next eight or nine months, I would have to see a pre-natal doctor. I explained to her that the pregnancy test was a mistake because my boyfriend couldn't have any more children. Then she gave me the same look the nurse and the doctor had given me when I told them Robert couldn't have any more children. They all acted as if they knew him personally. Just then, Robert came in and took me by the hand and insisted we walk out to his car.

"Let go of my hand. And why did you come way up here just to drive me home?"

"Just get in the car," he said. So I got in and, as he was pulling out of the parking lot, he said, "I have somethin' to tell you but promise me you won't be mad at me."

"I'm not promising anything. What is it?"

"You don't have to get another test because you probably

are pregnant."

Then my heart dropped to my feet. "Stop playing," I said.

"I'm not playin'," Robert said. Then I burst into tears and a very loud cry. "I'm sorry," he said.

"Sorry? That's all you have to say? You said you couldn't have any more children. Why? Why did you lie to me? You promised me! You're stupid! I hate you! Just stop the car and let me out! You're so stupid. Why did you do this to me?" As we pulled in front of my house I saw Monica coming home. I tried to stop crying and hide my tears but I couldn't. Actually I don't know when I stopped crying.

Monica stopped at the car window and asked me what was wrong. I said, "Nothing."

"I know something is wrong with you because you wouldn't be crying for nothing," she said. "Robert what's wrong with her?"

"She's sick," he said.

"Yeah and it's all your fault," I told him.

"What do you mean, she's sick? Are you pregnant?" Monica asked. I couldn't believe she came up with that so soon. I guess I'm the only stupid one around here. How come I couldn't see this coming? I could barely get the word "no" out of my mouth because of the crying. "Well, if you're not pregnant, what is it?"

"Nothing, I told you. Just go in the house, Monica."

Monica did just as I told her but she kept peeking out of the kitchen window.

"Why, Robert? Why did you lie to me and what else have you lied about?"

"I didn't lie. I really thought I couldn't have any more kids."

"You're so stupid. Just leave me alone."

"But, Cassandra, wait. I love you. I want to be with you. Can't you see that?"

"No, all I can see is that you're a liar. Leave me alone. I need to go and throw up."

"Actually I'm feelin' really sick too. Can I come in and use your bathroom?"

"No! Go home and leave me alone."

Then I got of his car and Robert pulled off. I went in the house and straight to the bathroom but I couldn't throw up. Then I went and lay down on my bed and started crying again. All kinds of things went through my mind. Why me? I'm only seventeen years old. What am I going to do with a baby? I don't even like baby-sitting. What about my education? What about my dreams of becoming a lawyer? Oh shit! What about my mom? She's going to kill me. I let her down. Now she'll know I lied to her. She's going to kill me. What now? Maybe I'll just take an overdose of something and I won't have to deal with her. I don't know what to do. For once I wish I could be someone else. Anybody else, it doesn't matter who. Then Monica came in the room with a peanut butter and jelly sandwich and a cup of milk.

"Do you want some?" she said.

"No thank you. I'm not hungry," I said, but I was really starving.

Why did that sandwich look so good? And that milk? I thought I could drink a whole cow right then. What was happening to me? Was I craving? I started crying some more.

"I know something is wrong with you," Monica said. Just then the phone rang and Monica picked it right up. It was Robert. Monica tricked him and said, "Cassandra told me she was pregnant," and before I could say, "No I didn't," Robert confirmed it by saying, "She told you?"

"So you *are* pregnant," Monica said. "Oooh, I'm going to go call Mom."

I jumped up and snatched the phone from Monica and begged her, "Please, pretty, pretty please, don't call Mom. I'll do anything you want me to."

"Like what?" she said.

"I'll do your dishes for you this week."

"And what else?" Monica asked.

"I'll do your homework for you too."

"Okay," Monica said quickly.

Then I got back on the phone. "See what you've done, Robert? I hate you." Then I hung up on him and I cried some more.

A few minutes later Mom came home from her part-time job. I knew I couldn't face her so I stayed in my room. Mom yelled down the hallway and said, "I'm home."

I yelled, "Hi Mom," but I hoped she wouldn't come in here. She'd know something was wrong. She yelled, "There's some spaghetti on the stove."

"Okay, Mom," I yelled back.

Then she said she was going to bed and asked me if I would come and set her clock for ten o'clock so she could go to her other job. I told her I would be awake so I would just wake her up.

Whew! I was glad she didn't come back here. I didn't know what I would have done. I didn't know what I was going to do. I felt so stupid. Mom worked so hard to give Monica and me the things we wanted and look what I'd done. She was going to be so hurt. And so was I as soon as she had gotten through with me. She'd never trust me again. I couldn't believe I had betrayed her, and all because of some boy. A lying boy at that. I hated him.

For the next month, I continued going to school and talking to Robert on the phone although most of the time I was hanging up on him. When I finally listened to what he had to say, he asked, "What are we gonna to do? When are you gonna tell your mother?"

"I don't know. Have you told your mom?"

"No, not yet."

"What do you think your mom's going to say?" I asked him.

"Oh she probably won't say anythin', or at least she won't be mad about it, her."

"How do you know she won't be mad?"

"Because she's real understandin'. She already knows everybody's havin' sex. You know my sisters already have kids and she wasn't mad at them."

"Oh yeah, I guess you're right. I'm still scared though. My mom is going to hit the roof. She's going to hate me."

"No she won't. My mom didn't hate my sisters," Robert

said.

"Well, you don't know my mom. I was supposed to start college this September. She's going to hate me, I know it," I said as I started crying again.

"Stop cryin'. It's not good for our baby," Robert said. Then I hung up on him again but he called right back.

"What do you want?" I asked him.

"Do you want me to come over?"

"No, for what?"

"I want to make sure that you and our baby are okay," he said.

"You think this is all a joke don't you?"

"No, I don't think it's a joke. I love you. How many times do I have to tell you that?"

"You don't even know what love is. And, anyway, if you loved me you wouldn't have lied to me."

"Well I do love you and it has nothin' to do with lyin', and besides, I didn't lie. I really thought I couldn't get you pregnant. But now that you are, why don't you marry me?"

"And where are we going to live, Robert? How are we going to live? You think you can support me and a baby?"

"Yeah, I can do it," he said.

"How? You won't have your maintenance job for long since it's only a summer job."

"I can do it because I can start workin' construction full-time with my father. I just don't do it now because I've been thinkin' about takin' a class down at the junior college by my house."

"But you've been thinking about that ever since you graduated last year. When are you going to actually enroll?"

"I don't know. I'll wait and see what you're gonna do about the baby."

"What do you mean, what am I going to do? What *should* I do?"

"Well I don't want you to have an abortion. I want you to have the baby."

Then I started crying again, so I told Robert I would talk

to him later about this.

"I'll be over this weekend," Robert said.

"Okay. I'll talk to you later. Bye."

I continued going to school and to work that week. That weekend Robert came over. We sat in his car for a long time. Then Monica came outside.

"So when are you going to tell Mom?" she asked.

"I don't know. Just leave me alone, okay?"

Robert turned to me and said, "Yeah, when are you gonna tell your mother? You can't keep waitin'. So you're about two months now, huh?"

"Yeah, I guess."

"I think you should tell her today," he said.

"I can't. I'm too scared. I'll tell her next weekend for sure."

"So have you been havin' mornin' sickness?" Robert asked.

"I'm not sure. Sometimes, in the mornings, I feel like I'm going to throw up but I never do. I don't know if that's morning sickness or not."

"Well, I think I've been havin' it for you because every mornin' I get up throwin' up. My sisters told me that some guys get mornin' sickness too."

"Uh uh, Robert you're lying."

"No, for real. They said that guys do get mornin' sickness sometimes."

"Well, that's good for you. You need to get something."

"Do you want to go to the park?" Robert asked.

"I don't care but let me go and tell my mom where I'm going." Then we drove up the street where Monica was playing and took her to the park with us. Robert and I sat on the grass and just watched Monica play with some other little children.

The next week was the same routine. I went to school and work and Robert called and some times I would talk and some times I would hang up on him. That Friday, when he called, he told me that he told his mother and then he asked me if I wanted to talk to her, and before I could say "no", she was already on the phone.

"Hi, Cassandra. How are you? Robert told me what's going

on, him. I think you should tell your mother because you need to start going to the doctor."

"Uh huh," I said.

"You *are* gonna keep it aren't you?"

I started crying and said, "I don't know what I'm going to do."

"You better keep it because that's my grandchild. And you need to tell your mother soon."

"Okay, I will." Then she put Robert back on the phone.

"Why did you do that?" I said.

"Do what?" he said.

"Never mind, Robert."

"So are you gonna tell your mom tomorrow like you promised?

"I don't know. Are you still coming over tomorrow?"

"Yeah, I'll be there."

The next day, Robert came over and we sat in the living room and watched television while Mom was in her room doing her bills. I kept getting up and walking past her door. I kept trying to stop but I couldn't. I told Robert I was going to count to ten and then I would go and tell her. But just like when I counted to ten two months ago, ten came and went at least a dozen times. Then Robert said, "If you don't go in there and tell her, I will."

I knew he was bluffing so I said, "Go right ahead."

Then he got up and went to her door and said, "Miss Grant, I have to tell you somethin'." I was shocked. I didn't think he was going to do it.

"NO ROBERT! DON'T!" I yelled.

"Yes I am," he yelled back.

"What is it, honey?" my mom asked Robert.

And as I put my hands over my ears, Robert said, "Cassandra wants to tell you that she's pregnant." I couldn't believe he just blurted it out like that.

"She's what?!"

"She's pregnant," he repeated calmly.

Then my mom started crying really loudly. "Is it yours?"

"Yes, Miss Grant. I'm the father."

Then Mom started crying even louder while yelling, "No! She's my baby. I can't believe this. My baby." Then she yelled, "Come here, Cassandra Ann Grant. Bring your ass in here right now," and I slowly walked to her bedroom door and stood next to Robert. "So you're pregnant, huh?" But I didn't answer her. I just started crying. "I don't know why you're crying now. How far along are you?"

"About two months," I mumbled.

"I'm sure you weren't crying about two months ago. So why are you crying now?"

"I'm sorry, Mom."

"Don't be sorry. You weren't sorry two months ago. So what about school? Have you lost your damn mind?" she said.

"I don't know," I mumbled.

"Get from in front of my door because I don't even want to look at you," she said.

"But, Mom, I'm sorry."

"But nothing. Just close my damn door."

I closed her door and then Robert said he was getting ready to leave.

"No you're not. You can't just tell my mother I'm pregnant and walk out."

"Well, what do you want me to do?" he said.

"I want you to stay here with me because I know she's not done."

"Okay. I'll stay a little longer."

Then we heard my mom call my dad. Between her crying spells we heard her say, "William, guess what? Cassandra's pregnant."

I don't know what my dad said to her but at least I knew he wouldn't fuss at me the way she did. A few minutes later, she called her best friend and told her too. Then I think she called every phone number in her phone book and cried as she told the rest of the world. She also called her job and told them that she wouldn't be in that night. Then my phone started ringing. The first call was from my dad.

"How are you doing, baby? Your mom told me about you. Are you okay?"

I started crying as I said, "Yes Daddy, I'm fine."

"Do you need anything?" he asked.

"No thank you, Dad."

"Well you better stop crying 'cause it's not good for you. And if you need anything, just call me and let me know."

"Okay, Daddy. I love you."

"I love you too, honey."

The next call was from my oldest sister Gwen.

"Mom just told me you're pregnant but I don't believe it. Are you really?"

"Yeah," I said.

"You mean Miss Goody Two-Shoes is pregnant? I don't believe it."

"Well, I don't feel like talking right now. I'll call you back later." So I hung up with her and took my phone off the hook.

It started getting dark outside so I walked Robert to the door and he said, "I have to go now but remember that I love you and I promise everythin' will be okay. I'll call you when I get home."

"Okay," I said.

Monica was coming in the house as Robert was leaving and she said, "So, did you tell Mom yet?"

"Yes, and she hates me."

I walked back into my room and put the phone back on the hook. Monica walked by Mom's room and slightly opened her door.

"Don't cry," Monica said from the doorway.

"Come here, baby," and she hugged and kissed Monica and told Monica that she loved her. I started crying even more because I knew Mom was only trying to make me jealous. "It's just going to be the two of us from now on because Cassandra's grown. She can take care of herself, or her little boyfriend can take care of her from now on," Mom told Monica.

Then I walked in Mom's room crying and she said, "Get out of here and go cry at Robert's house." I went in my room and started crying even louder. Then Mom walked down the hall to my room and slammed my door shut and hollered, "Shut up. I don't want to hear it." Then my phone started ringing as I wondered who it was going to be this time because I really didn't feel like talking to any one but Robert.

"Hello?" I said hesitantly.

"Hi baby," Robert's mom said. Robert told me that he told your mom. How are you?"

"I'm okay but my mom hates me."

"She doesn't hate you. She's just upset right now. Give her some time and she'll be okay, her. And you'll be okay too. A baby isn't gonna hurt you. You know all these girls out here have babies. I was upset with my daughters at first too but I love all my grandkids to death and I'm gonna love the one you're carryin' just as much. So you know you have to keep it. We don't believe in abortions in this family."

"Uh huh."

Then she put Robert on the phone.

"How are you?" he said.

"I'm fine, I guess."

Then I started crying as I told him that even though I was mad at him earlier, I was glad that he had told my mom because I couldn't keep hiding it. And even though she hated me now, it was going to come sooner or later. He told me to stop crying and that everything would be okay.

About a week passed and I kept trying to avoid Mom around the house. I also made sure all of my housework was kept up. I wanted to make sure I didn't give Mom anything else to fuss at me about. I knew I had hurt her and I would do anything, anything at all to make it up to her. So I thought about it and decided the only way I could make Mom happy was to have an abortion. I really didn't want to have an abortion because I think that's wrong. And if it weren't for Mom's anger, there was no way I would even consider it. I would just have to deal with being a mother. But if I had an abortion, maybe Mom and I could go back to being friends again. I knew she would never feel the same about me and we would probably never be close again but at least a baby wouldn't constantly remind her of how I hurt her. Then I could finish high school and go on to college as planned. So that was it. I really didn't want to but I was going to call and make an appointment for an abortion.

I looked in the yellow pages and called Planned Parenthood. I told them I was about 2 ½ months pregnant and I wanted to make an appointment for an abortion. But just as I started talking to them my mom walked in my room and asked me what was I doing. I told her I was calling Planned Parenthood and she asked, "What for?"

Then before I knew it I lied and said, "I'm calling for some birth control pills." Boy, how stupid. Why did I say that?

"It's a little late for birth control pills don't you think?" I know why you're really calling so just hang up the phone," she said.

"But Mom."

"But nothing. Just hang up the damn phone."

When I hung it up she asked me what was I really calling for and I told her the truth.

"If you have an abortion I will never speak to you again."

"I really don't want an abortion but I would do anything for you, Mom."

Then as she started crying she told me something that I would never forget. She said, "The first thing you need to learn about being a mother is to never let anyone hurt your child. That's your baby you're carrying in there," as she touched my stomach. "And you don't let anyone, not even me, come between you and that baby. Do you hear me?" she said.

"Yes. But Mom I don't want you to be mad with me."

"You mean the only reason you were calling was for me?"

"Yes." Then I started crying.

"You need to snap out of it. That baby is your number one concern. You need to call the hospital and make an appointment for your first prenatal visit."

"Okay." And as I took a deep breath I said, "But will you come with me?"

"I'll come with you to the first one and that's it. After that you need to make Robert go with you."

"Okay."

On my first visit to the doctor, I asked Mom what were they going to do. She said she wasn't going to tell me because I would soon find out. I guess I should have been scared but I wasn't. I felt like I could do anything with my mom there beside me. The nurse soon called me into the room. She weighed me, took my blood pressure and made me urinate in a cup. She explained that each time I came in I would have to give them a urine sample. Then she asked Mom if she wanted to come in the room with me but she said that she would stay in the waiting room.

"You need to completely undress," the nurse said as she gave me something to go across my lap and across my chest. Now I was nervous and embarrassed. I had never had a doctor's appointment where I had to completely undress. Then the doctor came in and it was a man and I was even more embarrassed. He told me he was going to examine my breasts first. His nurse asked me if this was my first breast examination and I said yes. Then the doctor showed me how to examine my breasts myself each month.

Then the nurse told me to put my feet in those little stirrup things. I couldn't believe it. How gross. "Open your legs wider," the doctor said. I couldn't believe it. Then the doctor explained what he would be doing and that he had to insert this spectrum thing inside of me. "Scoot all the way down here," the doctor said. So I did. I was so embarrassed. I was so glad Mom didn't come in here with me. I had no idea this was what they had to do. So he inserted that spectrum thing and it really hurt. When the nurse saw the look of discomfort on my face she held my hand and told me it was going to be okay. But easy for her to say, she wasn't the one lying on the table butt naked with her legs spread in the air.

The doctor asked me how long had I been sexually active and I told him just once, a few months ago. He said, "Well I guess you know that's all it takes."

"Yes," I said as I started crying. The nurse then asked me

if I was in that much pain and I told her no I was crying about something else. The doctor told me everything looked fine and I could go ahead and get dressed and he would be back in the room to talk to me when I was finished. When he came back in the room my mom came with him. He had the results of the urine test. He told me I was about three months pregnant and my due date was December tenth. He also told me that I needed to make an appointment to be seen every four weeks.

On the way home Mom told me that I was on my own from now on. She would not be going with me to any more of my appointments. She told me that was Robert's job. I said okay and told her I was just glad she came with me to this one. At least she was talking to me a little bit.

MOMMY DEAREST

My high school graduation was next month. I guess somewhere along the way I must have missed my prom, my senior breakfast and my senior trip to Disney Land. I don't know where the last three months went. I must have spent them all crying.

The day before graduation I stayed home from school. I needed to wash my hair and let Mom press it for me. It needed washing extremely badly. I had really been neglecting my hair because I was too afraid to ask Mom to do it for me. She used to press it for me every other weekend; it was like clockwork. She knew I would be washing my hair so she would always have that time set aside from her part-time jobs so she could do it. But I was too afraid to ask her then. Mom was a great hairdresser. All the girls at school used to wonder where I got my hair done and they were amazed when I told them my mom did it. So I washed it anyway and when it got dry I asked Mom to please press it for me. She looked at me and saw my hair all over my head. It looked like I had a big natural but she didn't care in the least. So she said, "I'm not doing your hair. Why don't you call Robert to do it?"

I started crying and said, "Please, Mom will you do it?"

"No I will not. And you better stop crying. Remember you're carrying that baby. I certainly remember everyday that you're carrying it. Every time I look at you it's a constant reminder."

"But Mom, I thought everything was okay now."

"I guess that's what you get for thinking. You should have been thinking a few months ago."

I guess I was wrong for thinking that Mom would ever

forgive me. Every time I thought things were getting close to the way they used to be she made me feel really badly. I knew she hated me just like I hated Robert.

I called one of my girlfriends up from school and asked her if she knew how to press hair and she said yeah she would be right over. Between the two of us we tried and tried to get my hair as straight as Mom would get it but we didn't even come close. My hair looked really bad. I couldn't believe it was my last day of school and I looked like Angela Davis.

Mom had graduation day off from work. About two hours before it started, I passed Mom's door with my hair looking like a mop and I asked her what time she would be coming.

"Coming where? I know you don't think I'm going to your graduation. You better ask Robert's mom to go with you." When I started crying again, she said, "And those tears are getting pretty old." But as I walked away from her door I heard her crying too. I wanted to go back into her room and just hug and kiss her but she would probably tell me I had the cooties or something. So I just walked away from her door. Then Monica told me she was ready to go. Just as we were walking out the door Robert pulled up.

Robert was looking really nice and here I was, this was supposed to be my day, and I was ugly, fat and pregnant. Robert asked me what was wrong with my hair and I told him what happened. I told him I couldn't take it any more. Mom was constantly reminding me of how I betrayed her. I just didn't know what I was going to do. Then Robert said, "Let's get an apartment together."

"Where? How? Why?" I said, but I already know why.

"Really Cassandra, I think we should. I really love you and I want to marry you so let's do it."

"When?" I said. I couldn't believe I was even thinking about it, but right then my only other choice was to stay with Mom and lately that choice just isn't working out. I told Robert okay and that I would look for us an apartment the next day.

Then Monica spoke up and said, "I don't blame you for leaving because I see how Mom has been treating you. I would go too if I could. So can I move in with you guys?"

"You know Mom isn't going to let you." But with tears in my eyes I told Monica I would still come and see her every day.

As we were walking to the graduation field I saw my dad. So Robert, Monica and my dad went one way and I went the other. "I will see you guys in a little while," I said as I kissed my dad and when he said, "I love you honey," I cried even more.

When I met up with the rest of my class I had dried my tears but I guess my eyes were really red. Everyone kept asking me what was wrong with my hair and what was wrong with my eyes. And whoever asked I told them the truth. "I'm pregnant and I've been crying all day." "You're what!" People would say surprised. Then soon I became the talk of graduation night. Just like my sister Gwen had said, "Miss Goody Two-Shoes was pregnant." Everyone was in shock and a couple of people even asked me if it were Marcus' baby.

Marcus' baby? I had forgotten all about Marcus. He was going to be mad that I was pregnant. As many times as he tried to get me to sleep with him, he was going to be really disappointed. And come to think of it, when Rochelle and I had that fight a couple of months ago, I guess we were both pregnant.

After my graduation ceremony my Dad kissed me again and said, "You look pretty honey." But I know I didn't, he was just trying to make me feel good.

"Well what do you want to do now?" Robert said.

"Do you want to go and get something to eat?" Dad said.

"Yes, I want a milk shake from McDonald's."

"Yeah let's go to McDonald's," Monica said.

So the four of us went to McDonald's. This certainly wasn't how I thought I would be spending my graduation night. As soon as I was done with my shake I said I was ready to go home and go to bed. So Dad left and Robert brought Monica and me home.

The next day Robert came over pretty early. I told him to bring a local newspaper with him, so he did. When Mom got up she saw us looking in the newspaper for an apartment.

"So you're moving out?" she asked.

And in a very low voice I said, "Yes, I think that would be best."

"Good. Give me the paper and I'll help you find a place."

Wow, she was so mean to me. I wasn't ever going to get pregnant again. So she really took the paper and started calling around for an apartment for me. She explained to people that the apartment was for her daughter who was seventeen and she also told them I was a fairly responsible teenager. Boy, she must have really wanted me to move out. She hated me.

"I think I found a place for you. I have the address so let's go check it out."

She drove us to this two-bedroom duplex on the other side of town. The man that met us there asked us what we thought. Robert and I looked at each other and said, "We like it." Mom and Monica said they liked it too. Between Robert's savings and mine we had just enough money to move in. So Mom wrote the man a check and we gave her all of her money back the next day. She also arranged for our PG&E and phone to be turned on. That next weekend Robert and I planned on moving in together.

As I was packing my things, Mom came in my room and noticed me putting my typewriter and my electric pencil sharpener in a box.

"Just where do you think you're taking those?" she said.

"I'm packing them with the rest of my things."

"Oh no you're not. Those things are staying here for Monica. I don't have the money to replace them and buy Monica new ones."

"But Mom, these were my Christmas presents."

"No they weren't. They were for you *and* Monica and since you're the only one that messed up, they now belong to Monica."

Monica just stood there shaking her head. We both knew they were mine but what's the point in arguing. I'd never argued with Mom before so why start now. I had to keep reminding myself that I should respect my mother but she was making it pretty damn hard.

"The only things you're taking from here are your clothes and pretty soon you're going to be to fat to wear them too."

"Okay Mom," I said.

I called Robert to ask him just where did he think we were going to get furniture. We hadn't thought about any of this. Furniture, cleaning supplies, food; where was that going to come from? Robert said he would be bringing his bed and an old couch that was in his mom's garage. I called my dad and he brought me two hundred and fifty dollars. With it I bought a dinette table, a twin bed and some linens from a garage sale and I even had a few dollars left to buy a little food. Between Robert, his dad and my dad, they got everything moved into our apartment within an hour. That was pretty easy because they really didn't have much to do.

That evening Robert and I sat on the couch. He put his arms around me as I lay my head on his shoulder. I still couldn't believe this was all happening.

"Well, we finally did it. We got our own place," Robert said.

Even though it felt good to be away from Mom I was still scared and I missed Monica already. Then I asked Robert, "What do you mean we finally did it? You sound like you have been planning this all along."

"No I haven't been plannin' nothin'. But we're a family now and you're just gonna have to get used to it."

"I guess you're right," I said.

"So do you love me?" Robert asked.

I turned and looked at him and said, "Yeah I guess so." Then Robert gently laid me down on the couch and as he started to get on top of me the phone rang. It was Monica.

"Cassandra, I miss you. Can I come spend the night if Mom says it's okay?"

"Sure," I told her. So she put the phone down and went to ask Mom. Ooops, I guess I was supposed to ask Robert if it were okay with him, but oh well, I'll try and remember to ask him next time. Then Monica came back and said that yes she could spend the night if I came and picked her up, so of course I did. Actually, since Monica was out of school for the summer she spent that night, the next night and a few more nights with us. Then one day Mom called her and asked if she had forgotten where she lived. So I told Monica she better go home because she definitely didn't want to give Mom a reason to be mad with her too.

I started working forty hours a week on my job since I was out of school. Then when I told them I was pregnant they told me I could only work until September because I could only have that job as long as I was in school. Meanwhile, Robert was supposed to start working full-time with his father but something happened and they told him that since he wasn't in the union he couldn't work at all. So Robert took a job pumping gas at a nearby gas station.

During the three months that we both had full-time jobs we managed to buy a television and put a few dollars into a joint savings account. We knew we would need some money for the baby very soon. I continued going to my doctor's appointments and Robert was right there with me. Instead of every four weeks, I was scheduled and appointment every three weeks then every two weeks. As time was getting closer and closer to December tenth I was getting more and more anxious, while at the same time I was getting more and more fatter.

What happened to my 120-pound figure? I couldn't believe it; I was up to 165 pounds. But that really shouldn't have been a surprise because I was eating everything in sight. Taco Bell was my favorite. Every single day I had to have Taco Bell.

As time got closer Mom kept warning me not to eat so much. She kept telling me it was going to be really hard to lose all the weight after the baby was born. For once it seemed like Mom was beginning to talk to me again. Or maybe not, maybe she just got a kick out of telling me that I was fat. But then one day she surprised me. She came over and took me shopping for the baby. We had a pretty good day.

It was December 3rd and I was beginning to feel those little cramps in my stomach but I didn't think I was in labor because I thought it was supposed to hurt really bad and it didn't. So I told Robert about the cramps and we decided to time them. They were coming about every twenty minutes. But it still wasn't hurting so I decided to call my sister Gwen. I told her how I felt and the first words out of her mouth were, "Fool you're in labor."

As I started laughing I said, "No I'm not. I can't be because it doesn't even hurt. So I think I'll go to bed and if I still feel the same in morning I'll go to the hospital then." So I got off the phone and went to bed.

The next morning Robert's dad came over bright and early to help Robert fix something on my car. Before Robert went outside I told him I still felt the same way but I promised to call the hospital for advice. The nurse told me to come in when my contractions were five to six minutes apart. Oh yeah, that's what they're called, contractions, not little cramps. I really don't think I'm ready for this mother thing.

A couple of hours later not only were my contractions every six minutes but they were more intense so I went outside to tell Robert I thought it was time to go. He looked at me and said, "We can't go now. Dad and I have completely taken your car apart and it's gonna take some time to put it back together." Taking Robert's car wasn't an option because we had a single car carport and my broken down car was behind his.

"Well you're going to have to do something. I'm ready to go."

Robert's dad looked at him and smiled and said, "I don't think you have a choice. When a woman says it's time to go, it's time to go. We're just gonna have to take her in my truck."

Any other time I wouldn't have been caught dead in his old 1960ish beat up truck, but all of a sudden it looked like a brand new Cadillac. Again this wasn't how I expected my ride would be going to the hospital delivering my first baby. Nothing about this pregnancy was how I dreamed it would be. Then again I had no dreams of ever becoming a mother. But all of a sudden reality finally hit me right along with those awful contractions and I realized there was no turning back.

After I got registered I went into a labor room, got undressed and then called my mom. She said she would be right there and she was. She must have flown down to the hospital. When she came in the room I asked Robert to leave, so he went into the waiting room with his dad. As soon as he left and Mom was there it seemed like my contractions got ten times worse. You know how things always seem to hurt more when your mother is around.

I think I was Kaiser's worst patient in hospital history. I yelled, screamed and hollered at every contraction. Mom was there holding my hand but that didn't seem to help this time. I managed to ask Mom what time it was and she told me it was going on ten o'clock. "Mom," I cried, "I have been here since this afternoon. Is this normal?"

"Yeah sometimes it takes a while," she said.

Then I yelled and screamed a lot more as I pleaded with the nurse to put me to sleep. I didn't really know what they would or could do to put me to sleep. I just knew I didn't want to have to feel anything. Then I pleaded with Mom to plead with the nurses to put me to sleep. Then the doctor came in a promised me if I didn't have my baby by midnight he would put me to sleep and do a cesarean.

Poor Mom, she couldn't take it any more. I think her feelings for me were finally coming back. She left the room for a few minutes and Robert came in. He asked me if it were really hurting that badly because he could hear me screaming all the way out in the waiting room. I told him sarcastically, "No it just tickles. Now get out of here and tell my mom to come back in," and she did.

It wasn't helping any but I was steadily watching the clock in between screams and about 11:30 the doctor came in and checked me again and said, "I think you're ready now." I thought, "No shit Sherlock." Then I said, I don't know where *you've* been but *I* was ready a long time ago." He and my mother just looked at each other and smiled. Then Robert came in the delivery room with a big ass smile on his face too. I don't know what everybody thought was so damn funny. There was nothing funny about lying on that table naked with my legs spread about ten feet apart. Where was the fucking joke? I must have missed it. Yes, labor pains even made Miss Goody Two-Shoes want to cuss like a goddamn sailor.

At 11:50 the doctor said, "On the next contraction just give me one more big push and that should do it." I can't believe it, at 11:57, three fucking minutes before they were going to put my ass to sleep, and on my very last push, out came my eight-pound two-ounce baby girl. The doctor asked Robert if he wanted to cut her umbilical cord and I immediately answered, "NO!" The doctor laughed and said, "Maybe next time, Mr. Johnson." And my mom and I looked at each other and we both said, "There won't be a next time."

Robert got to hold her first, then Mom, and then it was finally my turn. She was so pretty. The nurse asked if I had a name picked out for her yet and as I looked at my baby I said, "Yes it just came to me. I'm going to give her my mom's name, Amelia."

"I think that's wonderful. Grandma, you should feel really special. Let me take little Amelia and get her all cleaned up," the nurse said. Then Mom looked at me and as she started to cry she asked me why was I doing this and I told her because I loved her. Then she left the room in tears.

Then another nurse wheeled me into my new room. I was shocked because my dad and all three of my sisters were there waiting for me. I guess Mom had called them earlier. They stayed with me for about a half-hour then I thanked them all for being there, especially Mom. I told them it was late and I was tired so they could leave. Before Mom left she told me I did really well but, of course, she was lying. She said if I needed anything during the night to call her. Robert stayed in the room with me all night and slept in a chair next to my bed. Every time he would think about it he would kiss my hand and tell me how much he loved me but I was too tired to respond.

The next morning the doctor told me Amelia was nice and healthy and we would be able to leave the following day. Mom suggested when we left that we stay at her house for a few days, so we did. During our stay there, Mom showed me how to feed little Amelia, how to bathe her and everything else I could possibly learn in what turned into being a one-week stay. Mom really seemed to want us there but I had gotten used to being in my own place so after one week it was time to go.

When the three of us went home and we were truly on our own, everything seemed to flow naturally. I was expecting Robert not to have too much to do with Amelia since he was a guy and all, but he was actually quite helpful. He wasn't afraid to do anything for her. He fed her, changed her dirty diapers, bathed her and did everything that I did for her. He even got up in the middle of the night with her.

So if Robert's such a nice guy you're probably wondering why I called him a jerk in the beginning of this book. That's because he had me fooled at first too.

THE SURPRISE

A few months after Amelia was born I got a full-time job at the local phone company. Robert still had his job at the gas station, which worked out great because he was able to switch his hours to the night shift while I worked days so we wouldn't need a baby-sitter. Everything was great. That is, until one day I decided to surprise Robert.

I was able to leave work early so I stopped by a flower stand just to buy him a rose. I knew I didn't tell Robert I loved him that often but I liked surprising him with things like flowers. When I walked in, I didn't see Robert so I went straight to Amelia's room and she was asleep. Then the phone rang and Robert and I picked it up at the same time. I will never forget what I heard.

A female on the other end said, "Hi Robert. Are you busy?"

"Yeah, I mean no, because Amelia's sleep, her."

Then the female replied, "Oh. I was getting ready to say. I know you're not busy with your other honey."

"No, but I'll have to call you back later 'cause I think she's home," he whispered. Then they both hung up.

I yelled at Robert and asked who was on the phone. He lied and said it was his niece. I told him he was lying because I heard the whole conversation. I told him if he didn't tell me who was on the phone then Amelia and I were going to stay with my mom. I guess he didn't think I was serious until I started packing Amelia's bag. Then he told me it was Teri, his son's mother.

"You don't even have anything to do with your son so why

are you talking to his mother? Every time I tell you let's do something for him, let's call him, let's go and pick him up, you don't want to. As a matter of fact, I've never seen him. I've only seen the pictures of him at your mom's house. And why is Teri calling you her honey?"

"Just calm down," Robert said.

"No I don't want to calm down. Why is she calling you her honey?"

"Well the truth is, this is her first time callin'."

"So do you want her?"

"Hell no!"

"Well why didn't you tell her that a few minutes ago?"

"I don't know."

"Well call her back and tell her now. In fact, give me her number and I'll tell her."

"No, I'll do it myself," he said. So Robert dialed her number and as soon as I thought it was ringing I picked up the other phone.

"Hello Teri."

"Hi honey. So was that her?" she asked.

"Don't call my house any more 'cause I have too much to lose."

"Are you serious?"

"Yeah, I'm dead serious. I don't want to lose Cassandra so don't call my house any more."

"That's fine with me you pussy-whipped son-of-a-bitch."

Then they hung up and I guess Robert thought I was finished talking about it but he was wrong. I started looking through our drawers where I kept old bills when Robert asked me what I was looking for.

"Nothing in particular. I just want to see something."

"See what?"

"Nothing. I'm just looking."

Then Robert grabbed my arm and said, "I know what you're lookin' for; old phone bills."

"Yes you're right. I want to make sure you're telling me the truth."

"Why would I lie?"

"I don't know but it certainly wouldn't be the first time you lied to me."

"Why are you bringin' up what's in the past? I've only lied to you one time before and I've already told you why I did that."

"Why don't you just let go of my arm and we'll see."

"No. Why are you tryin' to check up on me? I'm not lettin' you go until you say you believe me."

"Well I guess you'll be holding my arm all night because if you have nothing to hide it shouldn't make a difference. And besides, you're hurting me. If you love me like you say you do you'll let go of my arm."

So he let my arm go as he watched me go through the bills. I found some of our previous telephone bills and there were a few numbers on them that I didn't recognize. I told Robert I was going to call every one of them until I found Teri's number. I started dialing the first number when he snatched the phone from me. Then he pointed her number out.

I couldn't believe it. Her number was all over our phone bill. And all of them were called at times just after I had left for work. I started crying and told Robert to get out and he left without a fuss. But as soon as he closed the door I wanted to tell him not to go because I probably had just run him straight into Teri's arms.

I immediately called my mother and told her everything. Well, not quite everything. I conveniently left out the part about Robert grabbing my arm. Mom asked me if I wanted to bring little Amelia to her house. She said the two of us could spend the night but I told her that no, we would stay home.

I could tell that Mom was really mad with Robert but she just said, "Let me give you a piece of advice. In the future, you need to call Robert's own mother and tell her what's going on because you need to talk to someone who loves him just as much as you do. If it were left up to me, I would move you and little Amelia back home with me and tell that bastard to stay out there with his other child." I told Mom I didn't know what I was going to do but I was going to stay home at least for tonight.

As soon as I hung up with Mom the phone rang. It was Robert's mother. She said Robert had just gotten there and she wanted to hear from me just what was going on. I explained to her that it was all about Teri. Then I couldn't believe what she told me.

"First of all, I've never liked Teri. She's a tramp and a troublemaker. That little girl is only trying to break you and Robert up and I'll be damned if I'm gonna let that happen, me."

Then she tried to convince me that Robert didn't like Teri either.

"How can you be so sure he doesn't like her? He has to have some feelings for the mother of his first child and I guess that's something that I'm just going to have to live with," I said as I started crying.

"The mother of his first WHAT?" she questioned. And before I could repeat myself she said, "You're the mother of his first kid. What are you talking about?" As I almost choked on the water I was drinking I told her I was talking about Teri and Daniel.

"Daniel!" she said in shock. "That's not Robert's baby. Teri was already pregnant when Robert met her and she's been a troublemaker from day one because she kept telling lies trying to get Robert to fight her ex-boyfriends. Robert knows that's not his baby."

"Are you sure?"

"Yeah, I'm damn sure that baby isn't his. He doesn't have our last name and you know how this family here loves kids. Don't you think that if he were my grandson he would be here all the time and I would have his pictures all over like I have my other grandkids? Now, have you ever seen that baby over here?"

"No, but you do have his pictures hung up."

"His pictures hung up where? Not here. There are no pictures of that boy here in *this* house."

"Yes there are. Robert showed me his pictures there."

Then she called Robert in the room.

"What's this shit about telling Cassandra that Daniel's your son? Boy, are you crazy? I told her that Teri's nothing but a troublemaker and I'll be damned if I'm gonna let that little tramp come between you and Cassandra. Why did you tell Cassandra that, her? You guys have that baby at home and that's where your ass needs to be, at home with your family."

Then Robert got on the phone and said, "I'm on my way home."

I said, "okay," and hung up.

When Robert got home he looked like a sad little puppy. His eyes were really red. I'm sure he had been crying too. But that's good for him. I just sat on the couch playing with Amelia and pretended not to look at him. After a few minutes he came over to the couch, took my hand, kissed it, then asked me to marry him.

"Marry you? You didn't sound like you wanted to marry me when you were on the phone a little while ago."

"Cassandra, I'm really sorry. I will never talk to Teri again because I don't ever want to lose you."

"So is Daniel yours or not?"

"He's not mine."

"Then why did you tell me that?"

"I don't know."

"You had to have a reason. You keep telling me you love me but you keep lying to me. First you lied about not being able to have children. Now this. So how many more lies have you told me?"

"I told you why I said that. I said it because I wanted us to be together forever. I wanted you to have my baby."

"So how many more lies have you told me?" I repeated.

"None. Can we just forget about this and start over from here?"

"We can try, but if you ever talk to Teri again it's over and I mean it."

"So now will you marry me?"

"No. Good night, Robert."

That night Robert wanted to have sex, so we did, but I really wasn't into it. I just did it to make him happy. I soon forgave Robert and we appeared to be really happy. Anything I wanted Robert would say, "go get it." Anything I wanted to do he would say, "let's do it." And anywhere I wanted to go he would say, "let's go." We did everything together. Whenever we weren't working you would find the three of us together. In fact, we soon earned the reputation of being called the three musketeers.

Then one day out of the blue I got another surprise. Marcus' sister called me. Remember Marcus? Well, his sister told me that he had been trying to get in touch with me but she didn't want to give him my number because she didn't want to start any trouble between Robert and me. I told her that Robert and I had our ups and downs but we were doing okay. Then she asked if it was okay to put Marcus on the phone and since Robert was standing right there, I asked him if it was okay if I talked to Marcus for minute.

"Go right ahead. I can't tell you what to do. You've probably been talkin' to him all along."

"What are you talking about? I haven't seen or heard from Marcus in about two years. I haven't seen him since high school. So do you mind or not?"

"No, go right ahead."

So I told Marcus' sister to put him on the phone and of course Robert stayed in the room so he could hear everything I said. But unlike him, I didn't have anything to hide. Marcus and I talked for a couple of minutes and he asked me how my daughter and the rest of the family were. Then he asked me if he could come over. I wasn't quite sure what he wanted or what he was actually asking me. I didn't know if he wanted to come and see me or if he wanted to come over and meet Robert. So I didn't give him a chance to say it was just me he wanted to see. I said, "Sure you can come over and meet my husband."

"Your husband? I didn't know you had gotten married."

"Well actually I'm not married yet but I probably will be

soon." Then I looked at Robert and he had a really big smile on his face. Then I asked him if it were okay if Marcus came over and met him and he said fine. So I gave Marcus my address and he came right over. I didn't realize Marcus was talking about coming over so soon.

Marcus was at my door in a matter of minutes. I introduced him to Robert and they shook hands. Marcus said, "I just wanted to meet the young man that makes Cassandra happy. You know she means a lot to me. She's like one of my sisters." And then, almost in a threatening voice, Marcus said, "And if anything ever happens to Cassandra you'll have to answer to me." Robert told Marcus he loved me and would never hurt me. So the two of them shook hands again and Marcus left.

As soon as I got a chance I called Marcus' sister back and told her about the two of them meeting. I told her that Marcus looked really nice, and that he looked like he had been working out quite a bit. Then she asked if Marcus had told me he'd been in jail.

"In jail?" I said.

"Yeah, he just got out a few days ago."

"In jail for what?"

"You mean you didn't see it in the paper when he was arrested for robbery?

"No! I know you're not serious."

"Yes I am. He tried to rob a store to support his drug habit but the storeowner hit him over the head with the butt of his gun and he got caught. He was in jail for a year and just got out."

"But I thought he got a baseball scholarship and had gone away to college."

"He did get a scholarship and was doing pretty well, but during one of his breaks at school he came back home and started hanging around the wrong crowd and got sucked in."

"I still can't believe it. Jail? Drugs?"

"But he's okay now. He's not on drugs and he got himself together and he looks nice now. You even said it yourself that he looks really good. You see he's so buff now."

"Well, yes, he is, but I didn't know he got that way by working out in jail."

"So now you're going to stereotype him too just because he's been in jail? You know that almost every black guy our age has either been in jail or is still there now. Or are you that naïve too?"

"No, I'm just really shocked that Marcus did what he did. I'm not stereotyping him at all. I still care about Marcus and I'm sure he knows that. Just like I know he still cares about me."

When Robert got back from the store I told him what I had just found out. Then he said, "Oh, so your old boyfriend is a convict. I knew there was somethin' I didn't like about him. I don't want him over here again."

"Well, if you suspected something about him, you should have pointed it out then, or at least said something to me. And you don't have to worry about him coming over again because it's not like he was coming over here to be with me. He had something he wanted to say and he said it. He has his life and I have mine."

"Just make sure that convict doesn't come over here again."

"Can we just drop it? I don't even know why I told you in the first place."

THE DISEASE

Robert and I continued working and spending lots of time with little Amelia. Over the course of the next few years we even managed to save a little money. Actually, I'd been saving a little of my own money all along. Especially after the Robert and Teri incident. No one knew about my personal savings account except my mom. I used to give her money to keep, or hold, or put in an account for me to save for a rainy day like she and my dad had taught me.

Then one day Robert asked me the question he had asked me over a hundred times before. Would I marry him? When I told him yes, you could imagine his shock.

"You will?"

"Yes, why not?"

"What about some rings and what about a weddin'?" Robert said.

"Well I don't really want a big wedding. As far as I'm concerned, we can just go to the courthouse and do it. And as far as some rings, I don't want anything fancy. We can go to the jewelry store downtown and pick out something."

"Okay, when do you want to go? Today?"

"I don't care. Let's just do it."

So we went to a local jewelry store and I picked out two simple wedding bands and Robert said they were fine with him. We put them on layaway and got them out three months later. Then I called the courthouse to see what we needed to do. We went to get our blood test done and went to the courthouse to get a marriage license. Now it was just a matter of picking out a date. Valentine's Day was the following week, so I told

Robert we should do it then. But he knew I didn't want anything fancy. Not a fancy dress, not a fancy wedding, and not a fancy reception.

Actually I didn't want a reception at all. Robert knew I was still shy and did not like to be around crowds. And I had already given up on my old dream of having this big fancy wedding. I guess I was perfectly content with the way things were. I felt like Robert and I were already married. I felt like we already had a commitment. I knew I would never mess around on Robert and I knew he would never mess around me. Everything I had been forced into seemed to be working out okay; motherhood and the whole family thing. But to make Robert happy, I agreed to legalize everything and become his wife.

I called the courthouse and made all of the arrangements. Valentine's Day it was. When I told my mom we were going to get married she didn't seem too enthused. In fact, she said she wouldn't be attending the wedding. Although this hurt me, Mom's reaction didn't surprise me because Mom hated to be around crowds too, regardless of the occasion, and I understood that.

When Robert told his family, everyone was excited and happy for us. However, they wanted us to have a really big wedding and reception but I declined. I told them of our plans to be married next week in the county building and they respected my wishes, but Robert's mom insisted on giving us a small reception at her house. I told her that was fine as long as it was a small one.

That next Tuesday Robert and I, and let's not forget about our little flower girl Amelia, were followed by my dad and my sisters to the county building where Robert's dad and one of his sisters were waiting. We went into the judges' chambers and in a matter of about two minutes we were married. As soon as I said, "I do" I started crying. Then Robert's father said, "I don't know what you're crying for now, it's too late to change your mind. You should have cried before you said I do." Then everyone laughed and so did I. I really don't know what I was crying for, nervousness I guess.

Then we all went to Robert's parents' house for a very small, intimate reception. When Robert and I cut the first piece of cake, Robert fed me a piece then everyone kept telling me to smash a piece in his face. But being Little Miss Proper, I fed Robert a piece of cake from my fork.

At my request we didn't stay at the reception long. I was already getting nervous being in a small crowd and being the center of attention. That wasn't my style and I was feeling quite uncomfortable. So I told Robert I was ready to get Amelia so we could go home. No one could believe we didn't have any honeymooners' plans but we really didn't. Robert had left everything up to me and I would have been perfectly happy with the three of us going home and playing Candy Land, which was Amelia's favorite game. To me, this was just another day, but Robert's mom insisted on keeping Amelia overnight, so I agreed.

When Robert and I got home all of a sudden he didn't need me to make all of our decisions. He seemed to have had an agenda of his own. And playing Candy Land certainly wasn't part of it. Or then again, maybe he did get some of his ideas from Candy Land. For instance, there was this lollipop game he wanted to play. And then he wanted to pretend we were the game pieces, which were all edible.

I think Robert has been storing up these ideas because up until now I thought I was happy with our sex life even though it was always the same old thing and the same old way. But tonight I realized what we had been missing. So I guess I really wasn't happy with our sex life after all. I was just content. Now I was happy.

That night, not only was Robert full of sex surprises but he also surprised me by telling me he wanted me to stop taking my birth control pills because he wanted us to have another baby. I told Robert I would think about it. But in reality, I knew I didn't really need to think about it because we were extremely fortunate that things had turned out the way they had. There were not too many teenage parents who stayed together. And there were not too many teenage parents that got decent jobs and kept them. So, I didn't want to rock the boat. Things were going good. However, I did tell Robert that it was time we bought a house and he said, "Okay," as usual. So I told my mom the next day and we started looking.

I really didn't know what I was looking for in a house and since it didn't matter to Robert, I guess I was on my own in deciding what to buy. I saw this one house that didn't look too bad on the outside so my mom called the realtor and made an appointment for us to see it. The realtor was really nice. She was black and not too much older than Robert and me. In fact, I went to school with her brother. As we started talking and getting to know each other she seemed like she was one of my sisters. I told her I was really interested in the house and asked what I needed to do to buy it. I told her Robert and I had saved about three thousand dollars and I told her I had about three thousand of my own money. She said she could get us in that house for less than six thousand dollars down and our monthly payments would be just a little more than what we were paying for rent. I was really excited and couldn't wait to show Robert the house.

When Robert saw the house he said it was nice and as long as I thought we could afford it, it was okay with him. Actually that was getting kind of old. Robert didn't seem to ever make any decisions. He always left everything up to me. But I guess that was good in a way because that was how I was able to save money of my own. And I certainly didn't want him to know that I had my own stash. So, I told Robert my mom would be loaning us anything over the three thousand we had saved together. And again he said, "okay." He didn't even want to know how we would be paying her back. He just knew I would take care of it. So my mom came with us to the real estate office to sign all of our loan papers. It seems like it took hours signing everything and when we finally got through I looked at Robert and cried and gave him a hug. I don't know why I was so emotional. The realtor and my mom told us how proud they were of us, to be buying a house at such a young age.

After we told the rest of the family and our friends about

what we had done, almost everyone seemed to be happy and proud of us, but a couple of our friends seemed like they started to get jealous. I don't know why they were feeling that way because we weren't trying to out do anyone. It just happened to be the right time for us.

One of those jealous friends was a long time friend of Robert's. They had been best friends since kindergarten. Once we moved into our new home things started to change. Almost immediately this friend told Robert he needed a place to stay for about two weeks so Robert asked me if it were okay for him to stay in our extra bedroom and I said sure. That turned out to be our first mistake after buying our home.

This friend not only moved in our house but he also tried to make his moves on me. One evening when Robert was at work this friend asked me if he could tell me something confidential and I said sure. He started telling me that he was attracted to me and that he had always been attracted to me even before Robert and I got married. I didn't know what to say because this was Robert's best friend. I tried to play it off so I told him I was flattered. Then he told me that I should be with him and that Robert didn't deserve me.

"What do you mean he doesn't deserve me? We have each other."

"You really don't have a clue do you? But you'll find out soon enough."

"I don't have a clue about what? What's going on?"

"Do you know that people in Antioch are making bets on your marriage? Everybody knows you're going to leave Robert."

"What are you talking about? And who's betting my marriage is going to fail? You don't know what you're talking about."

"Didn't Robert ask you recently to have another baby?"

"Yes, but what does that have to do with anything?"

"Well, all I'm saying is that Robert wants to get you pregnant because he's scared you're gonna leave him. So he figures if you have another baby that will keep you guys together longer."

"I don't believe you. And if Robert is supposed to be your friend why are you telling me this?"

"Because he doesn't deserve you. You're too good for him."

"And I guess I'm just perfect for you then."

"Well, I'm not sayin' nothing. You'll see."

"I think it's time for you to leave. You need to get your things and go."

"I was leaving today anyway, but don't be mad with me 'cause I'm only trying to help you."

"Thanks, but I don't need your help. Robert and I are doing just fine, thank you."

As soon as this so-called friend left I called Robert's mother and told her what he had said. At first she said she couldn't believe it either because he and Robert had been friends for so long. Then she told me to expect things like this to happen because Robert and I were doing so much better than our friends and to expect some of them to try to start things because they were jealous.

Then I called my own mom and told her what this friend had said. She suggested I tell Robert and to also keep my eyes open. She reminded me of how Robert had lied to me to get me pregnant the first time. I really didn't want to believe Robert's friend but Robert had to have told him about how he wanted another child. Now I was more convinced than ever. I was not having another child anytime in the near future, and probably not ever.

When Robert came home from work I told him what his friend had said. He played everything off by saying that it didn't surprise him because this friend had always been jealous of him, even while they were boys growing up. When I told Robert how he tried to come on to me, he said he knew I would never fall for him so he had nothing to worry about. He said it wasn't the first time they had tried to take the other one's girlfriend. I was kind of disappointed in the way that Robert handled the whole thing. I wanted him to say he was giving up his friendship with this person and that he was going to tell him off but he didn't do that either. So I decided to drop the whole thing because I had a so-called friend that stopped calling so much because she was jealous too.

Robert continued asking me to stop taking my birth control pills but I kept saying no. Then, one time I forgot to take them for two days in a row. The following month my body started doing some strange things. I missed my period and I started having this discharge. When this started happening I called Robert's mother and told her what was going on. She was happy. She said that if she were going to get another grandchild she was glad it was Robert's and mine. I told her not to jump the gun. I really didn't feel pregnant and Lord knows I didn't want another baby. I got so nervous that I didn't want to take a pregnancy test because I was afraid of the results.

When Robert came home I told him how I was feeling but he didn't seem too happy. I asked him what was wrong but he kept telling me nothing. I thought he would be ecstatic at the news that I might be pregnant but he wasn't. He asked if I already had a test done and I told him no, I was going to wait a few days to see if the signs went away. All Robert had to say was, "okay."

A couple of days went by and one evening when Robert came home from work he asked me if I had been to the doctor's yet and I told him, "No, not yet."

"Well, I think you should go some time soon."

"Why? If I'm pregnant it's not going to make too much difference whether I go now or next week."

"I think you should go as soon as possible and see what they say."

I could tell something was wrong because Robert wasn't excited at all. I wasn't excited at first either but I'd kind of psyched myself into thinking that being pregnant wasn't that bad of a thing. After all, we were married now and Amelia was already five years old. I guessed it was not that bad of a time, I thought. We could have one more baby and that would be it. No more. I was trying really hard to convince myself that being pregnant was not the end of the world. So I promised Robert that I would go to the doctor's tomorrow after work.

I went to the hospital the next day and advised the nurse of my symptoms. She said she would be doing a few tests including a pregnancy one and would have the results back the next day. But by the time I got home there was already a message on the answering machine from the nurse telling me I needed to come back in so I did. When I got there the doctor said he wanted to speak to me. I went in his office and he told me first of all that I wasn't pregnant and what a big relief I felt. "So what's wrong?" I asked the doctor. Then he started asking me questions like how many sexual partners I had. "Just one. My husband is the only man I've ever had sex with." Then the doctor asked me what would I do if I had a venereal disease.

"A what?"

"A venereal disease. You tested positive for gonorrhea."

I started crying, "you're not serious."

"Unfortunately I am very serious. But the somewhat good news is that we caught it in its early stage and I can give you a large dose of penicillin and that should clear it right up. I know you have a lot to think about right now but I need to let you know that once you have contracted gonorrhea or just about any other venereal disease, your body is very susceptible to contracting other diseases. So I suggest in the future that you and your partner at lease use a condom."

"But I've only been with my husband," I cried to the doctor.

"Well, then you really do have a lot to think about. Do you know if he's been treated yet?"

"No. I'm not sure."

As you can imagine, I left the hospital in quite a rage. I don't know how I made it home; I could hardly see straight. All kind of thoughts went through my mind. Who was she? Who had he been fucking? So that's what Robert's friend was trying to tell me. He'd known all along. I hated Robert. How could he do this to me? How could he do this to our family? I thought we had more than the average twenty-three and twenty-four year old, but we didn't have shit. We were no better than anyone else. I hated that bastard. And to make matters worse, when

I got home I called Robert's mother to give her the news and the first thing out of her mouth was, "I know my son hasn't been messing around, him. You were the one that said you were having female problems. He hasn't complained of any problems and besides you know where Robert is all the time. If he's not at work and he's not here, then he's right there with you and little Amelia. So if he does have anything he must have gotten it from you."

I couldn't believe that bitch. Robert was the first and only boy I'd ever had sex with and now she was accusing me. But of course she had to take up for her precious little boy. After all, he was her only son. That's her baby. So I just hung up on her. That fucking bastard, I can't wait for him to come home.

When I heard his car in the driveway I met him at the door.

"You liar! Who is she?"

"Who is who?"

"Don't play stupid. You know what the fuck I'm talking about." Then Robert grabbed my arm and yelled at me and told me I better not ever cuss at him again.

"So you've been to the doctor's? Do you have it?" he said.

"I shouldn't have anything. So who's the bitch you've been fucking? I hate you! How could you do this to me?" Then all of a sudden it seemed like I had said all of this before. I did! He's been lying to me from day one. "How could you do this to us? What about Amelia? What about our family?" Then Robert started crying too.

"I'm really sorry. I am so sorry I hurt you. Please don't leave me."

"Don't leave you? You're the one that left. Who is she, Teri?"

"No it wasn't Teri."

"Well who was it then? I want to know."

"I'd rather not talk about it right now."

"Well that's too bad. Who is she? I want to know now!"

Then after a moment of silence Robert said, "Do you remember last month when I told you my job sent me and two other guys to San Jose to pick up some supplies?"

"Yeah."

"Well we drove this big truck down there and on our way the two guys in the front of the truck was doin' some cocaine and then they pulled over to pick up this hitchhiker and before she got in the truck she asked them how could she repay them for the ride and she said she didn't have any money. Then they told her she could get in the back of the truck with them. So they all got in the back of the truck where I was and first the driver fucked her and then the other guy did her and then they kept tellin' me it was my turn. I kept tellin' them that I wasn't gonna do it but they kept pressurin' me so I did it too."

"You're so stupid. You threw our marriage away on a fucking hitchhiker? So what did she look like? Was she black? Was it good?"

"No she was white and I don't want to talk about it any more."

"You're so stupid. I hate you. I'm filing for a divorce."

"Please Cassandra, please don't leave me. I made a mistake. I'm sorry. I promise I will never do anythin' so crazy again in my life. That was just crazy of me. I don't know why I did it."

"So do the other guys have gonorrhea too?"

"I don't know. I don't want to talk about it."

"So if you fucked her and got gonorrhea she could also be pregnant. Did you ever think about that?"

"I told you that I don't want to talk about it any more."

"Well, you don't have to talk about it because tomorrow I'm going to file for divorce. So this is what your friend was talking about. That's why people have been betting on our marriage. It was only a matter of time before I found out. Well I guess whoever bet our marriage would fail can soon collect what they've got coming to them."

Then I went to the bathroom and since Robert wanted to follow me around the house that evening I gave him something to see. I took off my wedding band and flushed it down the toilet. When Robert saw me do this he grabbed my arms and he slapped me. So I started crying even louder and said, "And now you're a wife beater too."

The next day I called in sick. While I was at home I called several attorneys' offices. I couldn't believe how expensive it was to file for divorce. But I did finally find a paralegal service that wouldn't charge much to type up the papers but the only catch was that Robert and I would have to agree on everything because she couldn't represent either one of us in court. Since I had just spent all of my money on the down payment for the house, I was broke so I couldn't afford an attorney; the paralegal was my only choice. When Robert got home I told him how expensive it would be trying to hire an attorney so he agreed we could settle everything our selves and just pay the paralegal.

GUN SHOTS

During the next few months Robert and I didn't say much to each other but he sure had nerves because he would still ask me for sex. But I turned him down most of the time. The times that I did give in I didn't enjoy it because all I could think about was his being with another girl. Whenever we did have sex I would cry just thinking about it. All kinds of thoughts would go through my mind. Somewhere deep down inside I really didn't want a divorce. I guess I still loved him. But how could I ever trust him?

Is it possible he just made one mistake and he won't do it again? Divorcing him made me feel like a failure. I felt like I would be letting all young couples down. Robert and I would become just part of another statistic that says we were too young to have a baby and get married in the first place. I could no longer be a role model for other young mothers. And all because of Robert. I hated him. But if I hated him so much why was I already missing him. I don't think Robert would ever know how much I loved him and how much he had hurt me.

About four months after we filed for divorce we got a letter stating that our divorce could not be granted because we were still living together. I couldn't believe it. No one had told me we couldn't live together. We were only going to be there together until the divorce was final and then we were going to put the house up for sale and go our separate ways. Robert was happy the divorce didn't go through. So now what do I do? Was this a sign trying to tell me we should stay together? I don't know. I was so confused. I wished I were a teenager again. I didn't like this adult stuff but I guessed there was no going back. The decision was all mine.

One evening I got a baby sitter for Amelia and I told Robert I wanted to talk to him about my decision. I suggested we have dinner first, so we got out of the house and went to a nice restaurant. All throughout dinner I kept looking at Robert and trying to tell him what I decided but somehow I could not get the words out. He kept kissing my hand telling me how pretty I was and how much he loved me. And he kept telling me he didn't want to lose Amelia and me. So I decided to wait until we got home to tell him what I had decided.

When we got home for once I really shocked Robert. I started by taking his hand and leading him into our bedroom. Once we were there I made him sit on the bed and then I sat on top of him as I unbuttoned his shirt. Then I gently pushed his shoulders back, laying him on the bed. When he tried to ask me what was I doing I would give him a very passionate kiss to shut him up. Then I unbuckled his belt and unzipped his pants. He was all too eager to help me take his pants off. Then to his surprise I took off my dress in which I didn't have anything on underneath it. Then I sat on top of him and told him how much I loved him and didn't want to lose him either. Then I let my hair down and gave him another passionate kiss and he rolled me over and told me how much he loved me too as he promised he would never hurt me again. We had a beautiful night. Little did I know that was the first and the last of the beautiful nights.

For the next few months I tried really hard to forgive and forget what Robert had done. But every time we had sex I couldn't help but think about him being with someone else. And not only being with someone else, but also getting gonorrhea from her. So whenever we had sex I would cry. I would try really hard not to think about the past but I did anyway. Soon, Robert started getting agitated by my crying. He would tell me to just shut up because it was over and done with. He also would tell me that if it meant that much to me I should go out and have an affair too, and then I would see how it didn't mean anything to him and we would be even. I told him I wasn't trying to get even with him and besides two wrongs don't make a right. But Robert kept getting frustrated with my crying and I couldn't do anything to control it. I needed help.

When I suggested to Robert that we get counseling he refused. He said we couldn't tell a counselor what had happened because he and the other two guys could be charged with rape.

"Rape! What do you mean rape? I thought you said it was her idea. She volunteered you said."

"She did, but I don't want to talk about it."

"Well, if she did, then it wouldn't be considered rape and besides you said you guys didn't know who she was, so how can she press charges if she doesn't know who you are?"

"Will you just drop it? You need to go and have an affair with somebody so you can stop bringin' this up. Because I'm tellin' you now if you're gonna cry every time we make love then I don't want to be here. We're just gonna have to break up."

"Oh so now it's my fault? I'm sorry if I can't handle the fact that my husband, the person who I thought I would spend the rest of my life with, cheated on me."

"I didn't cheat on you. It only happened one time and it was a mistake."

"It doesn't matter how many times it happened. It happened at least once and *you* got gonorrhea. And not only that, but *you* brought it home. So don't even try to make it seem like it's *my* fault. So if you can't deal with me crying then maybe we should break up." Then we both just turned over and went to sleep.

That weekend Robert said he couldn't take it any more so he spent the night at his parents' house. So I decided to go for a drive. I took Amelia to the sitter's house and I drove to Fremont. While in Fremont I saw a Ford dealership so I decided to stop. Not only did I stop but I also bought a brand new convertible mustang that I saw on the showroom floor. I really didn't have any intentions on driving to Fremont and buying a new car. I guess I did it just to show Robert how I didn't need him. After all, I made more money than he did anyway and I had built my own savings back up.

That evening Robert came over just to tell me how he was going out with his friends, I mean, his so-called friends. I guess he was trying to make me jealous. So I told him to have fun but before he left I told him to look in the garage to see what I had bought. When he saw my new car he was shocked. He told me he would be back over tomorrow so we could talk.

The next day I took Amelia to the gas station with me, and guess whom I saw. Marcus. I couldn't believe it. I didn't even recognize him at first but he noticed me. He came over to my car and gave me a big hug. I asked him where he had been because I hadn't seen him since that time he came to my apartment and that had been about five years ago. He asked me where Robert was and I briefly told him what had happened.

"I told that fool if he ever hurt you I would fuck him up. Where is he?"

"I don't know where he is right now but he's supposed to come over later."

"So where do you live now? I heard you guys bought a house."

"I'm not going to tell you where I live."

And just then one of my neighbors drove up the street.

"Do you know him?" I asked Marcus. I figured he might know him because my neighbor had a reputation of selling drugs.

"Yeah, that's one of my partners."

"Well, I live next door to him and that's all you need to know."

"So when are you going out with me, since you and that nut aren't together any more. Let's go to the fair today. We can take your daughter if you want to."

"How about if I go and see if my mom will keep her for a couple of hours and then I'll call you."

"Okay, I'll see you later, sweetheart."

I took Amelia to my mom's and she actually volunteered to keep her for a little while, which was a switch. So I called over to Marcus' sister's house and he was there. He told me to pick him up at his sister's who lived only a few blocks away from my mom, so I did. Marcus and I talked about the times when we were in school. And I just had to mention that we had children the same age, and how his daughter's mother would probably have a fit if she knew we were spending the day together. You remember her, Rochelle, the one that I had a fight with in high school. Anyway, he told me that he and Rochelle never were together for any length of time. He said she now has three kids and that she's a crack head. So I asked him who the lady in his life was now and that's when he told me he was married.

Not only was he married, he was married to this woman who was twenty years older than we were and who had boys our age. He went on to tell me that they were married in name only and that he didn't spend much of his time at home. But of course I wanted to know why. I asked him what would happen if she saw us at the fair.

"If that stupid bitch sees us she better look the other way if she don't want to get her feelings hurt."

"If you feel that way then why are you with her?"

"That's all you need to know about me. What about you and that stupid nut you're with?"

"I don't want to talk about him any more either."

So we walked around the fair and Marcus was trying to pretend to be interested in the different attractions. Occasionally he would touch me on my butt or try to put his arms around me but with my little girlish smile I would tell him to stop. We walked around for a couple of hours and then he said he was ready to leave. I told Marcus I had a really nice time. It felt good to get out and not have to worry about my problems with Robert and I felt safe being with Marcus, just as I felt in high school. That is until everything went wrong after we left the fair.

On the way home Marcus asked me where was I going and I told him I was taking him back to sister's house. Then Marcus surprised me by what he said next.

"I'm not going back to her house yet." Then he looked at me and smiled. "We're going back to this motel that I know of. You're gonna finally give me what I've waited five years for." Then he touched me on my thigh and smiled even more.

"What are you talking about?" I said innocently, fearing that I already knew.

"You don't think I spent all day with you and I'm not gonna get something in return, do you?"

"Well, actually I thought we just spent the day together to keep each other company."

"Stop trying to act like you're innocent. You certainly can't use the excuse that you're still a virgin. You've been giving all my stuff to that stupid mutha fucker Robert and you know I'm the one you need to be with. Turn at the next exit. We're going over there."

Now I was really scared. Marcus was being really threatening. He had never used that tone of voice before with me. When I pulled into the motel parking lot I asked Marcus, "What are we doing? After all, we are both still married."

"I told you me and that stupid bitch aren't together and you don't need to be with Robert either." Then he looked at me and smiled as he told me to stop stalling and get out of the car so I did. Then he pulled me by the hand and went to the check-in desk. The clerk at the desk acted as if he knew Marcus personally. He just took his money and gave him a key. What have I gotten myself into? I certainly had not planned on this. But I have to admit I had always wanted to know what Marcus was like in bed. But if I weren't so afraid I definitely wouldn't have been there. I'm not sure what I was so afraid of. I knew Marcus would never in his life physically hurt me. When I turned around Marcus was completely undressed.

"Come on baby, take your clothes off."

So with his help I did. Then he lay me down on the bed and got on top of me. He was pumping up and down and telling me how good I felt and how he still loved me; however, I didn't feel a thing. As far as I knew he didn't even have a dick. And if he did, I didn't know where it was. I couldn't believe we'd waited years for this. I really didn't know what he thought he was doing, but whatever it was he was happy and I was glad of that. Talk about short and boring, I wouldn't have even had enough time for a V-8. So he got what he wanted and I didn't have to give up anything. So I thought, today wasn't so bad after all, but I was wrong because what happened that evening is something I hope no one will ever have to experience. It was an evening I will never forget.

When I got to Marcus' sister's house she was standing outside. She came over to my car and said that Robert had driven up the street about five times in the last half-hour. So I told Marcus to hurry up and get out of my car so I could go home. Right after Marcus got out and went inside Robert drove by again. I told Marcus' sister I would talk to her later and I made a u-turn and followed Robert home.

When I got home Robert opened the garage door and pulled his Camaro inside and instead of me pulling in the garage next to him I pulled in the driveway. Robert got out of his car and was walking towards mine and just as I opened my door to get out I heard this voice saying "hi" to Robert. I couldn't believe it. It was Marcus.

"Hi Robert. You remember me?"

"No. Who are you?"

Then Marcus walked towards Robert trying to shake his hand as he said, "I'm Cassandra's old friend Marcus. I met you at you guys' apartment a few years ago." But instead of Robert walking towards him to shake his hand, he turned around and went to the driver's side of his car and pulled out a machete and said, "Get off my property."

I was totally shocked. I asked Robert what was he doing and then Marcus told me to stay out of it.

"Get off my property, man!"

"What's with the machete? I just came over here to see how you and Cassandra were doing. So what's your problem?"

"You know damn well what's my problem. You just got out of jail and you're already startin' shit; goin' around town tellin' people that Amelia is your daughter and shit."

This was news to me so I asked Robert what was he talking about and again Marcus told me to stay out of it.

"Marcus, I don't know what's going on between you two but why don't you just leave," I said. But Marcus just stood there in the middle of the driveway with his arms wide open inviting Robert to use the machete.

"If you're a bad man, you would use that machete. But you're just a punk-ass nigga 'cause you're just standing there holding it like a little bitch."

I was standing there so scared of what was going to happen that I nearly used the bathroom on myself. I kept telling Marcus the same thing that Robert was telling him but he didn't seem to hear me. I kept telling him to just leave. Then I started crying and begging him to leave. Then he asked me if I was going to be okay and I told him yes, just go. Then he finally started slowly walking backwards out of the driveway but not without telling Robert exactly what he thought of him. Then Robert slowly walked towards him saying a few words too and waiving the machete in his hand.

When Marcus got out of site Robert grabbed me by my shirt and threw me up against the back of his car but this time the machete was directed towards me. I started screaming and the first words out of his mouth were why did I set him up.

"Set you up? What are you talking about?"

"I saw that nigga get out of your car. Why did you bring him here?"

"I didn't bring him here. I don't know where he came from. I was in my car by myself."

"Don't lie to me, bitch."

Then Robert grabbed my hair with one hand and put the machete up to my neck with the other hand. As I was screaming he kept telling me that he should just kill me.

"Stop screamin', bitch. I should kill your ass right here. And Marcus could raise your damn daughter 'cause I know she's his anyway."

"She's not his. She's your daughter. You can get a blood test if you want to."

"If she's not his, why did you just try to have me set up? Where's your nigga now? I'll tell you where he is, he got scared and left you behind, and you want a man like that?"

"No, I don't want him. I want you." Even though I was

lying I needed to tell him just what he wanted to hear. But Robert wasn't buying anything I was saying. He kept saying that I set him up. Then he started telling me about a mutual friend that he and Marcus had that was going around town saying that Amelia was Marcus' daughter. I kept trying to tell him it was all a lie and that I didn't even know whom this person was that was a mutual friend of theirs. But Robert kept banging my head up against his car and as he held the machete to my neck he kept saying he was going to kill me. So I kept screaming and he kept telling me to be quiet. Then he finally pulled my shirt and snatched me away from the car and told me to get my ass away from him before he killed me. So I did just that. I started walking out of the driveway when I noticed my car door was still open and my purse was still inside. So I asked Robert if I could just get my purse. You know black women can't go anywhere without their purse, but he told me to just get my ass out of his sight, so I kept walking. Then I thought, "Who cares about a damned purse." I was barely walking away with my life. But that wasn't the end of the evening.

I didn't know where I was walking. By now, it was starting to get dark and my mom was probably wondering where I was. There was a seven eleven a few blocks away, so I guessed I could go there and call my mom. But just as I got from in front of my house, I saw this person walking really fast towards me, and as he got closer I saw it was Marcus. He stopped me and said he heard me screaming. Then he looked at my hair and my face and saw that I was crying and he asked me if I was hurt but I guess I was too shaken and nervous to say anything. Then he saw my car door still open and asked me where was I going and where my purse was. I told him it was still in the car and that Robert wouldn't let me get it. Then he told me to go and wait next door and he kept walking towards my house.

Then the next thing I knew I heard a gun shot and as I screamed and almost fainted, from out of nowhere it seems, one of the guys next door caught me as I started to fall to the ground.

Then I said, "Who has a gun?" I didn't know if Robert

had a gun or if Marcus had a gun. And the guy next door said, "Shhhh." Then there was another gunshot and I screamed again. Then my neighbor called me by my name and told me it was going to be okay. I don't know how he knew my name. I didn't know his name; I just knew he lived next door. Then he asked me to go and wait inside of his house but I said, "No that's okay." Then there was another gunshot and I sort of fell into his arms. Then he walked me into his garage where there were about four of five other guys standing inside. They were all talking about how crazy Marcus was. They were all agreeing he was crazy because they said he had just gotten out of prison and was on parole and now he's over there getting himself in trouble again. I knew then Marcus had the gun but I wondered if Robert had one too. I didn't think Robert owned a gun but then again I didn't know he had a machete either.

Then my neighbor told me that he didn't know that I was the girl Marcus always talked about. He told me that Marcus would do anything for me. Then one of the other guys said, "Marcus is just fucking crazy and can't nobody tell him anything. He's hard headed." Then there was another gunshot and I just wanted to die. Two guys could be over there dead all because of me. Then all of a sudden Marcus came busting in the garage door, handed me my purse, and one of the guys asked him if he killed that "nigga." And as I could barely breathe, he said, "No, I just scared him a little bit."

I was standing there shaking, wondering what that meant. Then Robert flew by in his car making skid marks. "See, there he goes now," Marcus said. "I told you I just scared that punk but I should have killed him. If he wasn't the father of your little girl, I would have fucked him up." Then Marcus said, "You know the cops will be around here any minute so why don't you guys give me all of your dope so only one person goes down, 'cause you know they can't stand my ass anyway."

Then I thought, "What have I gotten myself into? I'm in the garage of a dope house with five guys, all of which probably have criminal records. Hell, some of them might even be wanted. And not only that, there was just a shooting at my house and my car is the only one there."

Then one of the guys said, "Shut up talking about some dope. Don't nobody have any dope around here," he said as he looked at me. Then Marcus took something out of his sock and put it in my pocket and said, "Keep this for me baby," and he left. He left me standing there with tears rolling down my face wondering how I got myself into this mess. Am I going to jail? Will I ever see my daughter again? What am I going to do with whatever it was that Marcus put in my pocket? Was I going to snitch? Was everybody going to jail because I had drugs on me?

Then sure enough the police pulled up and I got more nervous. One officer got out of the car and asked the guy next door what was going on and he said he didn't know. Then the officer said he got a report of gunshots in this area. My neighbor then said he heard them too and said he thought they were coming from over there, as he pointed in the direction of my house. So the police told him he better not be lying and they drove in that direction. Then Marcus' sister pulled up in my neighbor's driveway and said Marcus told her to come and pick me up and bring me back to her house. When we got to her house Marcus was there and so was his wife. Marcus' sister kept asking me questions trying to get my side of the story because there was no telling what story Marcus had told them. Then Marcus' wife stood up from the other side of the room and yelled at me saying, "What the fuck is goin' on? My husband came in here ten minutes ago and told me his ass was in trouble and now his ex-girlfriend show up in my sister-in-law's house and come to find out the two of you are involved in this shit together. What the fuck's goin' on?"

I just looked at her because I wasn't in the mood. I don't know why Marcus wanted me to come here in the first place so I told her she needed to ask her husband. Then she hollered, "I'm askin' you, bitch." Then Marcus jumped in her face and told her I was his first real love and he would do anything for me even if it meant "killin' some nigga." Then he went on to tell her that I hadn't disrespected her so he suggested she stop disrespecting me. He also reminded her that my name was Cassandra and not "bitch." Then he told her if anyone was a bitch it was her and that she was just jealous that I looked better than she did with her "skeezer looking ass." Then she just started laughing and said, "Shut up Marcus." But from then on she had nothing else to say to me.

Then Marcus came over to me and put his arm around my shoulder and asked if I were okay. Even though I was still shaking I said, "Yeah, I'm okay." Then I told him I was ready to go to my mom's house and he said okay and not to worry about anything and that he would call and check on me tomorrow. So his sister drove me to my mom's house. I told his sister I couldn't believe that after everything that had just happened, Marcus seemed so calm. He didn't seem like he was worried about anything but me. She agreed and said, "Yeah, I already know. Marcus always tells us how he will always love you."

Even though it was dark outside, when we got to my mom's house she was standing in the driveway with her purse in her hand like she was getting ready to go somewhere. As soon as I got out of the car she ran and hugged me and said that she was just going to look for me.

"Robert's mom just called me and said that Robert was in the hospital with a gunshot wound and that no one knew where you were. And you know that no one in his family has a car so she wanted me to go to the hospital and check on him thinking you were probably there too. So what in the hell is going on? What happened to your face? And what happened to your hair? Who did this to you?" But before I could answer her she said, "What are you trying to do, give me a heart attack or something? And what happened to Robert? Don't you think we should go check on him?"

But before I answered anything I asked her where my daughter was and she said Amelia was already asleep. Thank God, because I certainly didn't want her to hear what had happened or for her to see me like this.

Then Mom asked again, "Don't you think we should go and check on Robert?"

Then I started crying and sarcastically said, "Go check on Robert? I guess his mother didn't tell you that Robert was the one who did this to me, did she?"

"Robert did this you?"

"Uh huh. Robert beat me up and threatened to kill me with a machete but someone heard me screaming and came over and shot at Robert but I didn't know he was actually shot."

Then my mom almost passed out and I took her by the hand and told her I was sorry and we walked into the house so she could sit down.

"No, Robert's mother conveniently left that part out; that son of a bitch. And she's got her damn nerves asking me to go check on him and he did this to you. That mutha-fuckin' bastard. Hell no, I'm not going to check on him. Besides, you need to be in the hospital too. You look awful. I know you're hurting. Come on so I can take you to get checked out."

"No, I don't want to go to the hospital. I'll be okay. I just need to comb my hair and I'll be fine."

Then I tried to stand up and I felt really stiff and I guess Mom saw that.

"See, you can't even get up. Come on so I can take you to the hospital. Monica's back there in her room so she can watch Amelia."

Just then the phone rang and it was Robert's mother again. Apparently she asked Mom if she were going to check on Robert.

"Hell, no, I'm not going to check on him when Cassandra just came in here looking like she has just been in a fight with all the kids in the neighborhood and come to find out it was Robert that beat her up and tried to kill her."

Then I could hear Robert's mom screaming through the phone. She told my mom she didn't know I was hurt, and that Robert hadn't told her that. I told Mom that shouldn't be surprising because he lies about everything. Then my mom apologized for yelling but still told her no she wasn't going anywhere until she had taken me to the hospital. Just then I realized I still had whatever it was that Marcus had put in my pocket so I slowly stood up and went into the bathroom where I flushed whatever it was down the toilet without even looking at it. I conveniently left that part out when I was telling Mom what happened. Actually, I conveniently left out a lot. Although she kept asking a lot of questions, I kept my hands on my head and over my face as I kept crying. All I could think about was that Robert had just threatened to kill me and what would have happened to my daughter if he had. But since I was alive, what was going to happen to Marcus?

Then Mom asked me if I had made a police report against Robert and I told her "not yet." But as I sat there I realized that if I filed a police report against Robert I would have to tell them about Marcus and I knew he was on parole. And speaking of Robert, I didn't know if he were dead or alive. I was assuming he was alive because he left the house flying around the corner in his car. And besides, Marcus said he only scared him. He didn't say he shot him and I'm sure he would have told me if he did. But then again, maybe not, because I finally saw that Marcus would do anything to protect me. What was I going to do? What had I gotten myself into?

After I sat there a couple of hours just crying and thinking and thinking and crying, I finally asked Mom to call the hospital to see what had happened to Robert. They told her he had received stitches in his head and he would be released in a few hours. So I had Mom take me to my house to get my car before Robert was released. So we went to my house about four o'clock that morning. When I got there it seemed really creepy. The garage door was still open and so was my car door. I just jumped in my car, then let the garage door down and drove back to Mom's house. I was too scared to go inside. For all I knew, someone may have been in there.

THE THREATS

I called in sick from work the next couple of days and Amelia and I stayed at my mom's house. That Monday morning I called around trying to find an attorney so I could file for divorce, again. This time I wasn't going to deal with a paralegal. And I knew from experience that Robert and I had to be separated so I shouldn't have any problems this time. I also wanted a female attorney, someone that might be able to sympathize with what I was going through.

    I managed to scrape up fifteen hundred dollars, which was what this one attorney charged as a retainer fee. I met with her and told her everything that had happened and she agreed to take my case. She asked lots of questions like whether or not I wanted to keep the house and what type of visitation I wanted Robert to have. I told her I wanted this over as soon as possible and I didn't want a legal fight that would delay the progress of this divorce. So if Robert wanted the house he could have the house and everything in it. I just wanted to walk away with my daughter and a sound mind. She asked if I wanted to ask for alimony and I told her no. I could support myself but I did expect him to support his child, but if that became a big issue we could leave that alone too, I told her. I stressed to her that all I wanted was my daughter; nothing else was worth fighting for. She said she respected my decision and would type up the papers according to what I said but she advised me that if I changed my mind about anything, like keeping the house, just to let her know and she would make any necessary changes. I said okay and left her office.

    I stopped at a pay phone and called Robert's job just to

make sure he was there. Then I went to my house to pack some clothes. I guessed Amelia and I would be staying at Mom's house for a while. Shortly after I got home there was a knock on the door. I was so scared. I crept to the front window and saw that there was a police car. Now what do I do? What do they want? Am I going to get arrested for something? They knew someone was here because I left my car parked in the driveway. So I took a deep breath and opened the door.

"Can I help you?"

"Are you Cassandra?"

"Yes, what can I do for you?"

"Were you aware there was a shooting here the other night?"

"Yes."

"We have a search warrant to search your garage so we can start our investigation."

So I opened the garage door for them. I went in the garage and asked them just what it was they were looking for. One of the officers said that Robert named the person who had shot at him and that this person is on parole. So they needed to find as much evidence that would link him to my garage, such as fingerprints or the bullet casings. Then the officers started talking among themselves and one of them said that when they asked Robert what the connection between him and Marcus was and what could have been Marcus' motive, Robert would only say that they had a mutual friend. At that point, one of the officers looked at me and I felt as if I had a sign tattooed across my forehead reading, "That friend is me. I'm guilty." So I politely closed the door and went back into the house.

I hurried and got our clothes together. I wanted to leave before Robert got home and before the police could ask me any more questions. Then the police knocked on the door again and I jumped again. Lately, it seemed like I jumped and got nervous when I heard any little noise. But this time the police wanted to tell me they were done for today but they may have to come back. I said, "okay" as I quickly closed the door.

As soon as they left I pulled my car into the garage and

loaded it up with clothes and some of Amelia's toys and games. I wasn't able to get all of it but we should have enough to last for a while. When I got to Mom's house and she saw all of the things in my car, she tried to joke and say we couldn't stay at her house. But when she noticed I was still moving pretty slowly because my body was still stiff, she said she was just trying to make me smile and she said that, of course, Amelia and I could stay with her. She said we could stay as long as I wanted.

As we were bringing my things in the house, I stopped walking and started crying. Then I kissed my mom, thanked her and told her that I loved her. She told me she loved me too and told me to stop crying or else I was going to make her start crying. So I smiled at her and wiped away my tears. I felt that Mom and I were finally back to the way we used to be.

Later that evening Robert called and asked me what was I doing. I told him I was lying down and that I couldn't talk because I had just taken a pain pill, but he was determined to keep me on the phone. He asked me why I had him set up.

"Set up? What are you talking about?"

"Why did you bring Marcus over to the house to shoot at me?"

"I didn't bring Marcus anywhere."

"Yes you did. He got out of your car."

"What? You're crazy. Marcus didn't get out of my car."

"Yes he did too. I saw him. I can't believe you tried to set me up. You hate me that much?"

"Marcus did not get out of my car. You need to have your eyes checked. When I opened my door Marcus was walking up the driveway. So if he got out of my car, why was he walking on the driver's side?"

"Because he went around the back of your car, that's why."

"I'm afraid you're sadly mistaken. He did not get out of my car and I did not have you set up. But what were you doing with that machete in your car anyway?"

"What machete?"

"Okay, so now I see you're playing stupid. Well, that's fine because I want to let you know that I went and filed for divorce today. Amelia and I will be staying with Mom until it's final."

"For real you filed for divorce?"

"Yes, for real."

"Well I'm not gonna give you the house."

"That's fine. I already told my attorney that you could have it."

"Yeah right, you know you love this house."

"You mean, I *used to* love that house, just like I *used to* love you. And anything else you want you can have too."

"What if I said I want you?"

"You're so stupid. You want me all right. You might want me dead. So what was that machete doing in your car anyway? Were you just waiting for the right time to kill me?"

"No, Cassandra, I love you."

"You know what? I feel sick to my stomach when you mention the word love. You don't even know what it means."

"I really do love you. I just had that knife in my car for protection. Protection from anybody. If I wanted to hurt you I already would have."

"What do you mean if you wanted to? You did hurt me. Why do you think I have to take pain pills? I am hurt."

"No, I mean I could have really hurt you with the knife if I had wanted to but"

"But nothing, you did hurt me. And it wasn't a knife, it was a machete."

"Well, you deserved it because you tried to set me up."

At that point I just hung up on him. He had some nerves. Telling me he loves me then telling me I deserved what happened. And does he really think I set him up? That man is crazy. Then the phone rang again and it was him.

"What do you want?"

"I'm sorry, Cassandra. I'm sorry for everythin'. I want you back and I promise, I swear before God that I will never hurt you again. I love you."

"It's too late for all of that, Robert. You need to go on with your life because as soon as the divorce is final I'm going on with my life. Just me and Amelia."

Just then Robert told me to hold on because someone was

at the door, but as soon as he put the phone down, I hung up again. But, of course, he called right back. He said it was the police. They told him he had to go back down to the station tomorrow for some more questioning. He said they also told him that they hadn't found Marcus yet and that Marcus was looking at serving another fifteen to twenty years in prison. I asked Robert why they were giving him so much time and he said because not only did Marcus shoot at him but he also robbed him of five hundred dollars.

"He robbed you? What are you talking about? He didn't rob you."

"Yes he did so I guess now you're on his side."

"I'm not on anyone's side. I just didn't know he robbed you. And why did you have that much money on you anyway?"

"Because I had gone to the bank earlier that day and took out some money."

"What for?"

"Just because."

"So you mean you went and took our bill money out of the bank?"

"I just went and took some money 'cause I thought I would be needin' it. I was gonna put it back the next day."

"So what were you going to do with it for one day?"

"Nothin'. I don't want to talk about it."

"You don't want to talk about it because you're lying."

"So anyway the police told me that I have to go to the station tomorrow."

"So what are you going to do?"

"I'm goin' down there so that nigga can get locked back up. But don't worry, I'm not gonna give them your name."

"You're not going to give them my name because you don't want them to know what you did to me."

"So even if they knew they wouldn't do nothin' because I don't have a police record and I'm not the one they want anyway. It's your boyfriend Marcus. They've been wantin' to lock him up ever since he's been out. He's nothin' but a punk."

"Whatever."

"So is that your boyfriend now? You want to date a criminal like that? Is that why you filed for divorce, because you want to marry his sorry ass?"

"You know what? You're crazy. Good bye!"

Before I could get the phone on the receiver good, it rang again. It was Marcus' sister. She asked me if I had filed a police report and I told her no. She said the police had been to all of her relatives' houses looking for Marcus. She confirmed that Marcus was looking at fifteen to twenty years because they were trying to charge him with attempted murder and armed robbery. I told her I just found out about this robbery issue. She said that when Marcus shot at Robert the first time, Robert got on his knees and was begging Marcus not to shoot him. Then Robert offered to give Marcus all of his money and he threw his wallet on the ground to him but she said Marcus didn't take it. I told her Robert was supposed to go back to the station for more questioning tomorrow and she asked me if he were going. I told her I didn't know. She said I better do whatever it takes to keep Robert from going down there.

Robert called me back about thirty minutes later and said he had just gotten a phone call and someone told him if he went down and testified against Marcus they would kill all three of us. Robert, Amelia and myself. So Robert blamed everything on me. He said that I should be more careful in choosing the man I was going to marry. And again I told him I was not marrying Marcus.

"I know you won't because he'll be in jail where that son-of-a-bitch belongs."

"Yeah and the three of us will all be dead."

"Yeah right. Marcus would never hurt you or Amelia. I know you don't believe that threat, do you?"

Then I started thinking about what Marcus' sister had just said.

"Yes, I believe it. It may not have been Marcus that was making the threat. He has a lot of friends and relatives and I know they don't want him to go back to prison. He has the kind of friends that would probably do anything. Yeah, I believe the threat and I'm really scared."

"So you're admittin' your boy is a gangster and a big time drug dealer?"

"I don't know what Marcus is but I don't deny that he could be involved with some bad people and I think they're capable of doing anything."

"So you don't want me to go down there tomorrow, do you?"

"No, I don't."

"So you *are* takin' up for him."

"No, I'm not taking up for him. I'm just scared."

"Well, I'll make you a deal and we'll see just how scared you are. I won't go down there if you cancel the divorce."

"If I do what?"

"You heard me. If you cancel the divorce then I won't press charges."

"But they'll make you go down there and do it."

"No they won't. Not if they can't find me. So it's all up to you now. Either you cancel the divorce and come back home with me or I'll go to court and he'll get twenty years in prison. And if you're as scared as you say you are then you don't really have a choice."

"What kind of a deal is that?"

"It's the only one you're gonna get. So take it or leave it."

"So what's going to happen if I come back home?"

"Nothin's gonna happen. I already told you that I love you. I will never hurt you again, I promise. And if you want to we can move somewhere else and start all over. We can move anywhere you want to, even out of state if that's what you want. We can move to Washington and be near your brother; whatever you want. It's all up to you. So what's it gonna be?"

All of a sudden I had a gigantic headache. I put my hands on my forehead as I dropped the phone. I picked it back up and told Robert I couldn't think straight and I didn't feel good. Then he reminded me that I didn't have much time. In fact, I needed to make a decision by tonight. So I said, "Fine. I'll come back home but not tonight." He said that was okay with him because he wasn't staying home tonight either. So he went to spend the night at his mother's house. Shortly after I got off the phone with Robert someone called my mom's house and made the same threat to me that was made to Robert.

The next few days Robert stayed at his mom's house and he missed his appointment at the courthouse. When I went home to check the mail there were three different police cards stuck in our front door and several messages on the answering machine from the police. They were really looking for Robert. They desperately wanted to put Marcus back behind bars and for a long time.

I called Robert to let him know the police were looking for him. But all he wanted to know was if I had gone down and canceled the divorce and I told him that I had not done it yet. Robert said he wanted to go with me. What could I do? I agreed I would do it the next day.

On my way to my attorney's office I decided to stop and get the mail. Why did I do that? I wasn't home five minutes when I heard a loud knock on the door. I almost jumped out of my skin. I looked out the window and there was a police car blocking my car in the driveway. I went to the door and was asked if Robert were home and I told them that he wasn't. They asked if he had been home lately and I told them no. They asked me if I had gotten their cards out of the door and I said yes. Then they just looked at me as if I was supposed to keep talking but, of course, I wasn't going to say any more than they asked. I was so scared they might figure out that I was the person that Robert and Marcus had in common. In fact, none of the police ever asked me if I were there at the scene or if I were involved in anyway, thank God. Then one of the officers told me if I talked to Robert to let him know that it was imperative that he contacts their office.

"Uh huh," I said.

I met Robert down at my attorney's office and told him the police had just left the house. Then he told me if I wanted to put an end to all of this police stuff all I had to do was go inside and cancel our divorce. Like I really needed a reminder of why I was there.

Robert waited in his car while I went inside. I sat down, took a deep breath and told my attorney I wanted to cancel my divorce. She looked me straight in my eyes and asked me if I were being blackmailed.

How did she know? I just turned my head the other way and said, "No, I just changed my mind." Then she reminded me of how confident I was the other day. She told me that she felt I would be making a big mistake if I canceled it. I told her that I was just upset the other day and now I have calmed down and realize I don't really want a divorce. I told her that Robert and I decided to try and work it out. Then she asked me again if I were being blackmailed and I just said, "No." She was very hesitant on giving me the cancellation papers to sign but she did. As I signed them I got teary-eyed but I knew this was my only choice. As I turned to walk out of her office she told me that my check would be in the mail next week but I had forgotten all about my money.

When I left her office I went back to Robert's car and gave him a copy of the papers I had signed. He had this smile on his face as he told me again he was sorry for everything and he promised he was going to make it up to me. I really didn't believe him and I had no intentions of forgiving and forgetting that easy. In fact, I had no intention of forgiving or forgetting at all. I was only doing this for Amelia's and my safety.

Robert told me that his mom had made reservations for him to go out of town tomorrow so he would be staying at her house tonight. He said he would be gone for about a month and I asked him what he was doing about his job. He said he hadn't let his job know yet. He was just going to quit. I told him he should tell his job something because he was going to need it when he got back but he said he would just have to deal with that when he returned. In his little sarcastic voice he quickly reminded me of why he was going out of town and asked me if I would prefer that he stay home. I just rolled my eyes and told him I would talk to him later.

I could not believe the mess I'd got myself into. Let's see, I have my daughter's life and mine being threatened every day, along with an ex-boyfriend who will go to jail for about twenty years, and the only way to solve both of these problems is to cancel my divorce and take back a lying, cheating, and abusive husband. Life couldn't be more fucked up, excuse my language.

During that next month Marcus' sister called and told me that all of the charges against Marcus were dropped because they had no witness. Then Amelia and I moved back into our house. Shortly after we went back home Robert came back too. I tried really hard to forgive Robert for everything but I couldn't. My feelings for him were gone. Even though we were in the house together I had no love for him. We continued doing family things together like taking Amelia to the movies, to the parks, going on picnics, and we even took her to Disney Land but I still had no love for him. All of my feelings were gone. Even when he wanted to have sex I would just lie there. In fact, he told me several times that "fucking me was like fucking a dead woman," but oh well.

JURY DUTY

The following month Robert happened to be reading the sports section of the newspaper when he read that Marcus had been arrested on a parole violation. Robert immediately showed me the article as he laughed sarcastically and said, "Look what happened to your boyfriend."

That afternoon I sent Robert to the store to get us some ice cream and as soon as he left I called Marcus' sister. She told me the police went to Marcus' house and found a gun there. His wife tried to say the gun belonged to a friend of theirs but apparently the police didn't want to hear it so they arrested Marcus because he was not supposed to be in a house with firearms. Marcus' sister said their entire family had told Marcus he should have gotten rid of it because he knew the police were going to be watching every move he made but he wanted to be hardheaded. Although I hated to hear that he was back in prison, I was relieved that the gun that was found was not the same one used at my house and that his family didn't blame me for his ignorance.

After all of these things happening, Robert asked me if I wanted to move out of town. I told him that yes I thought I really needed to get away. I told Robert he needed to find a job first because his old job wouldn't take him back. So one day I took off from work and I rode around with him all day long putting in one application after the other. I felt like I was the one looking for a job because Robert said that he had bad handwriting so I filled out all of his applications while he just signed them. I even circled things in the newspaper for him and told him where to go to apply. I worked harder that day than I would have if I had been at my real job. But I guess it all paid off because Robert got a really good job a few weeks later.

I found a house about thirty miles away from where we lived and I told Robert I wanted to buy it. He said sure and that as long as we were together he didn't care where we lived. The house was beautiful. It was my dream house. It was a brand new two-story home with four big bedrooms, two of which were master bedrooms and it had three full baths. We put our other house up for sale and sold it in less than a week. We made a nice profit; nice enough to put a down payment on this new house without having to use any money out of our pocket. So we bought it.

A few months later I told Robert I wanted to have a pool put in the backyard and he said that was fine as long as I thought we could afford it. Robert didn't have a clue whether we could afford it or not. He always left the bill paying up to me. I must admit that money was the one thing we never fought about. Robert would either bring me his check or bring me the receipt from where he had deposited all but maybe twenty dollars of his check. I told Robert that we could afford a pool so I arranged for several contractors to come out and give us estimates.

We settled on this gorgeous in-ground pool that had an automatic pool cleaner, pool cover, two love seats and a waterfall. I felt that if I were going to stay with this man, I needed to have something in my life to keep my mind off of how much I disliked him. And besides, we were all good swimmers, and even though Amelia was young she could swim like a fish. One of the things we had done as a family was take swimming lessons together for the past three summers.

Well, that happiness lasted for me just until the wintertime. Then I was bored again. All of a sudden when Robert and I would have sex the only thing I could think about was how he had given me gonorrhea and how he had tried to kill me. Some nights I would just lie there and cry. As much as I tried to block the past out of my mind it kept coming back to haunt me. I told Robert I thought we needed to see a marriage counselor and he agreed but every time I got ready to make an appointment it seems like I got distracted. So I finally decided to set aside a day to call but again something got in the way. This time it was jury duty. But this wasn't your boring every day traffic jury duty; this was actually where I met someone who became a significant part of my life.

On my first day of jury duty I was sitting there hoping they wouldn't call my number when I noticed this nice looking guy sitting right next to me. We had been sitting there for at least an hour before I noticed him. I guess we noticed each other about the same time because we kind of did one of those double-take looks and then we said hello and introduced our selves. His name was George Lake and even though I was terrible at remembering names that one I would never forget. He was tall, bald-headed and had green eyes. He looked really nice.

As we sat there he told me he was hoping they didn't call his number and I told him so was I. We sat there making idle chit chat until lunchtime when we were excused for an hour and a half. He asked me if I would join him for lunch and I told him sure. Then he said he had just moved here from the East Bay so he didn't know of any places to go. I suggested a little sandwich place a few blocks away and of course I insisted on driving because I wasn't about to go somewhere and be stranded. He complimented me on my car and I just smiled and said, "Jump in. Let's go."

During the course of lunch I found out a lot about George. He was thirty-seven years old, and aerospace engineer, divorced, had two children, a nineteen-year old daughter and a six-year old son and had just bought a house in a town about twenty minutes away from here. Then it was my turn. I told him I was twenty-eight years old, married, but I made sure I told him I was very unhappily married, had a ten-year-old daughter and worked for a phone company. Then he said it was a shame that I was married because if I weren't, he would invite my daughter and me over to his house for a swim. Then I tried to make a joke and asked him if he heard me say the part about how I wasn't happily married. He laughed and said, "Yes, I heard you. So the invitation is still open." I guess I just wanted him to offer because then I told him thanks but I would have to pass.

Someone should have just slapped me. Why was I passing on George's offer? Not only was this guy good looking but he also had a job. He seemed like he had a lot going on for himself. But the truth of the matter was that even though Robert and I weren't getting along and even though I knew my marriage was over, I still couldn't see myself doing anything to hurt Robert. Even though we didn't have much of a marriage I still couldn't see myself cheating on him or forsaking my marriage vows. Boy, Robert's going to really wish one day that he hadn't screwed up because he's never going to find another woman like me.

When it cam time to pay for lunch George and I both pulled out money. Then he said, "I invited you out to lunch so I'll pay."

"Well, I've learned to never let a man do anything for me because I don't want to owe them anything in return." Then I smiled and said, "So I'll pay."

"I'll let you pay today with one condition," George said.

"I knew it. And just what would that be?"

"If I ever have the opportunity to have lunch with you again it will be my turn to pay."

"That's fair enough. It's a deal," I said.

Then with a smile on his face he said, "That way I won't feel like I *owe you* anything either."

So I returned the smile and shook my head. I couldn't believe this man. Finally I met some one who wasn't afraid to speak. And even though I had only spent one afternoon with this man he let me know there was more out there than just Robert.

On the way back to the courthouse he told me he was really shocked about something.

"Shocked about what?" I asked him.

"First of all I hope you don't mind me saying this but I think your husband is a fool. You're a beautiful black woman who seems very intelligent and it seems like you have a lot going on for yourself and for him to just let you go makes him really ignorant. If I had a woman like you I would hold onto you, I mean hold onto *her* forever and make her happy in every way imaginable."

Was this guy for real or was this what he said to every black woman he met?

"Thanks for the compliment. And, yes, Robert really is stupid, in more ways than one, but it would take more than five minutes to explain it to you." So we went back into the courtroom and sat for about an hour, only to find out that we had to return the next day. So George walked me to my car and I said, "Goodbye."

"This isn't good bye. I'll see you again tomorrow," George said.

"Okay. Then have a good evening," I said as he just smiled and watched me leave.

As soon as I got home I picked Amelia up from the baby-sitter's across the street and we went to the park for a little while. Then we went to the video store and rented a movie. After dinner we went in the family room and were watching the video when Robert came in and sat down and put his arm around me. I politely moved his arm and asked him not to do that.

"Amelia, tell your mother to let me put my arm around her," Robert said.

"Robert, don't even start it. And don't put Amelia in the middle of this," I said.

Then he laughed and got up and left the room. That was actually the only conversation Robert and I had that evening, which was fine with me because all I could do was sit there and daydream about lunch with George and all the nice things he said to me and how different he was from Robert.

So Amelia and I sat there until the movie was over and then she took her bath, read me a story and got ready for bed. Although it was pretty early for me, I too got ready for bed because I thought the sooner I got to bed the sooner tomorrow would come and the sooner I would see George again.

The next day George and I sat by each other again and he looked even better than he did the day before and he smelled good too. I wondered what it was that he was wearing. Should I ask? No, I'm a little to shy for that. I'll just let it be a mystery. So as I sat there deeply inhaling I didn't notice George asking me something.

"Huh?" I said. "Did you just say something to me?"

"Yes, I did, but you looked like you were deep in thought. Would you care to share what had your attention like that?"

With this silly grin on my face I said, "Um, it's really not that important."

"Don't be silly. If it's important to you it's worth listening to. So come on and tell me. What were you thinking about?"

I thought, okay, Cassandra, here's your chance. He's asking you a direct question and you're not used to lying so what are you going to do? How are you going to get out of this one? Are you going to tell him or are you just going to sit there and act like an immature little girl? I had all of these thoughts, plus some, before I blurted out, "It was you. I was admiring your cologne and was wondering what it was."

Okay so I said it. And now I was wondering how he was going to respond. He's going to think I'm immature, or I'm desperate, or I don't get out much. Then he replied with this sexy grin on his face, "Since you like it so much that's for me to know and you to find out."

Ooookaaay, so I'm thinking how do I respond now? Since I really *don't* get out much, I didn't respond at all. I just looked at him and smiled and told him we better pay attention to what's happening before they call our names. He smiled back and pretended to pay attention to what was happening in court. For the next couple of hours we just sat there looking at each other through the corners of our eyes and grinning.

When lunchtime came he asked, "So where are we going for lunch today?"

"Well, let's see. Since it's your treat today, I guess I'll pick out the most expensive place in town."

"That's fine. I'm sure you deserve the best." Then I had to tell him I was just joking but he said he wasn't. "Why is it so hard for you to accept a compliment?" George asked.

"Maybe it's because I don't hear them too often. So when I do, I wonder if it's for real, or if" then I paused and said, "Never mind."

George tried to get me to finish what I was going to say but I wouldn't. I think he already knew I was going to say that usually when a man gives a woman a compliment he wants something. And just like I told him yesterday, I don't take anything or accept anything from men because I don't want to feel like I owe them something in return. I didn't want to say this again to him because I didn't want him to think that I thought all men were just alike because I don't. It's just that I'd rather be safe than sorry. And, so far, he has had nothing but compliments for me, so in my opinion either he wants a lot or he's the exception to the rule. I guess you'll soon find out which one he was or is. You'll see what I mean because he still kind of has me confused. Okay I need to get back on track now.

George said he really didn't care where we went for lunch and that it was my choice. Then all of a sudden I had a flash back of Robert and how he could never make a decision so I kind of just spouted off and said, "Will you please just tell me what type of food you would like to eat and please don't leave it up to me. One of the problems I have in my marriage is that my husband leaves everything up to me and I know that picking out a place to eat seems so minor but I'm so sick and tired of making all the decisions. So can you just do me a favor and tell me where you would like to go for lunch or at least what you would like to eat? Is that so hard to do?"

Then George looked at me and said, "Damn, I'm sorry. You really aren't happy at home. Mexican. Let's have some Mexican food." Then he laughed and said, "And that's too bad if you don't like Mexican food because that's the choice I made."

Then I couldn't believe it but I put my hands on his shoulders and stood on the tip of my toes and kissed him on his cheek and said, "Thank you." He responded by saying, "You're quite welcome." From this point on I don't think I looked at him as being this handsome man any more. I simply looked at him as being a *real* man.

I really wanted to explain to him why I was so gracious but I didn't know if I could do that without coming across as being desperate or even hostile. I knew I had a lot of hatred for

Robert built up and that it sometimes came across as me having an attitude. But all I really wanted was a man to be a man both in the bedroom and out of the bedroom. Being a man in the bedroom is the easy part. But a man needs to know what makes a woman happy outside of those four walls. And it's so simple. Let a woman know she's special and she's appreciated and mean it. A man needs to make a woman feel like she's his partner and not his mother nor his secretary. Is that so hard to do or is that too much to ask for? Okay now that I've had my own little inner attitude adjustment I guess it's time to get back to lunch.

George and I went to a small and somewhat intimate Mexican cafe and no, I didn't do that on purpose, honestly. We were seated in a booth lit only by candlelight. I told George I didn't know what I was going to order because I always ordered the same old thing and I guessed I was bored with everything in my life. So George took the liberty of ordering for me. I don't know if George knew it or not but he sure was scoring a lot of brownie points with me. But I keep questioning myself as to whether or not George was all that, or if I would react this way with anybody other than Robert. I keep trying to tell myself George really wasn't all that and perhaps I was just infatuated because I'd been with Robert since I was sixteen and I didn't know what it was like to be in the company of a real man. That could be real dangerous; George better watch out.

During lunch I asked George how long had he been divorced and he said a little over two years and he loved the single life. Then he asked me how long I had been married and I told him I had been married for seven years but we have been living together since I was seventeen.

"I'm a firm believer in the seven year itch. If a couple can get beyond that seventh year then they've got it made," he said.

"I'm sure my marriage won't make it beyond this seventh year, so I guess I'm a believer too."

"So just what went wrong in your marriage?" he asked.

"I've been through a lot of not-so-common twists and turns and it's about time I get off the roller coaster because I know I deserve a lot better."

"Can you be a little more specific?" George asked.

I'm not sure if he really wanted to hear it but I gave him an ear full. When I was done all he could do was shake his head and agree that I had been through more than enough for one person. He said he didn't know how I kept going and I told him that my daughter was my strength. Then he told me something really scary.

"Your husband sounds like the type of person that would never let you go without a fight. So whatever you do, please be really careful."

I wasn't sure what it was that I had said to make him come to that conclusion but I told him that his point was well taken. Then I told him that we should change the subject because I didn't want to talk about myself any more. Then we both looked at our watch and realized it was time to go. The waiter brought the bill and as promised, George paid for lunch and then he smiled at me and said, "Now we're even."

We returned to the courthouse and listened as they called prospective jurors to the stand to be questioned. I looked at George and showed him that I had crossed my fingers hoping not to be called and then he put his hand on top of mine and said, "Now they definitely won't call you."

I looked at him and while blushing I said, "Thank you."

I wondered how this man was so confident? Did it come with age? Or again, was it because I didn't know any better? I'm not sure what it was but he held my hand for the next two hours and I couldn't believe I let him. What was he doing to me? Why did I feel so comfortable with him? I'd never felt this comfortable with anyone else. And it was only my hand. So why did I feel this way? Why was I making a big deal out of it?

I guess George holding my hand was good luck because at the end of the day, neither one of us was called, and actually everyone who wasn't called was excused from jury duty. I guess the saying, "be careful what you wish for," is true because now that jury duty was over I didn't have a reason to see George any more.

George looked as if he were disappointed too. He walked

me to my car and just stood there not saying anything. When I looked at him all I wanted to do was kiss him but something kept holding me back. So instead I said, "Thanks for the past two days. I really enjoyed your company."

"I really enjoyed your company too, sweetheart." Then he bent over and kissed me on my forehead and said, "Stay beautiful, Cassandra," and he walked away. I wanted to cry. I sat there and watched George disappear in the distance and then I drove off. For some reason, I felt like I had just lost my best friend.

MY NEW ATTITUDE

For the next few days I thought about George day and night and I wondered if he were thinking about me. Why didn't we exchange phone numbers or something? Well, I know why I didn't give him my number. It was because I was still at home with Robert. But I thought about him so much until I had to tell someone so I told my mother. My mother's first reaction was that she wanted to meet the man that had her daughter feeling this way. Then I told her it was impossible because we didn't exchange numbers or anything. Then my mom told me something that she had instilled in my head for as long as I can remember.

"Nothing is impossible. If you really want to find this man then go look for him."

"But should I? After all, I am still married."

Then my mom explained to me that all she wanted was for me to be happy and obviously I wasn't happy with Robert. Then she reminded me of some of the things Robert had done to me as if I really needed a reminder. And I thought to myself, if she only knew the other half of the things he had done to me that I never told anyone about, she would probably go looking for George herself. Then she also reminded me of what she had told me when Robert and I first started having problems. She said that if I ever had a problem with a boyfriend or husband, the best person to talk to was his own mother or someone who loved him just as much as I did.

"Mom, I guess the reason I'm telling you is because I don't love Robert any more and I'm very unhappy."

"Well, for Amelia's sake, if there is any love left for Robert you owe it to my granddaughter to try to work things out."

"But, Mom, how can you say that? I remember when you and Dad got a divorce and there were five children involved and that didn't stop you. And I know I didn't realize it then but I've learned that no one should stay together for the sake of children. Children will adjust. I did. In fact we all did."

Then my mom hugged me and told me I was absolutely right and whatever I decided to do, she was behind me one hundred percent. Then I looked at her and smiled and said, "Thanks for the pep talk and thanks for being behind me. Now I have to go so I can find George."

Then she smiled back and said, "That's not what I was talking about."

But I ignored that part and said, "Thanks again, Mom. I'll let you know when I find him."

As I was leaving she said, "Oh no, I've created a monster," as I blew her a kiss goodbye.

On my way home I started playing Miss Detective. How could I find George? Let's see, I know what town he lives in and I know approximately how long he's been there and I know where he works. So I'll start in the same place I met him.

I stopped at the courthouse, but this time I went to the County Recorder's Office to see if I could find his address from the title records. I told the clerk that I needed to find some property that a friend of mine had purchased and she asked me if I knew when it was purchased and I told her. Then she showed me which microfilm I could look on to find it. As I stood there nervous and shaking I couldn't believe it, I found his name and address on the first microfiche that I looked at. It had his name, telephone number, the date of purchase and other information regarding his house and lot size. I left there so happy you would not believe. But now that I had this information, what was I going to do with it? I couldn't just call him. He'd really think I was desperate. I think I'll just hold on to it. Somehow I feel close to him just having it.

When I got home Robert reminded me of how *I* was

supposed to make us an appointment to see a marriage counselor. I just got smart with him and rolled my eyes and said, "If you want to see a counselor so badly, why haven't you made us an appointment?"

"Because you said you were." Gosh, he sounds like a baby. *Mommy you said you were going to do it for me.* I bet George would never make me feel like I was his mother, but I guess I better stop thinking about George before I get myself in trouble. So I said, "Fine, I'll do it." I called and made us an appointment for the following week.

On our first session with the counselor she laid out some ground rules. She told us that we had to be perfectly honest and we could only discuss these issues in her office and not when we left the building. She told us that once we left the building if we had something negative to say about the other person we had to write it down and talk about it on our next visit, but if we had something positive to say we should say it. Actually, she encouraged us to think about the positive things we liked about each other. She told us to think about what attracted us to each other in the first place. After we agreed to the rules she said the first thing she wanted to know was why were we there. She asked Robert if he wanted to go first.

"The reason I'm here is because Cassandra asked me to come." Then I shook my head. Then she asked him to name three things he loved about me and three things he disliked. "I have no complaints. I have a beautiful wife and as far as I know everythin' is fine."

Then she asked me the same question and you would have sworn I was reading from a prepared list.

"Let's see, where do I start?"

"You can start anywhere you like," she said.

"Before I start, can you remind Robert that we're not supposed to talk about anything we say here until our next appointment?"

"Robert, do you have any questions about the rules?" she asked him.

"No, she can say whatever she wants to, her."

"Go ahead, Cassandra."

As I started crying I said, "Well, first of all Robert's abusive. He's had an affair, he's a liar, he has no backbone, he makes me feel like I'm his mother, he"

"Okay, Cassandra, three's enough. I can tell you're very upset but I want you to tell me three things you love about Robert."

"Um, I have to think about it. Sorry, I can't think of anything."

"Both of you need to think back to when you first fell in love and remember some of the things about the other person that you fell in love with. Robert, what did you fall in love with in your wife?"

"My wife is beautiful, smart, intelligent, and she's a damn good mother. She's everythin' I've ever wanted in a woman. But I know I've made some mistakes and she has too but she has to be willin' to forgive me because I would never ever hurt her again."

"Cassandra?"

"Well, the person I fell in love with was a lie. Robert lied to me from day one and has been lying to me every since. I have done nothing but try to forgive and forget but some things just aren't forgivable and some things I just can't forget. Besides, he's still lying to me. I feel like I have two children at home. Robert relies on me to do everything. I have to plan everything for our family. I plan everything from where we're going to live to what we're going to eat. Robert leaves everything up to me and he just sits back like a child and basically says 'okay mommy' to everything. I know he's capable of making his own decisions. After all, he didn't need my help in planning when and how he was going to have an affair."

"Robert, did you have an affair?"

"Yeah, but it just happened once."

"It doesn't matter how many times it happened. You got gonorrhea because of it and you expect me to forgive you."

Then Robert abruptly got out of his chair and stormed out of the room. I told the doctor that's what he does when he gets upset. He knew he was wrong, so that's why he left.

"Cassandra, just what do you want out of your sessions with me?" the doctor asked.

"I really wanted someone to tell me that things weren't so bad just so I would have a reason to stay because I can't come up with a good reason by myself. In the past, I have tried to hang in there for several reasons but mainly because I thought I owed it to my daughter, but now that I put things out in the open I realize I don't want Robert. I don't love him any more and actually this time I'm only with him because I was forced to be with him."

"What do you mean when you say you were forced to be with him?"

As I looked at the clock on the wall, I told the doctor that it was a long story and that she really didn't have time for me to get into it. Then she made me an appointment for the following week but said she wasn't expecting Robert to show up and neither was I. She asked me if I felt comfortable going home with him and although I really didn't, I lied and told her that, yes, I was comfortable.

When I got to the car Robert was sitting there waiting inside. On the way home Robert asked me if I really felt that way, referring to what I said about him during therapy, and I told him yes but I reminded him that we were not supposed to talk about it. Then Robert asked me if I really thought he would hurt me and I told him yes and reminded him again that we weren't supposed to talk about it. Then he asked if I were going back for another appointment and I told him that I had one scheduled for next week. Then he said he wasn't going back to her because she was on my side and that she didn't want to listen to him. He said that every female was going to be on my side and the only way he was going back was if I made an appointment with a male doctor. So I told Robert fine, I would make us an appointment with a male doctor.

A few weeks later we went to see a male counselor. At first I felt a little uncomfortable but I figured as long as I told the truth anybody should be able to understand my point after they saw what Robert was really all about. And besides, I know

Robert doesn't really want to go to a counselor. Whether it's a male or female, that's just his excuse, so I guess I'll call his bluff.

The male counselor started off by pretty much asking us the same questions as the other counselor but this time Robert did have something to say. He said he felt like he was my son because I made all of the decisions. Then I told him that I certainly didn't enjoy making all of our decisions but I was afraid of the personal choices that Robert had made in the past.

"I would love to be able to hand over my paycheck and know that all of the bills would be paid, extra money would be put in the bank and to know that we still had a little money around the house. I would love for someone to plan our family dinners and our family activities. Sometimes I get tired of just thinking. I will admit that Robert never complains about anything I plan, but that's not the point. If he would just take the initiative sometimes, it would relieve some of the stress from me and that's why I feel like Robert's my child."

"Just what do you two want to get out of your counseling sessions with me?" the doctor asked.

"I would like to be able to trust Robert again, love Robert again and forget the past but I can't do either of them."

"I wish Cassandra would forget about the past and forgive me and move on." Then he sarcastically said, "If she can't do that then I'm outta here."

"Fine. Then let's get a divorce," I said.

The counselor didn't really comment on what either of us had just said. He just sat there and looked at both of us talk as he kept moving his head back and forth as if he were watching a tennis match or something. Then he finally commented and said, "I want to see you both individually next week." I don't know what we were supposed to have obtained from that entire session. I personally felt like it was a waste of time.

On the way home Robert confessed that he really didn't want a divorce. He just said that to the counselor because he didn't want him to know our business. Daaah, was I missing something here? I thought that was the point of going to a therapist so they *would* know our business. Boy, Robert is so stupid. How did I ever get myself into this? Oh I remember, it's because he's a liar too. He's been a liar from day one. But I'm going to try not to dwell on the past. I need to come up with a plan for the future, for Amelia's and my future. I wonder if our future would include George? The following day I called his number.

"Hello," said a young female voice of about ten or eleven years old.

"Uh hello. May I speak to George please?"

"Just a minute. Mom, someone's on the phone for George."

Now what do I do? I certainly wasn't expecting someone else to answer his phone. George didn't mention someone living with him.

"Hello. Can I help you?" said this woman.

"Um yes. My name is Stacy and I'm calling from the County Office of Jury Duty. May I please speak with Mr. Lake?"

"He's at work. Is something wrong? Is he being summoned back to jury duty?

"I'm sorry but that information is confidential. Do you have a work number at West Coast Airlines that I can reach him on?"

"Yes, it's 415-555-7709."

"Thank you very much ma'am and have a good day."

Whew, where did that come from? Talk about ad-libbing. I think I did pretty well considering they really caught me off guard. George didn't mention them. So let's give Mr. Lake a call at work now that we have the number.

"Hello, this is George Lake. Can I help you?"

"Hi, Mr. Lake. How are you?"

"I'm just fine."

"You're wondering who this is, aren't you?"

"Yes, I am."

"Well did I catch you at a bad time?"

"No. Who is this?"

"Well, first of all this isn't a prank call. But you have three guesses and if I'm not your first guess then I promise I will never bug you again."

"Well, can you give me a clue?"

By this time I was feeling really stupid and immature. I should have probably hung up. Then I took a deep breath and said, "Your one clue is that you made a really big impression on someone and right about now I'm feeling really stupid and should probably hang up."

"Cassandra? Sweetheart, is that you?"

Then I picked the phone back up and said, "I'm sorry, I dropped the phone. Yes, this is Cassandra."

"I have really been thinking about you. How are things going?"

"I guess things are okay," I said.

"You guess? That means things really aren't okay. You need to talk, don't you?"

"No, I'm fine really. It's just that I went to marriage counseling with Robert yesterday and for some reason when I thought about my future I thought about you." I can't believe I just said that to him.

"Well, I'm really flattered that a beautiful young lady such as yourself would even give me a second thought. But I have a confession too."

"What is it?" I said as I put my hand over my chest.

"I've been thinking of you quite a bit too. I even looked your number up in the phone book but I didn't call it because I respect you and your situation even though it doesn't seem like a very pleasant one."

"Well, you wouldn't believe what it took to get your number."

"Whatever it took, I'm impressed, because there are hundreds of numbers at this company and you got straight to me. That's a sign of determination."

"Determination, snooping, investigating and a little bit of lying all rolled up in one package."

"Now you've got me curious. How about meeting me somewhere this evening and you can tell me all about your detective skills."

"That's fine. Where do you want me to meet you?"

"Since you've already made it clear that you won't come to my house, how about at the mall and maybe we can catch a movie or something."

"That sound fine with me."

"I get off at four o'clock. Is five o'clock too late for you?"

"No, five is fine. My daughter wanted to spend the night at her grandmother's tonight so Robert's taking her out there. Now I don't have to worry about her at all this evening."

"Okay, sweetheart. I'll see you at the movies at five."

"Okay, goodbye."

I got to the mall about twenty minutes early and I saw George as he pulled up a few minutes later. He got out of his car and walked near the cinema. Then I got out and stood right behind him.

"Hi stranger. Are you looking for someone?" I said.

Then he turned around and hugged me; I mean we hugged each other.

"Hi, beautiful. You sure are a sight for sore eyes. You certainly know how to make an old man's day."

"What do you mean *old* man? I think you're very attractive and besides, you're only nine years older than I am, so you're not old at all. What are you talking about?"

"Compared to you, I look like I could be your father. In fact, you look the same age as my daughter's friends. She's in her first year of college and she's always trying to set me up with her friends."

"So I remind you of your daughter's friends?"

"No, not exactly. I'm trying to give you a compliment but I almost forgot that it's hard for you to accept them. What I'm trying to say is that you could pass for twenty or twenty-one years old."

"Thank you. You're so kind."

"So would you like to go inside or would you rather go somewhere else and talk?" he asked.

"It doesn't matter. Whatever you feel like doing is fine with me."

"You better be careful making statements like that," he said with a smile.

"Why? I don't know what it is but I really trust you. And besides I'm a big girl. I think I can take care of myself."

"Since you're so bold, let's go for a ride and I'm driving this time."

"Okay, let's go."

Little did he know that inside of my car I had left a piece of paper with his name, and both of his telephone numbers, and I also wrote down the type of car I saw him pull up in. I did that just in case anything happened to me. You can't be too careful nowadays.

As we walked to his car, he put his arm around me and I wanted to melt. He was so built. He probably worked out every day. Then when we got to his car he opened and closed the door for me just like a real man. I guess I shouldn't expect anything less coming from him. Then he got in and drove to the marina. It looked really cold and windy outside so we sat in the car and talked. I told him I felt really comfortable around him and that I had never felt that way about anyone before and he told me he was really flattered. He told me that I was making him blush.

During the course of our conversation he told me that he almost dialed my number several times but he didn't want to start any mess at my house. I told him I appreciated it, so I gave him my work number. Then he said he wanted to spend more time with me and he wanted to get to know me better. He promised he would never pressure me to do anything. He said anytime I wanted or needed to talk to someone to give him a call day or night. After that evening we called each other almost every day at work. But that weekend it seemed like Robert wanted to stick to me like glue, so needless to say, I didn't get a chance to call George.

The following week I went to my one-on-one session with the therapist, which was a waste of about five minutes because all he said was that he wanted me to attend group counseling. He explained to me that the group was made up of all women who were going through the same thing. Robert had his one-on-one appointment the following day but he conveniently said he couldn't get off from work early enough to attend. Then I asked him why he didn't make his appointment for later in the day, and he said he didn't know. See what I mean? Must I hold his hand and make the phone call for him? Then I asked him if he was going to reschedule and he asked if I would do it for him and I said yes.

Now you see why I'm tired of thinking; I have to do all of his thinking too. But the only reason I'm doing it this time is because I really want him to go. He really needs help. So I got on the phone and made an evening appointment for him for the following week. But did he go to that appointment? No. This time he had no excuse.

"Robert, why didn't you go to your appointment this evening?" I asked.

"I didn't go because I don't need to go. There's nothin' wrong with me. So are you gonna keep goin'?"

"Yes, I am," I said sarcastically.

"Well you're the only one with the fuckin' problem so you're the only one that needs to go," he said.

I know he's just trying to start an argument but I refuse to give him one. So I just said, "Whatever."

Actually I was starting to like the group meetings. I learned quite a bit from them. When I first started going I used to cry just about every time someone mentioned the word divorce. Getting a divorce was a big step. And while attending those meetings I came to realize that what hurt me the most was the fact that my daughter would not be raised in a house with both of her parents.

For me, getting a divorce not only made me feel like I had let my daughter down but I felt like I had let all other teenage couples down. Even though I wasn't a teenager any more, I felt like my marriage and divorce would become just part of the statistics that says teenage couples doesn't last. And all of this because of Robert. I hated him. It was all his fault. But I learned so much about myself in these meetings. These meetings were what helped me turn my life around while boosting my self-esteem. Actually, because of the meetings and my frequent conversations on the phone with George, I must admit they may have created a monster.

I came to realize that I definitely didn't love Robert anymore. Actually, I'm not sure if I ever did, but that didn't take George or a psychiatrist to figure out. I also came to realize that I didn't need Robert for anything. My daughter and I could make it on our own. And to think that at first I couldn't even stand to hear the word divorce. Huh. Now I can say it all day long, divorce, divorce, divorce, divorce. I had to give my own self a pat on the back as I walked out of my meeting with an attitude that no one could touch. You go girl!

That evening I went straight home and told Robert I was filing for divorce. At first I guess he lost his hearing because he kept asking me, "What did you say?" I told him that he had heard me right the first time. "Tomorrow I'm filing for divorce."

"So, what about Amelia?" he said.

"What do you mean, what about Amelia? She's going to be with me."

"What if I want joint custody?" he said sarcastically. I know he really didn't want her.

"Fine, Robert. If you want joint custody you can have it. My intentions are not to hurt you or Amelia. We just have to face it that our marriage just didn't work out."

"Well, what about your precious house?" he said.

"What about it? As far as I'm concerned, tomorrow we can put it up for sale."

"Yeah right, you know you love this house. How many of your friends have a house like this and with a pool too? In fact, bitch, if you knew you wanted a divorce, why did you just have the pool put in?"

"First of all, you know my name. It's *Cassandra*. And I know you're just trying to start an argument but it's not going to work. And did you hear what you just said? You wanted to know why *I* had the pool put in. That is one of our biggest problems. I've had to make all the decisions around here and you've just kicked back and watched. Well, you know what? Tomorrow you can just kick back and watch me go file for divorce."

"Every since you've been goin' to those little stupid meetins' with your psychiatrist you've been gettin' smart with me but you better shut up before I knock your teeth down your fuckin' throat. So that's who told you to divorce me, isn't it? Isn't it? So now you're listenin' to the white man."

"Don't try to blame what you've done on someone else. You said you wanted a male counselor so I got one. And don't tell me about listening to the *white* man because if you hadn't fucked that *white* girl we probably wouldn't be going through all of this."

"So is that all you can talk about, what I've done? I thought that was old and done with."

"It is. And, no, we don't have to talk about that or anything else as far as I'm concerned. And besides, I'm tired so I'm going to make sure Amelia's ready for bed and then I'm going to bed myself."

"Go right ahead, bitch. But remember you're still my wife and we're still gonna have sex."

"You know what, you're crazier than I thought. No we're not going to have sex. So I'll just sleep downstairs if you want me to."

"It doesn't matter where you sleep 'cause I'm gonna be right there."

"If that's the case, then I'll sleep upstairs where I've been sleeping but if you touch me you'll go straight to jail."

"Yeah right, you'll really tell the cops that I raped you. Come on, don't fool yourself because no one will believe a man raped his wife."

"You mean soon to be ex-wife. And yes they will, and not only that, I'll tell them how you and your friends raped that other girl too. You see, I don't forget things very easily. So it's your choice. Good night Robert."

Talk about attitude. I had a big one and it felt damn good and I was proud of it.

HOME FOR SALE

The following day was a busy one. As I promised, I filed for divorce and I made an appointment with a real estate agent to put the house up for sale. When I went to the attorney's office I was well prepared. Thanks to Robert always handing over his check, I was able to bring copies of his most recent pay stubs right along with mine. I also brought in copies of all of our bills so I could request that everything be paid off with the proceeds from the house. My attorney was really impressed that I was so well prepared so I didn't tell her that I had already been through this twice before.

When she looked at our pay stubs she asked me if it was correct that I made that much more money than Robert and I told her yes. Then she said I probably wouldn't get much child support so she suggested I file for alimony too. I told her I didn't want him to give me anything, but that I just wanted him to help take care of his child. Then she kind of talked me into not disallowing alimony all together but to request to reserve it until a later date.

When Robert got home that evening I told him what I had done and I also let him know that a real estate agent was on her way over to talk to us. At first, Robert didn't believe me. He didn't believe me about the divorce or about the house until the doorbell rang promptly at six o'clock.

"That's her. That's the real estate agent," I said with this grin on my face. "I guess you'll believe me now, huh?"

Even though at first I was putting up this front trying to make Robert feel guilty, all of a sudden, I guess since it was really happening, it felt kind of weird showing the agent around my house and then sitting there listing all of the amenities we had put into it. I looked over at Robert and he had these tears in his eyes and for a minute all I wanted to do was cancel everything and go and hug Robert and tell him everything was going to be okay. Sike!

What I actually did was excuse myself to go into the bathroom to wipe away the little tears that were beginning to form in my eyes. Then I started thinking about all the things Robert had done to me and how I had promised myself in one of my group meetings that I had already had my last cry. Then I walked out of the bathroom with my newly formed attitude and told the agent I was ready to proceed. Then she said if this wasn't a good time for us she could reschedule. I told her there was no need to reschedule. "Let's do it now. In fact, the sooner the better," I said. Then Robert excused himself and went into the bathroom too. We waited a few minutes for him then I told the agent to proceed without him. I told her that anything Robert missed I would explain to him later. So the agent and I went through most of the paper work ourselves.

When Robert finally returned, his eyes were bloodshot and I knew for sure that he had been in there crying. But, oh well, he should have thought about how much he had to lose a long time ago. He came back and sat down and I told him we had already gone over everything and now all he had to do was sign and initial everywhere I had already signed and initialed, and he did. He's so stupid. He didn't have any questions, of course, because again, he was leaving everything up to me, as usual. I guess Robert really trusted me. Deep down inside he knew I would never intentionally hurt him, not even now. And he was right. Too bad I couldn't say the same about him.

That night was a long one. I thought about all of the things Robert and I had accomplished at such a young age but I wasn't going to dwell on the past. And Robert was just that; past history. It was time for me to start thinking and making plans for Amelia's and my future. Where would we live? Do I take her out of her current school? Should I move to Washington near my brother to get away from everything? Then I thought about my job.

I know I am very fortunate to have started working with a great company at the age of eighteen. My job is very stable and I know there is always room for advancement. So why would I be ready to give that up? Just to get away from Robert? I don't think so. He would probably love to see me quit my job and get on welfare but he's going to have to keep on dreaming. So if he doesn't decide to move away himself, then he's just going to have to see Amelia and me prosper on our own.

Well, several months passed and it was really strange because we hadn't sold the house yet. I questioned my agent about what was going on. I asked her if we should lower the price and she said that she felt it was already moderately priced. I just wanted it sold so I could go on with my life, yet Robert seemed perfectly content that it hadn't sold yet. My agent said she didn't understand why it hadn't sold either because there were several people that had come to look at it. There were two couples in particular that came over one day and Robert and I showed them the house ourselves. I told my agent those two couples seemed very interested. So when my agent decided to call the two of them to see what their thoughts were, she got an ear full from both of them.

They both said that Robert followed them out to their cars and told them that we were *thinking* about going through a divorce but we really weren't sure yet. He said we only had the house on the market to see what kind of response we would get if and when we were really ready to sell it. My agent then questioned me to see if that were really true. I explained to her that, yes, we were going through a divorce and that Robert was grasping at straws, or should I say thin air, trying to save our marriage. I told my agent I wanted this house sold NOW, so I suggested that in the future she arrange for any potential buyers to see the house when we were not home, so she agreed to that.

At this point I didn't even think I could be any madder at Robert so I'll just say it again, "He's so stupid." That evening I told Robert I knew what he had done but of course he denied every bit of it. Liar. Then I told him there was nothing he could do to stop this divorce so I suggested he just live with it. I guess it was finally sinking in because then he started saying things to me, just trying to get a reaction.

"Cassandra, you know I'm seein' someone else, don't you?"

"I really don't care what you're doing."

"Well, how would you feel if my friend Tamika and I just buy you out of this house?"

"I don't care who buys it. I just want it sold so I can go on with my life."

"You mean you don't care if another woman lives in your house?"

"Once you guys buy me out, it won't be my house anymore. It would be hers."

Even though that's the first time he's mentioned another woman, he really doesn't get it. He should know not to bother me because this attitude is here to stay. If I were losing something of some value, I might be upset but she's the one that's getting the short end of the stick, and I do mean the short end. So I just smiled and asked him if they had already been pre-qualified for the loan and he said no.

So I proceeded in telling him that I thought it was a good idea if he and his friend could keep the house. That way, Amelia's things could stay here and she would already be in a familiar environment. I also told him they should go and get pre-approved as soon as possible, like tomorrow, before some other couple got interested in the house. I guess I just burst his bubble. I bet he won't mention that again. His little scheme to try and hurt me just backfired in his face.

After a couple of days passed I decided to ask Robert about his little plans.

"Robert, were you and Tamesha able to qualify for the loan?"

"Me and who?"

"Your friend Tamesha."

"No, her name is Tamika, and we went down to get the loan but they wouldn't let us have it."

Yeah, sure, he went down and applied for a loan. He was so

stupid he wouldn't know where to go or what to do but I'll play along anyway.

"So why weren't you guys able to get it? What did they say?" I knew I was just encouraging him to lie but that headache belonged to Little Miss Tamika now, so let's see what else he could come up with. Then he started smiling and with him that was a dead give away that the next thing out of his mouth would be a lie.

"They told us we didn't make enough money. So are you satisfied now?"

"No, I really wanted you guys to get it. You think maybe you can add someone else's name to the loan as a co-signer, like someone in your family or maybe someone in her family?" *Like someone in his family would really be able to qualify for a loan.*

"You know nobody in my family could get a loan, nobody out there even has a job." I knew that but I just wanted to hear him say it. "So why are you so concerned about me and Tamika gettin' this house anyway?"

"I've told you already. I think it would be a little easier on Amelia if one of us stayed here. Her school is just right around the corner and the day care is just across the street. I think it would be perfect if one of us could stay here." Notice how I mentioned twice, if *one* of us could stay here. I was just setting him up to watch him fall for it as he always did.

"Yeah, I agree it would be better for Amelia. So why don't you and your boyfriend try to get a loan and buy me out?"

Okay, so he took the bait just like I knew he would. First of all I had never mentioned a boyfriend to Robert. He was just trying to see if he could catch me in a lie, or see if I would volunteer some information. But that only worked on him, the stupid one, not on me. See what he said to this.

"Actually I did mention it to my friend and he said he wouldn't mind being a co-signer on a loan for me but he just bought his own house so he has no interest in moving in." Now let's see if Robert can take what he dishes out. "And he has a really good job so I know with both of our incomes I wouldn't have a problem buying you out of this house. So name your price."

Then Robert looked at me fuming, as he picked up the closest thing to him, which was a candleholder, and at this point I didn't even get scared, as he got ready to throw it at me.

"Go ahead and hit me with it and you'll go straight to jail."

"You stupid bitch. I can't stand your ass. That's why Amelia's not even my daughter. You little tramp. So who's the nigga you're fuckin' now?"

"I don't know. Let's see. Maybe it's Tamika's brother. But then again, maybe not, because I really like older men. So maybe it's her father or better still, maybe it's Amelia's father."

Then Robert turned around and threw the candleholder at the wall, putting a hole in it. Then he picked up the match to the candleholder and threw it into the wall too.

"Robert, what are you doing? Why are you tearing up the house?"

"I don't give a fuck about this house. I'll burn this mutha-fucka down before I let you stay here with another nigga."

"First of all, there is no one else. I only said that because you wanted me to accept you and your friend staying here and you said it would be okay if I stayed here with someone else, so I made up a friend too and look how you're acting. And you know damn well Amelia is yours. You know you really shouldn't say things you don't mean. One of these days you're going to regret having said things like that, you just watch."

"I'm sorry. You just make me so mad sometimes. I'll fix the wall tomorrow."

"You're always doing something you say you're sorry about. You should never have done it in the first place. And it's getting really old hearing you say that Amelia isn't yours."

"I said I'll fix the wall tomorrow. And I know Amelia is mine. But if I didn't love you so much I wouldn't act like this."

"Yeah, right. Good night, Robert." Once again, he proved to be so stupid.

THE MONTEREY TRIP

The next six months or so were pretty much the same between Robert and me but things certainly progressed between George and me. Robert brought up Tamika's name several times but he didn't get any response from me. I didn't bring up George's name to him because I knew what kind of response I would get from him.

George and I started doing a lot of things together. He showed me things I had never seen before with Robert. We went out to eat a lot. We went to parks I had never heard of. And since George had a bad back we frequently visited hot tubs. We even drove down the coast to Monterey one weekend. I'll have to tell you in detail all about this beautiful Monterey weekend.

It had been ten months since I had filed for divorce and put the house up for sale and I was beginning to get a bit frustrated. During these ten months the only thing that kept me sane was the fact that I saw George quite a bit. In fact, I felt myself falling in love with him, which really wasn't hard to do.

I knew there was something special about him the first day we met. He was always there for me and seemed to know exactly what I needed. He told me everything I wanted to hear and even things I didn't want to hear but he was usually right. I could talk to him about anything and everything and what was so good about our conversations was the fact that we didn't have to always agree with each other, but we always respected the other's views. We were able to talk about everything from gun control to birth control. When we discussed birth control

I told George that since I wasn't sexually active I had been off the pill for about six months.

We talked about everything. We even discussed the possibility of one day having more children; or should I say the unlikelihood of ever having more children. This was the one subject that George and I completely disagreed on. I wanted more children some day and George didn't want any more ever. We talked about what would happen if we ever got together. One of us would have to do a complete about face. And from the way George talked about not ever having any more children, it sounded like I would have to be the one to rethink the issue, but I'd cross that bridge if and when we ever got there.

George understood how unhappy I was with my home situation so he told me if I were able to get away for the weekend he would love to drive me down the coast to Monterey. Rather than ask Robert to keep Amelia for the weekend I asked my mother. Mom said that yes, she would keep Amelia under the condition that I let her meet this man with whom I was going away for the weekend. I had been telling her bits and pieces about George and me spending time together and at first she told me I shouldn't be seeing him since I was still with Robert. But then, she saw this big smile on my face every time I mentioned George's name so she started loosening up and told me that she really wanted me to be happy and to just be careful.

I told Robert I was going out of town that weekend because I was so stressed out and that I needed to do some thinking. The first thing he wanted to know was if I was going to be alone. So I did one of his numbers; I lied and said yes. Then he wanted to know where Amelia was supposed to be all weekend and I wanted to tell him that since she was his daughter too she was going to be with him but I knew that would only start something. So I told him that my mom would keep her but she couldn't watch her until that afternoon, so he would have to bring her to my mom's house. He agreed really quickly. Actually, it was almost too quick. He was probably thinking that now he could spend the entire weekend with Tamika. If there really was a Tamika.

So I called George back and told him my mom would keep Amelia but that she wanted to meet him first. He said okay. George asked me if I minded if we went in my car so we could let the top down and enjoy the ride and I told him that would be fine. George's mom and my mom lived in the same town so we agreed to meet at his mom's house so he could leave his car there.

When I got to his mom's house she was not home, so he parked his car and I drove us to my mom's. I introduced him to my mother and they talked for a long time. My mom told George that she was finally getting to meet the man that I had been talking about for the past year. She said she was beginning to wonder if he really existed or if he were just a mere figment of my imagination. Then she embarrassed me and asked George what his plans and intentions were for her daughter this weekend. She was acting as if I was sixteen years old but I let him answer the question anyway. He gave her a little bit more information than I think she was asking for.

He confirmed that we had known each other for a year now and said he really respected me and that he knew all about my situation. He told her he would never take advantage of me and as far as that weekend went, he said his only intentions were to take my mind off of everyone else and to pamper me and make me feel special. Then Mom asked him how he planned on doing all of that. He told her that he planned on doing it without sleeping with me and if it would make her more comfortable we could stay in separate beds or separate rooms. Then I jumped in the conversation and told George that he didn't have to promise my mom all of that. Then we all laughed and he handed Mom a piece of paper and told her it was the name and number of the hotel in which we would be staying. I kissed Mom and told her we had to go. I handed George my keys, he let the top down, and we took off.

It was a beautiful day outside but the wind was tearing up my hair. I kept trying to hold my hair back in a ponytail with my hands, but then George told me to loosen up and let my hair go. He told me I was beautiful even if my weave was all over my face. Yeah right, like I had ever had a weave. So I let my hair go and I put my hands down but I didn't just put my hands anywhere, I put them on George's leg and he just looked at me and gave me this sexy smile. So I proceeded in massaging his leg, then his thigh, then he told me not to start something I wasn't ready to finish. I told him that maybe I was finally ready to finish.

"What do you mean by that?" George said as if he didn't know.

"I mean that even though I'm not divorced yet, I'm ready to try and make you as happy as you've made me."

"You've already made me happy, sweetheart. Just spending time with you makes me happy and I will always be there for you. I will always be your friend with or without sex," George said.

My friend I thought. Is that all he wants? That smile I had on my face every since I'd picked him up quickly turned upside down right along with my stomach. Here I was in love with this man and all he wanted was a friendship? I guess the only way to find out for sure was to ask him point black. But was I really ready to get my feelings hurt? Well let's see.

"So are you saying that all you want is a friendship?"

"No. Is that what you're over there thinking? Is that why that beautiful smile disappeared?"

"Yes," I replied. I couldn't believe he was so attentive towards me. I guess that was one of the reasons I fell in love with him.

"No. I'm sorry. I guess what I said didn't quite come out right. The truth of the matter is I want much more than a friendship but only when you're ready."

Then my smile came back but the only parts I seemed to hear were the words *much more*. I continued rubbing George's thigh and then I got bold and starting unfastening his belt buckle. Then with a big smile on his face he said, "Stop trying to seduce me in the car. It's not going to work. I told you I'm bringing you to Monterey so you can relax and take your mind off of things. You certainly don't want to complicate things by..."

By this time I had his belt buckle and his zipper undone and my hand was inside his pants. Then his head dropped back and I said, "I'm sorry you didn't finish your sentence. What were you going to say?" And for once he was speechless. So I took advantage of the situation. "Well, since you don't have anything to say, I have something I need to say to you. Actually, I have two things I need to say, but first I need to move my hand," and so I did. Then I looked at him and I said, "George, I love you."

He sarcastically replied, "Sure you do."

Then I said, "But loving you is the easy part. I also need to tell you that I'm *in* love with you too."

Then, all of a sudden George pulled over on the side of the freeway in the emergency parking only lane and parked the car. I asked him what was wrong; if everything were okay. Then he reached over and put his hand behind my head and pulled me closer to him and gave me the most passionate kiss I had ever experienced in my life and followed it by saying, "I love you too."

Talk about speechless. What do I say now? You would have thought this man had just asked me to marry him or something, because I felt like I was the happiest woman alive. Then George looked at me and said it again. "I love you but I know you've gone through a lot this past year and I don't want to complicate your life any more than it already is. I want this weekend to be a weekend you and I will never forget. I want it to be special. We'll have plenty of time in the future to do other things. And, besides, I promised your mother that we wouldn't have sex."

Then I laughed and said, "No. If I remember correctly you promised my mother that you wouldn't take advantage of me. So let's get back on the road and get to Monterey."

Then he laughed and said, "Okay, Miss Cassandra. Whatever you say."

I guess he didn't know me very well and he had better watch out because I didn't remember promising my mom anything. Then he fastened his pants and we drove off. That didn't stop me though because I continued massaging his leg and his thigh and looking at him out of the corner of my eye as my hand went higher and higher up his leg.

As soon as we got into Monterey he stopped and asked for directions to our hotel. George didn't know it but he was continuing to score brownie points because it took a real man to ask for directions instead of driving around in circles pretending to know where he was going. Or like Robert would have done, just assumed that I would have door-to-door directions already in hand because I would have planned the entire trip. Anyway, that's enough thinking about Robert. This was a Cassandra and George weekend. I mean, make that a Cassandra and George *special* weekend and no one was going to ruin it.

When we arrived at our hotel I was stunned. The hotel was sitting right on the beach and the balcony of our room was overlooking the water. The weather was beautiful. It was about 85 degrees. George changed into some shorts with a tank top and I changed from my skirt to some shorts with a bikini top and a see-through cover up.

George suggested we take a walk along the beach. He brought along a small blanket for us to sit on once we found the perfect spot. George had thought of everything. As we were walking hand in hand, a golden retriever approached us with a tennis ball in his mouth. He dropped the ball right in front of George so George felt obligated to respond. He let my hand go so he could throw the ball for the dog to fetch. Well, that one obligation turned into two, then three and then four fetches. Since George looked like he was having such a good time, I decided to take the blanket from him and I made a place there for us to sit.

I sat there for what seemed like a half an hour watching George and the dog play ball. George said, "Baby, I'm sorry but this dog won't let me stop. He's so cute."

I looked at George as if to say, "Who did you come here with, me or the dog?"

He said, "But I better stop playing fetch because I have someone here with me that is much more pleasing to the eye."

I'm thinking, flattery will get you everywhere, and George

is scoring more and more brownie points. I told George I really didn't mind him playing with the dog because they both looked like they were having a lot of fun. Besides, the beach was so beautiful. I could just sit back all day and watch people go by.

The atmosphere was perfect. Besides the nice weather, there were all kinds of people there. There were couples that you could just tell were in love. There were families who were picnicking. There were children building sandcastles and there were individuals who were walking up and down the beach. Even with all of that going on, it was not crowded. Everyone seemed to have his or her own space. It was simply beautiful.

George finally decided to join me on the blanket as someone else took over the fetch game. As he sat down, he reached for my hand and kissed it. I didn't know whether to melt right there in his arms and give him another brownie point or to just expect to be treated this way. But I was not one for taking anything for granted so I just kept adding up those points. George then placed his head on my lap and I massaged his back and his shoulders. He must have liked my massages. Then I whispered, "I love you" in his ear and he responded sarcastically again with "No, you don't." Then there was silence for a few minutes.

"Oooh, honey, this feels good," George said.

"So you like my massages, huh?"

"No. I'm talking about my head in your lap that feels good," he said. Then he turned his head around to see me blushing as he gave me another passionate kiss. About five minutes later, when the kiss was over, I just sat there trying to gather my thoughts, which seemed like such a difficult task. Well, maybe the kiss wasn't really five minutes but I just couldn't seem to think about the time or anything else right then.

I started having a conversation in my head with myself. I was now an angel and a devil. The angel in me thought, "Okay, Cassandra, get a grip."

But the devil in me thought, "I'd like to get a grip all right, but not on my thoughts."

And the angel said, "He brought you here to sit back and relax."

And the devil, "Well I came here to lay down and screw."

I'm not sure what all of that was about but I guess I was probably somewhere in the middle. I came here to relax and take my mind off of my home life and so far that's working. But in the past, I'd also wondered over and over if I could ever make love to George while still being married to Robert. I don't know why I still gave Robert that respect, but I really did think that if the opportunity presented itself at that point, I could do it. And what an opportunity we had. A beautiful day, no children, and a hotel room on the beach. George had better watch out. And Robert who?

George voluntarily took his tank top off so I could really massage his back. I kissed his back, then massaged, then kissed, then massaged. I would really like to spoil George, I thought. I wish I knew what he was thinking. Then George sat up, put his tank top back on and told me it was my turn and I looked at him and smiled and said, "Okay, but I'm not taking off my top." Then he smiled back and said, "You have to take this big shirt off," referring to my cover-up. So as he helped me, I took it off. I tried to get George to take his tank top back off but he wouldn't. He kept referring to himself as being fat but I didn't think this man had an inch of fat anywhere on his body.

Then I lay down on the blanket with my head on his lap. He massaged my back and my legs until I felt like I couldn't stand up. He asked me how I felt but I think my mouth was also numb because I tried to talk but nothing would come out. Then he moved my hair to one side and kissed my neck and said, "Never mind. You don't have to say anything. Just lie here and relax." So we stayed on the beach a little while longer until George said he was getting hungry.

We went to our room to freshen up and then we walked about a half-mile to a really nice restaurant that was also on the beach. It was also beautiful and we had a nice dinner. When the waiter came to bring the check, he had a long stem red rose in his hand and as he handed it to me, he said that it was from

George. I looked at George, gave him a kiss on his cheek and thanked him. I don't know when he had the time to do that. All I knew is that he sure was getting points, and I wondered what he'd cash them in for. Then I told him to give me the bill so I could pay for it and he said, "Absolutely not." He just smiled and said that I could pay tomorrow.

After dinner we walked around Monterey and window-shopped because by now most of the gift boutiques were closed. George told me there was a shopping mall nearby and promised that we would go shopping tomorrow. So we made our way back to our room and I asked George if he wanted to watch a movie and he said sure.

He went to take a shower first and when he came out he was only wearing a muscle tee-shirt and a pair of boxer shorts. He looked so good. Then I took my shower and came out in a pair of black and gold silk pajamas that I often lounged around in at my house. I didn't want to pack anything too revealing or too sexy just in case Robert went through my over-night bag before I left. When I came out of the bathroom, to my surprise, George kissed me and we stood in the middle of the room for a moment just holding each other. He told me that I was really beautiful and sexy and he asked me what was I trying to do to him. I just blushed and said I wasn't trying to do anything, but you know I was lying.

George sat on one side of the bed and I sat on the other. It was as if we had been doing this for years, like we knew what side of the bed the other one wanted. George asked me if I had enjoyed myself and I told him that today was beautiful and I didn't want it to end. He asked me if there was anything I wanted or needed to talk about and I told him that no, I just enjoyed being in his company. Then he told me again that he would never put me in a situation that would make me uncomfortable and I told him I appreciated that. Then I scooted over to the middle of the bed and started massaging his back again. I told him that I felt extremely comfortable around him, and that it was a type of comfort that I had never ever felt before. Then George asked me if I needed the lights on and I told him no. So he got up and turned them off, took off his tee-shirt and his boxer shorts and lay down in the bed.

"I hope you don't mind me taking off my clothes, but I usually sleep nude," he said. As I started to stutter, I told him it was okay. "Your back rubs feel so good. Do you mind doing it again?" he asked.

"Of course not," I told him. I was just glad that I could make him feel good because he did so much for me.

Neither one of us watched the movie that was on. In fact, George soon fell asleep so I got up and turned the television off. I continued to rub his back for a while and as I lay there next to him I kept thinking that I knew I was ready to take our relationship to another level. Tonight was the perfect time for us to make love. So needless to say I wasn't getting any sleep.

George woke up a couple hours later and when he turned over and saw that I was still awake he apologized for falling asleep on me. I told him there was no need for an apology. Then he asked why was I awake and I told him the truth. I told him I was lying there fantasizing and hoping that tonight would be the night we would make love. I explained to him that I was ready and I told him that I fell in love with him without sleeping with him so I knew our relationship could only get better. Then he gave me another passionate kiss and we lay there for a moment holding each other tight.

Then George reminded me of how often I prided myself on not having an affair on Robert and how I valued my marriage vows whether it was a good marriage or not. Then he also reminded me of his promise to my mom. I jokingly said, "First of all, you can forget about your promise to Mom because I'm grown." Then my Miss Thang attitude came out and I said, "And secondly, you can forget about my marriage vows to Robert because I certainly have." I told him that I was tired of being faithful to Robert while pretending not to be in love with him.

"Cassandra, I understand how you feel but what I don't want to happen is, say tomorrow when you get up, or maybe even next week or next month, for you to look back at this day and have any regrets and be mad at me for destroying your family values. I respect your values as I respect you. I would like nothing more than to make love to you right now, the way you deserve to be loved. You just don't know how much I'm fighting it."

Then I touched him in his private area and said, "Yes, I do know how much you're fighting it," and as I stuck my tongue in his mouth I told him to stop fighting.

Then he moved my hands and said, "Wait a minute, this isn't fair. I'm trying to do what's right and you're making this incredibly hard."

And I touched him again and said, "You're absolutely right. It is incredibly hard."

Then he laughed and said, "That's not what I'm talking about."

"Fine. Have it your way," and I moved my hands from his private area as I turned over.

Before I could get turned all the way over George reached over and turned me back. From that moment on George and I made the night more than a fantasy. It was more than incredible. We lay there and kissed and caressed each other's body and George explored places on my body that had never been touched and I think he knew that. That night was when I realized the difference between making love and having sex. George and I made love that night with no sex involved. It was beautiful. A night I will never forget.

The next day George and I walked around the mall as he had promised. We also walked around downtown Monterey and visited all the little specialty shops. George was wearing a really nice pair of sunglasses that I admired. He asked me if I had a pair and I told him that I left my sunglasses at home but they weren't nearly as nice as his were. Then he insisted on stopping at a sunglass store where he bought me a pair that matched his. I couldn't believe the price he paid for them. When the cashier rung up the price and gave him a twenty-percent discount it was still more than a hundred dollars so I said, "Wait! Let me get a different pair."

"Don't be silly. I want you to have a pair just like mine. Do you like them or don't you?"

"Yes they're nice *but*."

"But nothing. You deserve them." And looking at the cashier, he said, "We'll take them."

"I'm not sure what to say. Thank you," I said to him in a really soft voice.

"Don't try to get quiet on me now. You certainly didn't have a loss for words last night," he said as he smiled and kissed me on my forehead.

When we got back to the hotel it was nearly check out time. I told George that I didn't want to leave. I thanked him for the weekend and told him I would cherish it forever. Then he thanked me for spending the weekend with him and told me he would never forget it either. We drove home with the top down and with our matching sunglasses on. We looked as if we didn't have a care in the world but in reality I was going back to a miserable life at home with Robert. Something has to change soon.

SPOUSAL ABUSE

Well guess what? That next weekend I got my divorce papers in the mail. I was ecstatic. As soon as I opened the letter and saw what it was, I immediately called George and told him the good news. But for some reason he didn't seem as happy as I thought he would be. However, he did tell me that we would have to celebrate. Then I told him I had to go and that I would call him from work on Monday because I just saw Robert pulling up in his car. Even though we hadn't sold the house yet, having these papers was still a big relief. I don't know what took it so long to become final but it didn't really matter anymore. It was finally over.

As soon as Robert came in the door I gave him his final papers.

"I guess you're happy now, bitch," he said.

"You can call me whatever you want, but yes, I'm very happy. Aren't you?"

"So now you can keep screwin' the nigga you were with last weekend, huh?"

"I don't know what you're talking about."

"Don't lie to me, bitch."

"Whatever you say, Robert. You're so damn smart. Whatever you say."

"And don't cuss at me," he said.

"You have your nerves. You call me out of my name all the time but when I say *damn* you get offended. You know what, you're so stupid. These papers couldn't have come a minute too soon."

"Don't get smart with me because I'll kick your ass right here and right now."

"Well, if that will make you feel like a man then go ahead and do it."

"So what are you tryin' to say, I'm not a man?"

"No, what I'm trying to say is what we think about each other really doesn't matter anymore."

"You're right, bitch, because the only thing that matters to me is what Tamika thinks and I don't care about your fuckin' feelins' anymore anyway. She's more woman than you'll ever be."

"You only wish. And if she's all that why don't you move in with her? You can take your things right now and go be with her." Then I handed him the phone. "Here, call her right now and tell her you're a free man and that you'll be right there."

"She'll know in due time and besides, I'm not leavin' this house. You think I'm crazy enough to let you have the house so you and your man can stay here. I know that's why you want me out. So why don't you call your man and tell him you're movin' in with him."

"I already did. I called him as soon as I opened your papers. So he knew before you did." Then Robert pushed me into the wall.

"So you're admittin' you got a man. So is that the nigga you've been fuckin' all summer long, huh?" Then he pushed me again. "So is that the nigga you went out of town with?" Then he slapped me and punched me in my face several times, and then I started yelling.

"Stop it, Robert! Stop it! You're hurting me!"

"Well I hope his dick was worth it, bitch. Why don't you call your man to come and rescue your ass now?"

"Well, one thing's for sure. He doesn't have to hit a woman to make himself feel like a man. And thanks to you he's all the man I'll ever need or want. And another thing; I finally figured out why you call me 'bitch' all the time; it's because that's all you grew up around. You fuckin' bastard."

Then Robert pushed me into the wall again and said,

"You're not even worth goin' to jail for, you bitch," and he walked upstairs.

As soon as he got all the way upstairs I called 911. I whispered and told them what had just happened. She asked me if he was still in the house and I told her that yes he was upstairs. She asked me if he had any weapons and I told her none that I knew of. Then I heard him coming back down the stairs so I hung up. He looked at me and said he was sorry but I told him that it was a little too late for that and he asked me what was I talking about. I told him that he couldn't beat up on someone and then say I'm sorry and expect everything to be okay. Just then the doorbell rang.

"That's for you, Robert," I said.

"Who is it?" he asked me.

"Never mind. I'll get it for you. It's the police," I told him. Then I opened the door and said, "There he is, over there, officers."

"What seems to be the problem?" one of the officers asked Robert.

"I don't know. I was sittin' here watchin' TV with my wife and the next thing I know you guys rang the doorbell."

Then I started crying and told the officers he was lying. I told them it all started when we got our final divorce decree in the mail today and that Robert had just beaten me up. Robert told them I was lying and that I hadn't cried all day until they showed up. Then the officers asked me where had he hit me and I told them all over. I told them he had slapped me several times, threw me into the wall and hit me with his fist. Then one officer asked me if I had any bruises and I told him I didn't know but we could look.

When there were no visible marks on my arms, Robert laughed and said, "I told you she was lyin'. She's a big liar."

Then the woman officer said, "Let me see your face," so I turned to the side and there was a scratch and a very visible handprint. Then the male officer asked Robert where that came from and Robert said he didn't know and maybe I did that when I was putting on my makeup. Then I cried even more as I told the officers that I don't even wear makeup. Then the male officer told Robert he was under arrest and walked over and handcuffed him.

"Can you just handcuff me when we get in the car? My daughter is outside playin' and I don't want her to see me like this."

"Officer, he's lying again. He doesn't even care about his daughter because if he did he would have thought about her before he did what he did to her mother."

Then the female officer told him that he didn't deserve any special privileges as she gave him a little nudge out the door. The male officer escorted Robert outside while the other one stayed behind. She gave me a card with a telephone number for the local battered women's hotline and shelter. She told me she noticed the "for sale" sign in the yard and wanted to know if I had a place to go. I told her that, yes, I had planned on staying here. Then she suggested I pack some things for Amelia and me because she said even though they were bringing Robert down to the station, more than likely he would be released in a few hours. She also explained that I could get an emergency restraining order that would be in effect for this weekend just until I could go and apply for a permanent one on Monday. I told her to do whatever she could. So I signed a paper for the emergency restraining order and they left.

As soon as they left I looked in the newspaper for a place for Amelia and me to move. I took the first place I found available, site unseen. It was an apartment complex and I was told to bring in the first month's rent plus a deposit so I nearly drained our joint checking account, while there wasn't much left in the savings account anyway.

When I got to the apartment complex I was a little disappointed. It was definitely a step down from the way I had grown accustomed to living. In fact, it was several steps down. But then I thought about how my mom fought back and struggled after she and my dad divorced and I remember her saying that it really didn't matter where we lived, that all that mattered was the fact that we were all together. So then this place didn't seem so bad anymore. And besides, it was only temporary. I knew it would be a struggle for a while because I had my car note and Robert and I had lots of other bills together. I knew I couldn't count on him to help with anything but Amelia and I would make it as long as we were together.

When I got home there was a sarcastic message from Robert on the answering machine saying that he would be home shortly and once he got there he wasn't leaving again. So I immediately packed some clothes and Amelia and I left for the weekend. We headed for Mom's house before Robert got back. Amelia had several questions along the way.

"What's wrong, Mom? Why are we going to Grandma's?"

"Well honey, your dad and I are divorced now, so you and I are going to be moving soon."

"How come my dad can't move and let us stay at home?"

"Well that's a good question honey, but the truth is your dad has refused to move until we sell the house and I no longer want to stay there with him. Would you like to stay there with him for a little while?" I secretly crossed my fingers and prayed that she said no.

"No, Mommy. I don't think my dad even likes me. He doesn't do anything for me unless you ask him to. And you guys think I don't know what's going on. I saw the police take him in the police car today and I know why they did. It was because he hit you, didn't he?"

As I held back the tears I said, "Don't worry, everything is going to be okay. I promise."

"I know he hit you. And you guys think I'm asleep at night but I hear him cussing at you all the time but I don't say anything. I just lay there and cry," she said.

Then I had to let the tears go as I said, "Amelia, I am so sorry. I really am."

"Sorry for what, Mom? You didn't do anything. It was him."

"I'm sorry you've had to hear that, honey. And I'm sorry I have to take you away from that house. But Momma will promise you this; you and I are going to make it by our selves and as far as that house goes, one of these days I'm going to buy you a bigger and better house and it will be all ours. No one will be able to make us leave." Then with a little smile on my face I said, "Okay, honey? How does that sound?"

And with a grin on her face she said, "That sounds good, Mom. I love you."

"I love you too, sweetheart. Oh yeah, one more thing. When we get to Grandma's house I'm not going to tell her what happened today, okay?"

When we got there I didn't want us to walk right in with our bags so I left them in the car. Mom immediately kissed Amelia and then she asked, "What are you guys doing here? I didn't know you were coming down today."

"It's nice to see you too, Mom." Then apparently she saw a bruise or something on my face.

"What's wrong with your face? Someone hit you?" she asked jokingly.

Then Amelia said, "Yeah Grandma, my dad hit her." Then I looked at Amelia and gave her the evil eye.

"Your dad did what?"

"My dad hit her today and the police took him away so we're going to stay with you for a while."

"Cassandra, is this true? Are you okay? What's going on? And where is that son-of-a-bitch now?"

Then I looked at Amelia and back at Mom and said, "Can I talk to you about this later, Mom?"

"No, you can't. Amelia, why don't you go in your mom's old bedroom and play with one of your toys in there."

"You just want me to go in there so I can't hear what you guys are talking about but I already know what's going on."

"Amelia, do what your grandmother told you and remember what I said, honey. Everything is going to be okay."

As soon as she left the room my mom got started. "Now, what in the hell is going on?"

"We got our divorce papers today, Robert got upset and hit me, so I called the police."

"Yeah, today a letter came in the mail for you here and I

figured that's what it was. I was afraid something like this was going to happen when he got his copy. You're going to mess around 'til that son-of-a-bitch kills you, huh? So where is he now?"

"He's probably at home. The police did take him to the station but they told me he would probably be out in a couple of hours."

"Come here and let me see your face. Where else did he hit you?"

"Mom, I'm fine."

"That's not what I asked you. You're not fine. I can see a bruise on your arm from here and I don't even have on my glasses and your face is a mess too."

"Thanks, Mom. I love you too."

"Stop trying to change the subject. Where else did that son-of-a-bitch hit you? It's times like this when I wish your brother or your cousins weren't so far away. I'd have one of them kick Robert's ass. And where is George? Have you told him? He doesn't seem like the type to put up with Robert's bullshit."

"See, Mom, that's why I don't tell you things. I'm fine, really. And no one else needs to get involved. Robert's just mad because of the divorce but he'll get over it. You watch. He's going to get everything he deserves. That's a promise."

"So have you told George?"

"I called him after I got the mail but I haven't talked to him since. I really don't want him to know what happened because I don't want him to get involved either. Robert's not worth it."

"But aren't you scared of Robert?"

"I know Robert's crazy but I have a restraining order that's good until Monday, and then I'll go to the police department or the county building and get a permanent one."

"Cassandra, I'm just so scared that one of these days he's going to hurt you really badly or kill you. Then what?"

"Mom, don't worry about me. I'll be fine. And oh yeah, I found a place for Amelia and me to stay and I'm going to try to move in on Monday too, while Robert's at work."

"Do you really think he'll let you go just like that?"

"No, but if other people are there helping me move then I'm sure he'll be okay because he's a coward. I know him like a book. When other people are around he acts like a perfect angel. So I know he'll act decent then."

"Well, I'm going to call his mother and let her know what's going on and maybe she can keep him out there so you can get packed and get some things moved. Have you guys decided on who's taking what?"

"No, but I'm not going to argue with him. Whatever he wants he can have."

"Ill be damned if you're going to just let him have everything. You've worked hard for your shit and there have been times when he wasn't working at all."

"I know, Mom. I just want things over with. No loose ends and nothing to argue or fight over."

So Mom called his mother and told her everything that I had just said plus some of her added extras. I don't know where she got the part about him jumping on me. Did I look that bad? And I don't know where she got the part about me having to take off from work on Monday and Tuesday to get packed and moved because I was already off those two days because I had to work next weekend. But, I guess she got her point across because Robert's mom called back about thirty minutes later and said Robert would be staying with her for the weekend.

I wish she would keep him there with her forever but I already knew he was not going to let me stay in the house without him. He was too afraid that I would do exactly what I had told him. I said I would put an ad in the paper for a roommate and I would keep the house. I told him I would give him his equity and keep the house myself but he's afraid I could really make that happen. Then I told him he could do the same thing; get a roommate and buy me out. But no, he'd rather sell it than to do anything civilized like that.

THE MOVE

The next day I asked Mom if she would watch Amelia for a few hours. She would be really upset with me if she knew I was going home to pack. She would have insisted on coming with me or at least made me promise to bring someone else with me, someone like George. But again, I didn't want to get anyone else involved in this, not even them. So I went home and packed us some clothes. I made several trips back and forth to our new apartment. I also took some pots and pans and bed linens. I even made sure I left enough for Robert. But if Mom were there, she would have made sure I didn't leave anything for Robert. I wasn't able to take any furniture though because I forgot to order a moving truck the day before, so there were none available until that Monday.

I figured I would take the waterbed furniture that was downstairs in our spare bedroom because that was a gift from my mother. I would have liked to take the bedroom furniture that I was use to sleeping on because it was a really nice set. I had gone all the way to San Jose to find the perfect bedroom set, but oh well, I'll leave it for him. Then I figured I'd take Amelia's bedroom furniture and leave him the twin beds in the other spare bedroom. I didn't know what he would do with them but I was trying to be fair. Why I was being fair, I don't know. Maybe it was because I'm a firm believer in what goes around comes around and you better be ready to reap what you sew. I guess that's enough of my preaching though.

As far as our living room set went, we bought that one year when we went to Washington to visit my brother. I knew Robert was not going to want me to take that because he thought it was my pride and joy. I didn't know if he'd want the dining room furniture but I was not going to argue over it either. So I figured instead I would take the washer, dryer and refrigerator. Actually, the refrigerator was a house-warming gift from my mom and dad. Even though they'd been divorced for many years they were able to come together when it was something involving one of us children. Too bad Robert and I would never be like that. He was too stupid. And too bad his parents never gave us anything because that way it would be easy. He'd take what they gave us and I'd take what mine gave, but of course he would end up with nothing. Which is the way he was going to end up even years after this divorce if he didn't change his tune. He was so stupid.

Well, speaking of stupid, I see his car. Here he comes now. Okay, Cassandra what are you going to do? Should I call the police? Maybe I should have brought my mom with me. Oh well. It's too late to worry about that now because he's on his way in the door. And besides, all I have to do is be nice to him and tell him what he wants to hear and then he will be perfectly fine. So I guess I'll play this little game with him until I get out of here.

"Where have you been? I've tried to call you all night and I left messages," he said.

"I stayed at my mom's house."

"And what's all that stuff in your car?"

"Um, um, I was getting some things together for me and Amelia."

"What kind of things? Where are you going? I thought we were gonna stay here until we sold the house."

"No, I think it's best that we not stay here together, so Amelia and I are moving."

"Where are you movin' to? With your man?"

"See, that's why I can't stay here with you. You're always assuming I'm with some man. I already told you there is no other man. It's just time you and I go our separate ways."

"But until we sell the house, how am I gonna pay for the house and the rest of the bills around here? Are you gonna help?" Robert asked.

"Robert, you know I will help with everything I can. But since I have to move somewhere else I can't help with the house note here too. If you get a roommate you can make the mortgage payments until the house is sold and we can keep up the bills together."

"You know I can't get a roommate. So now what?"

"You can get a roommate if you try, or you can let me and Amelia stay here and I will get a roommate."

"I've already told you that I'm not leavin' this house."

"That's fine Robert, do what you want to. We'll just have to move. No big deal."

"Where are you movin' to?"

"I don't know. Somewhere around here so Amelia can stay in the same school, at least until next summer when school is out."

"And then where are you goin'? You movin' in with your man?"

"I told you I'm not arguing with you anymore. I'm getting ready to go."

"No, wait, Cassandra. I need to tell you somethin'."

"Well, tell me. I'm standing right here."

"Sit down a minute, okay? Last night I stayed at my mom's house and I missed you so much. I don't know what I would do if I ever lost you." I'm thinking, HELLO, you've already lost me and you got your papers yesterday to remind you everyday of what a butt hole you are, but instead of saying that to him I just listened. "I'm really sorry for what I did yesterday and I promise on a stack of bibles that I will never hurt you again. Just don't leave me, okay?"

"Robert, it's too late for that and besides, you have already made me that promise before. Several times in fact. And you have broken that promise just as many times as you've made it. So please, I don't want to hear it anymore."

"But I love you and I don't want you to go. Let's just go upstairs and make love, okay?" I can't believe he just asked me that. I haven't made love to him in a year so what makes him think I'm going to do it now? And besides, he hasn't mentioned

Amelia's name once since we've been here. He hasn't asked where she is or how she's doing. It really hurts but Amelia was right yesterday. I don't think her dad cares about her either. He just uses her to have a connection to me. But in the future, anyone that loves me will also love my child. So in reality it's impossible to make love to someone you don't love. He's so stupid.

"Robert, I don't think that's a good idea. Making love won't solve any of our problems."

"But I need you, Cassandra. You don't know how bad I need you."

Well, I can just about imagine how much he needs me. But what he doesn't realize is this is just the beginning. He doesn't have Miss Goody Two-Shoes to plan his life for him anymore. And wait a minute; he couldn't possibly need me because he has Tamesha and she's more woman than I'll ever be, remember? So I just ignored his last statement.

"Robert, it's really time for me to go but before I do, can we at least see how we are going to divide the furniture when I move?"

"What do you mean, divide the furniture? If you're the one that's leavin' then you choose to leave everythin' here." Okay, so now I see he wants to be difficult, like I really didn't see that before now. He knows I'll be more than fair. He just wants to get me upset, so I can make him upset, and then in his eyes he'll have a valid reason to break his promise and physically hurt me again. But I'm tired of being his punching bag.

"Robert, let me just tell you what I want. You can have our bedroom set upstairs and all the linens that go with it. You can have everything in the twin bedroom. You can have the dining room furniture and everything in two of the bathrooms. I think I should have Amelia's furniture, the bedroom furniture that my mom gave us and the washer, dryer and refrigerator."

"You can have the two bedroom sets but you're not taking anythin' else."

"Robert, why are you trying to be so difficult?"

Then he grinned and said, "I'm not bein' difficult and

besides, divorces aren't supposed to go all smooth the way you want it to. Somebody has to be difficult."

What he just said didn't make any sense but I think I know what he was trying to say. In his eyes someone has to act a fool so it might as well be him.

I just rolled my eyes and said, "Whatever Robert. I'm leaving now."

Then he laughed sarcastically and said, "Go ahead and go, bitch, but you're not takin' anythin' else with you." So I just walked out. I had a few things in my car that I wanted to drop off at the apartment but I noticed Robert following me so I drove to my mom's house instead.

When my mom saw all of the things in my car she got upset because I didn't take someone with me. I told her I reserved a moving truck for tomorrow. A couple of the guys I grew up with on my mom's block agreed to help me get moved. George agreed to wait at my apartment so he could take over from there because I didn't feel comfortable having him go to my house.

The next day everyone showed up on time. We were going to try to move everything while Robert was at work. They got everything loaded into the truck that Robert and I had agreed on. Then they asked me why wasn't I taking the washer, dryer, refrigerator and living room furniture and I told them how Robert said I couldn't have it. Then they sort of laughed at me and asked me if I wanted it or not. Just as I started explaining to them how I was trying to be fair, Robert pulled up. This time I wasn't nervous at all.

My friends that were with me didn't like Robert anyway and wanted any excuse to beat him up like he had done to me. One of the guys told me over and over what a coward Robert was because he wouldn't fight a man. So I got bold and told my friends that, yes, I wanted those things.

"Yes, I want the washer, dryer and refrigerator. Amelia and I need them."

Robert came in the house and asked me what was going on and I wanted to say, "What the hell does it look like?" but instead I said, "I told you I was moving."

Then one of my friends said, "Cassandra, where is your washer and dryer?" and I laughed and said, "Oh I forgot to tell you guys that the washroom is upstairs."

"The washroom is where?"

"It's upstairs."

"What kind of house is this? I've never seen a washer and dryer upstairs."

"I know. It's one of the things I like about this house. It was really convenient having it there, but oh well."

"Maybe it was convenient for you, but it's not so convenient when you're the one that's moving it."

As they were walking up the stairs Robert spoke up and said, "Hey man, Cassandra was leavin' the washer and dryer here."

"What are you talking about, Robert? You know I'm taking them for Amelia and me," I said, lying.

"Cassandra, stop lyin'. You know we've already talked about this."

"Yes, we have, and I'm not going to argue with you. Amelia and I need them so I'm taking them."

Meanwhile my friends had already strapped the washer up to the dolly and one of my friends told Robert he better get off the stairs because they were on their way down. Then Robert came over to me and whispered, "That's all right, bitch, because you're not gettin' the dryer to go with it."

So I followed my friends out to the truck and told them what Robert said. On their next trip inside the house Robert told them I wasn't taking the dryer when one of them replied, "Come on, Robert, get out of the way. Stop tripping. You know Cassandra needs the washer, dryer and the refrigerator for Amelia. Man, don't you care about your daughter?" Then they just walked right past him and proceeded to get the dryer. Then Robert whispered to me again and said that I wasn't getting the refrigerator. So, when they got the dryer loaded on the truck, I told them what Robert said but I told them I didn't want any trouble so I would leave the refrigerator. They assured me that it wouldn't be a problem getting it. They really wanted a reason to let Robert see what it was like to get hit by a man.

"Are you sure you don't want us to go in there and get it, because we will. It's not a problem at all," as they balled up their fists just ready for a fight.

"No. I'm sure. Let's just go. I don't even need to go in there for anything else. Let's just go."

"We'll go but what I really want to do is go in there and kick his ass. He's a punk and you know you're like a sister to us."

"I know I am. Let's just get out of here."

They reluctantly got in the truck and followed me to my apartment. When we got there I introduced them to George. Then one of my friends asked me if I were afraid that Robert might have followed us over here. George told them that he would take care of Robert, so I had nothing to be afraid of. Then my friends proceeded to tell George what a coward Robert is and how stupid he was.

I told George, "See, I told you Robert's a butt-hole."

The three guys got everything unloaded from the truck and George thanked them and tried to pay them for helping me but they told him that wasn't necessary because I was like the sister they never had. When they left, George asked me what was going on with Robert. I told him it was all over now and there was no reason for him to get involved.

MR. WONDERFUL

George set up Amelia's bedroom furniture and hooked up the washer and dryer when he noticed I had no refrigerator.

"I don't want to talk about the refrigerator. I will go and get a used one from somewhere tomorrow."

Then he set up my waterbed to the point of filling it up but I didn't have a water hose so he went to the hardware store and bought one.

As the waterbed was filling up, George asked, "What time does the rental truck have to be turned in?"

"By noon tomorrow."

"Well, I won't be able to take off tomorrow so I'll go and gas it up for you now."

It was taking George a long time to get back and as I started getting really worried he pulled up. He told me that my friends had left something in the back of the truck and for me to go and see what it was. When I looked in the truck, I hugged George so tight; I didn't want to let him go. There was a brand new refrigerator in the truck with a big red bow on it. When I finally let him go he laughed and said, "So that's what I have to do to get a hug from you?"

"I'm sorry, George. I just wasn't thinking."

"You should be sorry. I've been slaving away setting up all of your furniture and you hadn't even stopped to give me a hug or say I love you or anything."

"I'm really sorry and stop trying to make me feel guilty."

Then George hugged me from behind and kissed my neck and said, "Why? What's going to happen if you feel guilty?"

I turned around and smiled and said, "I don't know. What do you want to happen?"

Then he looked at me and said, "Don't give me that I don't know stuff. You were full of ideas in Monterey, now weren't you?"

"Well, actually no. If you recall, you were the one full of ideas. I was the one with only one idea." Then I said sarcastically, "But no, you turned me down because you had to keep your promise to my mother." Then he kissed my neck again. "Come on, George I have to finish putting up this stuff first. But oh yeah, can you come with me to turn the truck in now so I don't have to do it in the morning?"

"Sure, we can do it now. Do you feel comfortable leaving your bedroom window open with the water hose sticking out of it?"

"I guess so. Actually, the truck rental place isn't too far from here so we'll be right back."

When we got back I couldn't believe George. While I was hanging up clothes, George was making up Amelia's bed with the linens I had left in her room. Then I put up all of Amelia's clothes, so her room was the only one in the house that was complete. Actually, there weren't that many rooms to complete in the first place. My apartment had two bedrooms, one and a half baths, a combined living room and dining room and a kitchen with a small washroom in it.

I went over to George and hugged him from behind as I thanked him for everything and told him I loved him. Then I told him I was tired and since he had to go to work tomorrow we should stop and sit down for a moment. That's when I realized I had nothing to sit on but Amelia's bed. I had no living room or family room furniture and I had no table or chairs.

"I'm sorry but I have nothing for us to sit on."

"That's okay, honey. Don't worry about it. We can get some blankets and lay on your living room floor and watch television."

Then George asked if I minded if he took a shower and of course I told him that no, I didn't mind. I told him while he was in the shower I was going to find my phone and call Mom to let her know everything was okay.

"You mean you didn't forget to have your phone turned on like you forgot to reserve the truck," George said sarcastically.

"No, I did not. My phone is one thing I don't think I could ever live without. Actually, I had the phone and PG&E transferred over here. Robert probably doesn't know it yet but he has no phone and his gas and electric will be turned off tomorrow. And he's so stupid, I'm sure he doesn't know how to call and have it turned back on in his name. He'll probably get one of his sisters to call for him."

"You mean all this time you had the utilities in your name?" George asked.

"Yep, every last one of them. And even though I don't have to pay water and garbage here, I called to have them turn that off too."

"Miss Cassandra, I don't believe you. You have everyone believing you're this little angel and feeling sorry for you while I see you've really been taking care of business."

"I've never said I was an angel. I've said I wanted to be fair and I think I've been more than fair with Robert. If he wouldn't have had me take care of all the bills and everything else while we were together he might be able to handle his own business now. But oh well, his problems are no longer my problems. He said he wanted the house, so now he's got it. Let's see how long he keeps it."

"You go girl, with your bad self. I'm beginning to see a side of you I've never seen before," George said.

"That's because you've never had a reason to see it."

"In other words, I better not ever piss you off or I'll see it again?" George asked.

"All I'm saying is don't take my kindness for weakness." Then George said I was scaring him so he decided to go and take his shower. I guess my Miss Thang Therapist attitude was beginning to surface again.

I found my phone and called Mom to check on Amelia and to let her know everything was okay. She volunteered to keep

Amelia for the night and of course I didn't argue. I spoke to Amelia for a minute but all she wanted to know was if she could spend the night with her grandmother and I told her sure. I just let them think it was their idea. Mom asked me if I was scared to stay home alone and I told her that, no, I would be fine. I also told her to call me if she wanted to and then I laughed and told her that I had kept the same phone number. She said she didn't want to know any details about the phone, but that she just wanted me to be careful.

George came out of the shower with a pair of boxer shorts and a tank top on.

"Where did you get those clothes from? That's not the shirt you had on earlier."

"I know. I brought a change of clothes so I wouldn't have to drive home dirty and musty after going to work and helping you get moved all day."

I wonder if he really expected me to believe that. He didn't want to drive home like that; he only lives about twenty minutes away. But I'll let him think I believe him. I know this isn't his way of bringing his clothes over here little by little. So, I just looked at him and smiled.

"Why are you looking at me like that," he said. "Do you think I'm trying to take over and bring my things here too?"

"No, honey. I don't think anything of the sort." Then I hugged him and said, "I'm going to take a bath. I love you."

While I was in the tub I kept wondering why couldn't I have met George when I was in high school. Why did I have to waste so many years of my life in order to truly fall in love with someone? I was so glad I was able to fall in love with George with out having sex with him.

When I got out of the tub, I was so tired I didn't even try to find something sexy to put on. I just put on the first thing I found which was a big old pair of cotton pajamas. I couldn't believe George; he was still nice enough to tell me that I still looked sexy. He must have been blind. Then I looked on the living room/dining room floor, well, actually on the living room/dining room carpet, where George had spread several blankets out and made it like a bed. He had also finished filling up the waterbed.

"All we need now is some popcorn and everything would be perfect," George said.

"I think I can arrange that. If that's all you want is popcorn."

"But since you didn't have a refrigerator I thought you didn't have any food."

"That's where you're wrong. I took a few things out of the cabinet that Amelia likes to snack on and popcorn just happens to be one of her favorites. And oh yeah, I had one of my friends take the microwave from the other house too."

"Remind me to never make you mad with me, okay? And that reminds me, I have something I need to tell you," he said very seriously.

"Well, if it's something that would make me mad with you, just save it for some other time because I'm too worn out to get mad tonight." Then I kissed him and said, "I don't think I could ever get mad at you anyway." So I popped George some popcorn and we sat on the floor. I mean we sat on the blankets and started watching television.

George told me to lie down as he put a pillow down for me. He said he knew I had a long day and he wanted me to relax while he massaged my back. There's something about George's massages that makes me forget about anything and everything that's going on in and around my life. When George touches any part of my body I get weak. Even when it's just a quick little hug. I'm not exactly sure what it is, besides the fact that I'm totally in love with this man. I don't think I could ever love a man more than I love George and I hope I never have to try. George has been there for me at times when I've needed him most and hopefully I've been there for him as well. I tell George constantly how I feel about him because I don't want him to ever doubt my love.

My back massage was slowly and gently turning into a body massage. What was this man trying to do to me? If he only knew what power he has over my mind right now, it could be dangerous. Whatever he wants from me he can have. I'm trying really hard not to say anything because I really don't want him to know that he has that much control. He could ask me anything in the world right now and I would say yes; that is, if I could speak. I keep telling myself, "Okay, Cassandra, get a hold of yourself." But instead with George's help, he must have been thinking what I was thinking, so I turned over and said, "George." But before I could get the words "make love to me" out of my mouth, he covered my mouth with one of his fingers and said, "shhh."

Then he said, "Cassandra, will you make love to me?"

As if he really had to ask me. He was such a gentleman, even then. Then I kissed him and I guess that answered his question. George proceeded to kiss my entire body and I couldn't begin to tell you what happened next. That is, because it was indescribable. But what I can tell you is that I now know what it's like to have made love to the most fabulous lover in the world. I know what it's like to win the lottery with no money involved. I found out where cloud nine is. And now I also know what it's like to have an out-of-body experience and an inner body experience all in the same night, if you know what I mean. Oh, and of course we used a condom.

I'm going to have to do something extra special for George. He has done so much for me. I don't know how I can begin to pay him back. Not including what he's done to me and for me tonight, he's done so many other things. He's bought me so many gifts, the sunglasses, the Monterey trip, the refrigerator. How can I begin to thank him? His ex-wife must be a fool. But I thank her anyway.

Later on that night I think I partially paid George back. I woke him up from a deep snore by kissing on his chest. At first I thought something was wrong because as I was kissing him he abruptly sat straight up.

"I'm sorry, honey. Did I startle you?" I asked him.

"No, sweetheart. I'm the one sorry. I must have been having a nightmare," he said.

"Well, do you want to talk about it?"

"No, sweetheart. Why don't you go to sleep? You have got to be tired."

"Don't worry about me. You just relax and go back to sleep if you want to."

Then I continued kissing George's chest and then the rest of his body.

"What are you trying to do to me?" George asked.

"Who me? Miss Innocent Cassandra? I'm not trying to do anything."

"Cassandra, you better stop whatever it is you're doing because you're going to make me lose control. Oh Cassandra, I can't talk right now."

So whatever it was Miss Innocent Cassandra did to him I knew he enjoyed it. And I guess I did it right. He had no complaints.

George eventually made me lay my head on his chest and he kissed my forehead. Then he said, "Damn girl. Why did you make me lose it like that? Cassandra, I hope I've satisfied you at least half of how you've made me feel tonight."

"Are you kidding? It was that, plus some," I said.

That morning I must have been burnt out because I didn't even hear George when he got up and left. However, he did manage to leave a note on a receipt he found on the kitchen counter saying, "Thank you! I love you too! I will see you this evening." This man is too good to be true. So what's wrong with him? What ever it is, do I really want to know?

That evening George stopped by on his way home but he didn't stay long because I told him I had to go and pick Amelia up from my mom's house. As soon as he came in he gave me a kiss on my forehead and told me I shouldn't have done that.

"I shouldn't have done what?" I said with a grin on my face.

"Wait a minute. I left something for you on the seat in my car. I'll be right back," he said.

He came back in and handed me one red rose and a small jewelry box.

"What is this, George? You have to stop buying me things."

"Okay, fine. Give it back," he said.

"No, it's too late now." Then I smiled and said, "I mean in the *future* you have to stop buying me things."

"So go ahead and open it. Then I'll let you go and pick up your daughter."

I opened the box and it was a pair of diamond earrings.

"George, they're beautiful. You're going to make me cry. You have to stop buying me things for real. I want you to know that I love you for you and I don't want you to ever doubt that."

"Cassandra, trust me. I know exactly how you feel and I'm not sure that I deserve your love. But you deserve everything I've given you, plus some. And when the day comes that I can't buy you things then that's the day I'll stop. So let me see how they look on you. You're beautiful. Now give me a kiss and you go and pick up Amelia and either I'll call you later or you call me when you get back. Okay?"

"Okay, George. I love you."

"I love you too, sweetheart."

GRANDMA'S HOUSE

Just as I was walking out the door the phone rang. It was my mom saying she would bring Amelia home so she could see our new place. So I gave her directions as I tried to pick up a few things to try and make it more presentable.

When Mom and Amelia arrived they both seemed a little disappointed. Well, actually Mom was very disappointed but she tried not to show it too much. She asked me if I was sure we could adjust to such a small place. I told her it wasn't a matter of *if* we could because we would. Then she wanted to know where the rest of the furniture was and I had to tell her Robert kept it. Then of course she had a few curse words for him as she told me how I was being much too nice. I told her that they were all material things and how those things didn't matter to me. I also reminded her of what she said when she and my dad were going through a divorce. When I reminded her that as long as I had Amelia with me nothing else mattered, then she agreed and saw it my way.

Amelia at first seemed a little disappointed too. Her bedroom was much smaller than it was at the other house. In fact, all of her furniture wouldn't fit in her current bedroom so I had to store some of it on the patio. Then I showed Amelia that there was a park and a playground right outside of our back door, but she wasn't too enthused. Her main focus was if there was a pool or not and I told her "Not." But I did tell her we could spend a lot of time at the local city pool where we had taken swimming lessons year after year and she seemed to be happy with that. In fact, with a big smile on her face she said, "Okay, Mom, that's something we can do together. Just the two of us." And that one comment made all the difference in the world.

With Amelia's help, I was determined to make our little apartment a happy home. And besides, it was only temporary. I had already promised Amelia that. I guess Amelia's comment touched my mom too because now Mom wanted to come back over on my next weekend off. She wanted to first hit all of the garage sales to find some pictures to go on my walls and any other odds and ends that she could find.

"Okay, Mom, that sounds good. Drive careful and call me when you get home."

My dad came over the next evening and as usual he didn't have any negative comments; at least none that he said out loud. Dad is so mellow nothing ever seems to bother him.

At my request he took a tour around the apartment and said, "This is nice, honey. Is there anything else you need?"

Then I told him I left a lot of things over at the other house.

"Well, I don't want you going back over there to get anything. What is it you need right now?"

I hadn't realized it before but I left things like the iron and ironing board, the vacuum cleaner, the mop, the broom and cleaning supplies. Then Dad gave me his checkbook and told me to write myself a check for two hundred dollars. "I hope this helps, honey," he said.

Then I kissed him and told him, "Yes, it does help. Thank you."

This seemed so weird because every since I was seventeen and moved out on my own I hadn't had to ask my parents for anything. Actually, it was quite the opposite. I'd helped my mom out financially quite a few times and I'd helped Dad in other ways. But I guess there's a first time for everything and if Robert and I didn't sell the house soon, I might be asking my parents for a lot more. But my promise to myself was to someday be able to pay them back for everything.

That evening Robert's mom called and asked if Amelia could spend the weekend with her. I asked her if she were calling for herself or for Robert and she said she was calling for herself. She told me that no matter what went on between Robert and me she didn't want Amelia to feel left out. Actually, that was one of the things I was afraid of. I thought since she had all of her daughters' children around her all the time that Amelia would somehow be forgotten, being that Amelia was her *son's* child and Amelia was the only grandchild who lived out of town.

Even though we only lived about forty-five minutes away, it is going to be somewhat difficult because, although Robert had a large family out there, they all shared one car. So I agreed to bring Amelia out there and drop her off this one time. And I'll probably end up dropping her off quite frequently because I know Robert's not going to do it and I really want Amelia to keep in touch with that side of her family.

That weekend the weather was awful. It was raining off and on and I really didn't want to drive to Robert's mom's house but I got in my car and took my time and drove out there anyway. When I got home there was a message from George asking if he could come over. I called him back and told him yes.

George spent the night and we made beautiful love all night long. Well, at least we tried to, but the phone frequently interrupted us. Someone kept calling and either breathing really heavily or just calling and hanging up. I know it was Robert. He's still stupid. He needed to get a life because I certainly had. My life was going to be just fine right here with Amelia and George.

The next day Robert called me from his mother's house and admitted that he was playing on the phone last night. He told me that he knew I had company.

"Yeah, so what? What's it to you?"

"Well, since you're such a little smart bitch I'm gonna put your daughter outside on the porch in the rain and let's see if you can stop screwin' your man long enough to come and get her."

"Robert, why are you talking so crazy?"

"I'm not crazy. You're crazy, bitch. And I don't give a fuck about Amelia. She's not my fuckin' daughter anyway. She's probably Marcus'. And if she's not his, she's probably that guy's you were fuckin' last night. So how long have you known him?"

"What I do is none of your business."

"Well, you better come and get your daughter because I'm putting her outside now."

"Let me speak to Amelia."

"Hi honey. What were you doing?"

"I was in my grandma's room watching TV."

"Is everything okay? Is your dad okay?"

"Yes. Why?"

"Oh, just because he doesn't sound too good and I was thinking about coming to pick you up tonight. Is your grandmother there?"

"No, she's gone to bingo but she should be home in a few minutes."

"Okay, tell her to call me when she gets there. Are you sure your dad is okay?"

"Yes, he's fine."

When I hung up I called the Antioch police department and told them what Robert had said and I told them I wanted to pick Amelia up. I told them about the restraining order I had against Robert and they asked me if I thought Robert would give Amelia to me without a fight and I told them no. They also asked if I thought Robert was serious with his threat and I told them that I wasn't sure but I didn't want to find out. I think he would do anything he could to try to hurt me and make life more difficult for me. So the police told me to bring my copy of the restraining order with me and to call them from a pay phone as soon as I got in the area so they could escort me to Robert's mom's house to pick Amelia up.

I really don't like to get other people involved in my problems but I called my sister Sharon and asked her to ride with me and she agreed. We called the police from a nearby Seven Eleven and they followed us to Robert's mom's house. When we got there Robert came to the door and when he saw

I had the police with me he got ugly. He tried to push one of the officers out of the way as he was yelling and trying to get to me. Then the other officer immediately told me to get back in my car. Then my daughter and her grandmother came to the door and one of the officers told Amelia's grandmother what was going on. She told them that I should have known Robert wouldn't have hurt Amelia.

I guess she always has to take up for her precious son. In her eyes, he can do no wrong. And when he does she'll always find a way to justify his actions. So my daughter was standing right there watching the police hold her father back as he cussed me out. I wish she didn't have to see this. I thought those days were over when I moved out. Then Robert told the police that since Amelia was his daughter too, he had a right to keep her with him sometimes. Then they told him he was right but when he speaks of putting her in danger then he has no rights. Of course he denied ever having that conversation with me. Amelia was soon escorted to my car and we took off. The next day Robert called my house several times trying to apologize but I hung up on him each time. If he thinks he's sorry now, just wait. And anyway, where is Tamesha?

MRS. WONDERFUL

The following weekend Amelia went to a slumber party at my sister Sharon's house so I called George to let him know I was alone. I asked him if he wanted to go to the movies and for the first time ever he told me he was pretty busy and he wouldn't be free until later on tonight but he promised to come over when he became available. Then I asked him if there was anything I could do and he said no. I reminded him that since I was a free woman, I was now able to come over to his house without feeling guilty but he wouldn't take me up on that offer either.

Well, for the first time George didn't keep his promise to me. I sat at home all evening waiting for him but he never showed up. I picked up the phone several times to call him back but every time I got close to dialing all of his numbers I would hang up the phone.

I guess I was still in shock. George was always there when I needed him. Whenever I would call he would always be there for me. And now all of sudden he had something to do and he didn't even tell me what it was; however I didn't ask him either. From day one we had been able to talk to each other about everything so I was sure that he would tell me what was going on as soon as he got a chance. So I went to bed.

The next afternoon George came over. When I asked him what happened he just looked at me and didn't respond. Then I took his hand and led him into my bedroom.

"What's wrong, honey? You don't seem like yourself. Is something bothering you? Have I done something?"

"Yes, as a matter of fact, there is something. But before I tell you I want you to know that I love you."

"Honey, I already know that. So what's wrong?"

"Cassandra, I know I haven't really expressed to you how much I love you. But I want you know that what ever happens between us I really do care about you."

"George, stop it. You're scaring me. All the times I've told you that I'm in love with you, do you think I was joking? So whatever it is that you have going on, we'll get through it together. You've been there for me for the past year and I really appreciate that. So I promise you that I'll always be here for you."

Then I started unbuttoning his shirt and he stopped me and said, "Are you sure you want to make love to me?"

"Of course I'm sure."

Then instead of starting on his shirt again I started on his pants and he didn't stop me. As he sat there on the side of my bed undressed from the waist down, I also undressed myself. I sat on his lap and attempted to unbutton his shirt again but he stopped me again. Then he flipped me over on my back and started kissing me. Somehow between the kisses I managed to ask him to take his shirt off and he did. At first, I wondered what the big deal was with him leaving his shirt on. Then I found out what the big deal was. Right in the middle of making the best love ever, I opened my eyes and there was a tattoo on his chest as big as day that had a female's name along with a date, which happened to be just two years ago. Then, all of a sudden, I pushed his shoulders up and said, "Honey, who is Gloria?"

"Let's not talk right now. This feels so good. Girl, I don't know how you do it but when we're making love you make me forget everything else."

"But who is Gloria?"

"Honey, come on, stop talking. I love you, baby."

"George, I love you too, but who is Gloria?"

Then George starts making love to me like there's no tomorrow. He gave me a really passionate kiss and for a while I almost forgot what I had asked him. But then I remembered.

"George, for the last time, who's Gloria and why do you have her name and that date tattooed on your chest?"

"Do we have to talk about this right now? This feels so good."

"Yes we do. So get off of me."

George got up and got dressed while he kept trying to avoid the question. Then he reminded me of my promise that what ever it was we could work it out together.

"Um, Gloria is my wife," he mumbled.

"Your what?"

"She's my wife. But before you get upset let me tell you that we only live together for financial reasons. There's nothing else between us."

As I stood up naked I hit him with a pillow and cried, "She's your what?"

"Cassandra, I'm so sorry, honey. I never meant to hurt you."

Then I started getting dressed and said, "You never meant to hurt me? Well, you had a whole fucking year to tell me you were married. So that's why you never pressured me for sex. You were getting it from your wife."

"No, Cassandra. It was nothing like that. You were going through so much of your own mess I didn't want to bother you with mine."

"Well, I thought we could talk to each other about anything. So you didn't think it was important enough to tell me you were married? I can't believe I've been so stupid. I can't believe I fell in love with a married man."

"Cassandra, come here. You're not stupid at all. It's all my fault."

"You're damn right it's your fault. I really thought our relationship was something special but you've lied to me from day one. I remember you told me you were single and invited Amelia and me over to your house for a swim. How were you going to pull that off?"

"It wasn't a matter of pulling anything off. At first I didn't think it was necessary to tell you because I didn't know our relationship would progress to what we have now."

"Okay, I understand you didn't know at first, but what

happened to at second, at third, at ten, at eleven, at twelve months later?"

"Gloria and I are basically roommates and she sees who she wants to see and I see who I want to see. And when I first met you she was away on a business trip, or maybe she was on some trip with her man, I don't know. So you really could have come over."

"Oh, so you two make it a habit of cheating on each other and you can feel free to use the house as long as the other one is out of town? Is that the way it works?"

"No, it's nothing like that. She and I are married in name only. I haven't slept with her in over a year. In fact, we sleep in separate rooms. And you of all people should be able to understand that."

"Well, I might have been able to understand that if you would have told me a year ago. I don't know what to believe now. And now that you're caught you're probably still lying."

"I'm not lying to you, Cassandra. I love you. In fact I'm *in* love with you too."

"Well, that's the first time I've heard that from you. But you don't even know what love is. If you loved me you would have told me a long time ago. So, like Tina said, 'What's love got to do with it?' I can't believe I've been so stupid. Me, Miss Family Values, I can't believe I fell in love with a fucking married man."

"Cassandra, do you know how funny you sound trying to cuss? And did you hear what else you said? You said that you still love me. Do you?"

"I'm glad you think everything is a joke. So when I call Gloria and tell her the joke maybe you can explain the punch line to her because I don't get it."

"Cassandra, please believe me. I never meant to hurt you."

"Oh, so now all of a sudden it's no longer funny. I'm sorry, but why don't you tell me how am I supposed to feel?"

"Well, before I told you, you said that what ever was bothering me we would deal with it together. So can we at least try and work things out?"

"And how do you suppose we do that?"

"I don't know but if you really want to be with me, if you really do love me, we will work this out together. So do you love me like you say you do or not?"

"Don't even try to make me feel guilty or sorry. And unlike you, I'm not going to lie about it. Yes, unfortunately I do love you. But don't use my love to try to change things around. You just want to have your cake and eat it too. But you've eaten all the cake you're going to eat here. So leave me the fuck alone and go home to your wife. And you can take all of your gifts with you too."

"Cassandra, I don't want anything back from you. I bought you things because I wanted you to have them. They're yours. But please don't shut me out. No matter what you think of me right now you have to believe that I love you. And you can't deny that you love me too."

"Please just leave me alone and go home to your wife. And don't worry about me. I will be just fine. I promise you. So would you like me to call your wife for you and let her know you're on your way? Oh, or is she out of town?"

"Cassandra, I don't care what you say. I'm not leaving you here like this. I would never walk out and leave you crying like this."

"Well, you might as well leave now, because thanks to you, I have a year's worth of crying to do. But like I said, don't start worrying about me now."

"Cassandra, that's what you don't seem to understand. I have loved you for a long time. And no matter what you say we're going to get through this. And I'm not going to leave here until I know you're okay. So what else do you want to know?"

"What else should I know? So how many more wives and children do you have out there? You've told me about your daughter Connie and your first wife. Then you told me about your son George Jr. and his mother. So is Gloria George Jr.'s mother or is she wife number three and are there even more children out there too?"

"Yes, Gloria is my third wife and no we don't have any

children together. She has a daughter by a previous relationship and she can't have any more children which is one reason why we got together, because you know how I feel about having more children."

"Okay, so what are the other reasons you got together with her?"

"Gloria and I have been married now for almost three years. We met through some mutual friends and at that time we both were going through some critical times in our lives. Both of our fathers had just passed away in tragic accidents and we were there to console each other because no one else could imagine the pain we were going through. And after that things happened so quickly. I had only known her a few months and then we were married. It might seem strange to you but we both thought that because we had the tragedies in common we could build a relationship based on that and we tried but we were both wrong. Our relationship only lasted until we, in our own little way, stopped grieving. Then we realized we had nothing else in common. Sex was never that great with her and neither was anything else. But I don't mean to talk about her, we just found ourselves in a situation that we didn't want to be in and just haven't done anything about it."

"So do you love her?"

"I care about her but I have never been in love with her. Like I said, we really did get together for the wrong reasons."

"But you still could have told me a long time ago."

"I'm sorry. I am truly sorry."

"I can't believe I've put myself in this situation. But why am I taking the blame for you? You're the one who put me in this situation."

"Cassandra, just stick with me and I promise I will make it up to you."

"I can't believe it. How could my life be so wonderful this morning and so totally fucked up this evening?"

"Cassandra, believe me, I know I've hurt you, but please, give me a chance to make it all better. Come here and let me hold you."

Okay, I'm thinking what do I do now? I really want George to hold me but he can't just apologize and think everything is going to be all better. I know I have to be strong because if I let him get away with this he'll think I'm weak and who knows what he'll try to get away with next. He can't even begin to understand how much he has hurt me. I can't believe I've had an affair with a married man. There go my values right down the tube. But maybe he really does love me and maybe he really didn't mean to hurt me and maybe I should give him another chance. NOT.

"Cassandra, I asked you to come here so I can hold you."

"Hell no. Get out and go home and hold your wife."

George left and I know he didn't want to leave any more than I wanted him to. Even though he should have no doubts about the way I feel for him, he'll learn not to take my love for granted.

Then I started crying again and I'm not sure when I stopped. I couldn't believe I'd been so stupid. And how did he get away with his little secret for so long? I know why I'd never been to his house; it was my choice. Going to his house went right along with not having sex with him until my divorce was final. But why didn't I see the obvious tattoo sooner? I know they say love is blind but I thought I had my eyes wide open. So what happened? How did he pull this off?

Well, let me think about the times in which I've had the opportunity to see this tattoo. Let's see. There were the hot tub trips but of course it was always pitch black inside the rooms, which is why he didn't mind getting completely undressed. Then there was the hotel room in Monterey but I remember him sleeping nude that night so how come I didn't see it then?

That dirty dog. I remember now. He came out of the bathroom with his tee shirt and shorts on but later he asked me if I needed the light on and when I said no he turned them off, got undressed and got in bed.

Then the day I moved into my apartment he spent the night but, again, he came out of the bathroom with his tee shirt on. When he woke up that night and found me kissing his chest he nearly had a heart attack but he said he had just had a nightmare. Nightmare my butt. He was scared I would have found his little secret then. That dirty dog. So that's how he pulled it off. He didn't. He left it on until dark.

THE ROLLER RINK

The next few weeks I kept avoiding George's calls or maybe it was only the next few days but it seemed like weeks. He kept leaving me messages saying he was sorry and he was begging me to return his calls but I didn't. I really did love George but if I let him get away with this, he'd only hurt me again. I know it. The best thing for me to do was just plan my life around Amelia and me. So that's what I did.

The city pools were closed for the winter so we took up a new hobby of roller-skating. I did what ever I could to spend more time with Amelia and less time thinking about George. Every chance we had, Amelia and I would drive around to different roller-skating rinks in the bay area.

One weekend, out of the blue, I decided to drive Amelia and one of her little girlfriends down to a skating rink in Fremont. It took us about an hour and a half to get there but I didn't mind the drive because we sang and played games the entire way. When we got there I noticed it was quite different from our local skating rink. There were a lot more people and a lot more men there.

I sat on the bench for a while and watched the girls skate. Then all of a sudden this tall, dark, bald headed guy came and sat down next to me. And in this deep voice sounding like Barry White he said, "So how are you doing today?"

"I'm doing fine. How are you?"

"I'm doing good. I have my daughters for the weekend so I decided to bring them skating."

"Oh, that's nice."

"We come here quite a bit but I've never seen you here."

"No, you sure haven't. We don't live around here. I woke up this morning and decided to bring my daughter and her girlfriend down here for a change of scenery."

"So where did you drive from?"

"We live in Fairfield."

"Boy, that's sure a hell of a drive for a change of scenery."

"I know, but we do things like this quite often. Anything to make my daughter happy."

"So are you married?"

"No, I'm divorced. And you?"

"I'm single."

Then he held out his hand for me to shake and he said, "Well, today must be my lucky day. My name is Chris. Chris Scott."

"I'm Cassandra."

"Cassandra, you sure are beautiful. So is there some lucky man in Fairfield waiting for you to come back home?"

"No, my daughter and I live alone."

"Well, I have custody of my younger daughter out there; and my older daughter lives with her mother in North Richmond but I still see her often. I love spending time with my girls. They're my pride and joy."

"That sounds so nice. I wish my ex would spend more time with my daughter but he doesn't. If he can't see me he doesn't want to see her either. So I try to over compensate for his absence by being Mommy and Daddy both."

"That's a damn shame. I hate stupid men who don't see their kids for whatever reason."

"I feel the same way but unfortunately it happens all to often. You really should be commended for spending time with your girls."

"Bullshit. I shouldn't be commended. People think that when men spend time with their kids they deserve an award or some shit, but that's their job. Take you for example. Don't you feel that being a mother is a full-time job?"

"Yes, actually it's like having several full-time jobs."

"Well, men should feel the same way."

"You're absolutely right, but in reality, men like you are the exception rather than the rule. But that's enough of that subject because it makes me mad every time I think about how my daughter doesn't have her father in her life."

"So, Cassandra, what else would you like to talk about?"

"I don't know."

"So is there a local skating place there in Fairfield?"

"Yes, but I'm tired of going there."

"How about if I brought my girls to Fairfield next weekend to visit your skating rink?"

"That sounds fine."

"So can I get your phone number?"

"Sure. You seem like a nice guy."

So Chris and I exchanged numbers and we continued to sit there on the bench watching the girls. Then here came all of them. We introduced the girls to each other and come to find out, his oldest daughter, Eboni, was only a few months older than Amelia and his youngest daughter, Marissa, and I shared the same birthday. What a coincidence. I was really impressed that he was so attentive to his girls. Seeing a man spend time with his children really turned me on. And Chris's deep voice was pretty sexy too.

The next time Amelia and his girls came over to the bench, Chris offered to take us all out for pizza and I accepted. I followed Chris about two blocks to the pizza parlor and we all sat there looking like we were one big happy family. Chris must have been feeling what I was feeling because right after we sat down he told me how nice it would be to have a good woman in his daughters' lives. And for a whole thirty minutes or so I even forgot about George.

When it came time to pay for the pizza I offered to pay half and Chris accepted. I didn't mind paying but he was certainly not George in those regards, that's for sure. When we got ready to leave, Eboni asked Amelia for her phone number so they exchanged numbers also. Then Chris told me to call him as soon as I got home to let him know we had made it in. As I was saying "okay" all of the girls giggled and blushed.

When I got home there were more messages from George on my answering machine, again begging me to give him a call. I really wanted to call him so badly, but instead I called Chris. Chris and I talked on the phone for hours. We learned a lot about each other. I learned that Chris had two habits that I don't particularly care for. He smoked cigarettes and he drank occasionally. Chris couldn't believe it when I told him that I had never smoked before nor had I ever drank alcohol, not even when I got married, I told him. It appeared though, that we still had a lot in common.

We were the same age. We both loved spending time with our children. We both wanted more children some day but agreed not until we were in a loving, stable relationship.

Chris told me his children were by two different women. His oldest daughter was conceived with his high school sweetheart while they were also seniors, just like I was with Amelia. His youngest daughter's mother was white. He went on to tell me that she was on drugs and that was why he had custody and that was why he was looking for a good woman for his girls. I told him how I loved children and that really seemed to turn him on.

"Maybe one day we could have a child of our own," Chris said.

"Maybe. You never know," I replied.

Chris and I talked on the phone several times during the next week and we agreed to meet at the Fairfield skating rink on Saturday afternoon at one o'clock. I knew I was going to have an expensive phone bill because every time George called and left me a message I would in turn call Chris. I was trying really hard to avoid George because I really did love him but I didn't want to be used and I certainly didn't want to be hurt any more. Then all of a sudden there was a knock on my door.

ANOTHER LIE

"What are you doing here?" I said to George.

"I'm really sorry for just popping up. Do you have company or something?

"No, I don't have company or something. What do you want?"

"It's cold out here. Can I come in and talk to you for a minute? No, let me re-phrase that, because that's all you'll give me is a minute. So can I come in for a while and talk to you?"

"What is it that we have to talk about?"

"Cassandra, please. It's cold out here. I'm begging you."

"Well, you've been doing quite a bit of begging lately. Why should this time be any different?"

Then Amelia hollered and asked me if I could close the door because she was cold. So I told George he had five minutes and that was all. Then I looked at my watch and realized I had on a watch he had bought me. And as I started taking it off I said, "Here, you want this back?"

"Cassandra, stop it. The only thing I want back from you is your love."

"Well, I'm sure you can get plenty of that at home."

"Cassandra, please just hear me out. You said I have five minutes, so just listen."

Then there was another knock on the door.

"Maybe that's your wife. Maybe she followed you over here."

I answered the door and it was one of Amelia's friends from school asking if she could come over. Amelia grabbed her jacket and I told her I would pick her up in a couple of hours.

"Okay, George, now you have four minutes. So what's so important?"

Then he walked over and hugged me but I didn't hug him back. Then he kissed me on my forehead and told me how much he missed me. Now I wish Amelia hadn't left because as much as I pretended that I didn't love George and no matter how much I pretended I didn't want to be with him, I still did. But I know that only makes me a weak woman. The only way for me to say no to him was not to be around him and I think he knew that.

"So are you just going to stand here and hold me or do you have something to say?" I asked George.

"Yes, I have something to say."

Then I sat down on the living room floor and George joined me.

"Cassandra, I've been doing a lot of thinking."

"Yeah, so what. Am I supposed to be impressed?"

"Cassandra, what I've been thinking about is children."

"Yeah, again, so what?"

"What I mean is I know I've told you all along that I didn't want any more children but like I told Gloria yesterday, I've changed my mind."

Then with tears in my eyes I pushed him and said, "Oh, so what are you trying to tell me? Now you and your wife are planning a family together? So did you come here to hurt me even more?" Then I stood up and told George, "Get out of my house and get out of my life."

"Cassandra, you've got it all wrong. Didn't I tell you that Gloria couldn't have any more children?"

"And why should I believe you? And what's your point?"

"I really mean it. She can't have any more children. That's one reason why she and I got together because neither one of us wanted any more."

"Now, I'm really confused, George. So why would you tell her you want more children if you know she can't have any more? That must have made her feel like crap."

"Well, she told me to go on and have some and then she said not to look at her to do it. Then I told her I was involved with you and that I wanted children with you. So she and I decided last night that it was time for us to go our separate ways. I told you that she and I both knew our relationship was over a long time ago. We just never openly said it."

"I can't believe you would tell her something like that. She's your wife. You don't care who you hurt, do you?"

"I didn't mean to hurt her nor did I mean to hurt you."

"Oh, you didn't mean to hurt us? What, it just comes naturally?"

"Cassandra, you know what I mean."

Just then my phone rang.

"Hello."

"Hello Cassandra. This is Chris."

"Hi Chris. What's going on?"

"I'm calling to see if we were still on for tomorrow."

"Yes, we're still on for tomorrow. Amelia and I are really looking forward to it. In fact, if you want to come over a little earlier than we had planned I'll cook lunch for us all."

"That sounds good. What are you going to cook?"

"I don't know. Actually I can't stand cooking but, for you, I will make an exception."

"Oh, I feel special now."

"That's my intent, to make you feel special. But, anyway, I have company right now but he'll be leaving really soon, so can I call you right back?"

"Yeah, but I'm going to pick up my daughter in a few minutes so if I'm not here just leave me a message, okay?"

"Okay, I look forward to talking to you later. Good bye."

George was trying to pretend like he wasn't listening to my conversation but I know he was. As soon as I hung up the phone George said, "So, who is Chris?"

"Chris is a friend of mine that I recently met. I mean he's an *unmarried* friend of mine that I just met."

"So, you're seeing someone else already?"

"That depends on what you call seeing someone. I met Chris and he seems really nice and, in fact, he wants more children too. So what do you know, you're not the only one who wants to have more children."

"Come on, let it rest. I came over here to tell you that I love you and that I want you to have my baby."

"So am I supposed to feel privileged or something?"

"You know you're doing a great job at convincing yourself that you don't still love me but you're not convincing me at all. So stop pretending and come here."

Then George grabbed my hand and pulled me close to him; actually he didn't have to pull too hard. In fact, I nearly knocked him over, leaning on him so hard, so I said I was sorry but he only laughed. Then George asked me to look him in his eyes and tell him I didn't love him any more.

"Cassandra, if you can do that, I will pick up my jacket and walk out of your life for good." He knows I can't do it. I wonder if he really wants a baby. Why do I let him get to me like this? Because I still love him that's why.

"Cassandra, will you answer that one question for me?"

"What's the question again?"

"Do you still love me?"

"What do you mean, do I still love you? If I said no, it would mean I never did love you and you know that is not the case. But don't try to turn this around. The real question is do *you* love *me*? Or better still, are you *in love* with me? And if you can't answer yes to *both* of them then you do need to pick up your jacket and walk out of my life forever."

Then I couldn't believe it, and as my heart almost stopped, George walked over to his jacket but instead of putting it on he brought it to me and told me to look in his pocket.

"Look in your pocket for what? And you haven't answered my questions."

Then George reached in his jacket pocket and pulled out a jewelry box. Inside the box was a half-carat diamond ring surrounded by two hearts. Then he got on his knees and said, "This is for you, Cassandra. Yes, I love you and yes, I'm *in* love with you. I'm truly sorry for hurting you but I promise I will never hurt you again. So do you forgive me?" Then George put the ring on my finger and took my hand and led me to my bedroom.

"George, this isn't right. You know what we're doing isn't right and now I know it too."

Then George put his finger over my mouth and said, "Shhh" as he undressed me. Then like a fool, I unfastened his belt and his pants but I conveniently left his shirt on. Then George and I made love like we never had before. Actually, this time it really was different. This time, Mr. Protection didn't use a condom. I guess he really did want a baby.

When George left I felt so guilty. I couldn't believe what I had done. I had to make sure I didn't let it happen again. I knew it was going to be hard but I had to do it. But how? Just then, Amelia called and said she was ready to come home so I went to pick her up.

FAMILY OUTINGS

When we got back I called Chris. He and I talked on the phone for nearly two hours. He asked me why wasn't I involved with anyone. So I told him about George but of course I left the part out about us just sleeping together. He couldn't believe I was involved with George for so long and didn't know he was married. I told him I couldn't believe it either but it happened. Then Chris asked me what was I looking for in a man and I told him at this point I had to start with the basics. I was looking for someone first of all, who was single, honest and had a job. I told him that since I loved children, I wanted someone who also wanted children. Then Chris told me he wanted the same thing in a woman. He and I really seemed to have a lot in common.

Chris said he wanted more children some day but only after he found the right woman. He told me he'd never been engaged or even close to being engaged. He had his first baby by his high school sweetheart but then shortly after his daughter was born they grew apart. Actually, he said it was his fault for their breakup. He said he used to hang around with the wrong crowd and soon he became a part of that crowd. He spoiled his baby's mother by buying her everything she could ever want or need but then he realized it was time to get out of the fast life before he ended up dead. When he stopped giving her the things that she was used to, she didn't want him anymore. They broke up and she continued that lifestyle with someone else.

He told me again that his youngest daughter's mother was white and she was quite a few years younger than he was. He met her at a local grocery store where she used to bag groceries. She told him she was eighteen and had been kicked out of her mother's house for dropping out of school and for doing drugs so they became friends and he took her in. Six months later she was pregnant with his child and back on drugs. As soon as Marissa was born, he kicked her mother out and he got custody. Chris seemed like a really caring and sensitive man and I think I could really like him if I could only stop thinking about George.

The next day Chris and his girls came over but they were an hour early. So instead of cooking lunch for them some how they talked me into cooking breakfast omelets. I reminded Chris of the fact that I did not cook. In fact, I couldn't stand cooking. Amelia and I went out to eat every chance we got. But I'll fake it for now. After all, how hard could it be to cook a few omelets? I pulled out a brand new set of glass pots and pans that I had just bought and I was ready to go.

I put my little cooking oil in one of the small pans to get it hot and then, just as I was pouring the eggs into the pan the whole thing blew up. I mean the whole pan; eggs and all exploded right there in front of my eyes, Chris' eyes, Amelia's eyes and his daughters' eyes. Of course, I screamed and then Chris came running over to me. He grabbed me and asked if I was all right.

As he and I stood there in the middle of the kitchen floor I started laughing to keep from being embarrassed and then everyone else started laughing. When Chris saw that I was really okay he put his arms around me and kissed me. Then the girls started giggling and Chris said, "I thought you were kidding when you said you didn't cook but I see you were serious. I've never seen anyone blow up the whole kitchen just trying to fix some omelets. From now on I'll do all the cooking, okay?"

Then I kissed him on his cheek and the girls started giggling again and I said, "I'm sorry, but it wasn't me. It's these new pots I bought."

Chris just stood there shaking his head looking at the big mess I had made. There was glass everywhere. I told Chris instead of staring at it he could help me clean it up and he did. After we got it all cleaned I told everybody I would try it again but they wouldn't let me, not even Amelia. They all laughed and told me it was okay. In fact, no one seemed to be hungry anymore.

We soon left my house and we all squeezed into Chris' car and went to the skating rink. As soon as we got there, of course the girls said they were hungry and I told Chris I would buy hot dogs and snacks for everybody and he said okay. We stayed at the skating rink several hours and then Chris suggested going to a park so we went to a local one. Amelia and Eboni decided they didn't want to hang out around us so they took off walking and giggling together like they were long lost best friends. We kept Marissa with us. It was really fun pushing her in the swing and playing with her in the sand. I missed doing these things with Amelia. She was at that age now where she wanted her independence and I gave it to her as long as I could see where she was and what she was doing at all times. Well, actually I wasn't *that* bad.

Amelia and Eboni soon returned because they were getting cold. Actually, the weather had changed and it looked as if it was going to start raining soon. So we packed all the children back into the car and were headed to my house when Chris saw a video store along the way.

"How about if we pick up a couple of videos to watch before I take my girls home?" Chris said.

"That's fine with me."

While we were in the store, Chris whispered in my ear that he and his daughters were having such a good time he didn't want to leave me, so I smiled. From the looks of all the videos he was picking out you would have thought we were going to be locked in together for the entire winter.

When we got back to my apartment and everyone got settled in, I said that I was getting ready to start dinner and, almost in harmony, everybody yelled, "NO." Then Amelia and Eboni somehow managed to slip away into Amelia's room while Marissa kept drifting back and forth between her big sister and her daddy.

Chris finally left me alone to cook. I promised him I

wouldn't blow up the kitchen again. Actually, if he would have stuck to the plan I could have cooked my little spaghetti surprise earlier. But, no, instead he had to change the plans on me and arrive in time for breakfast. That would teach him. So now, I'd have to try and make it up by cooking one of my spaghetti specialties. Well, actually, it was my only specialty. Okay I can't lie, it was really Prego's specialty but that will be my little secret.

Dinner went well. Everyone had at least seconds so I guess Prego helped me redeem myself. After dinner all three girls went back into Amelia's room. I think the two oldest ones were trying to escape from doing the dishes but I let them think they were getting away with something. I started cleaning the kitchen myself, then Chris offered to help and I accepted. I told him I was surprised he offered and he said it wasn't a big deal. He reminded me that he was used to domestic chores since he was a single father. In fact, we finished cleaning the kitchen pretty quickly. It was as if we had been doing it together for years. He washed, I dried and put them up and he cleaned the cabinets and swept and we were done.

Before we sat down to start watching the movies, we called several times for the girls to come and join us but all we heard was laughing and giggling so we soon stopped calling. Chris and I originally sat down on a couple of beanbags but then he asked me to come closer. So I moved my beanbag right next to him and he asked me to come even closer.

"If I get any closer to you I'll be in your lap," I told Chris.

"Well, that's fine too," he said as he grinned.

Just as I was about to sit between his legs the phone rang. At first I didn't want to answer it but since I hadn't talked to my mom in a few days I decided I better get it; at least that's what I told Chris. But, of course it wasn't Mom. It was George.

"Hi, sweetheart. How are you?"

"I'm fine."

"Are you busy?"

"Yes, as a matter of fact I am."

"Do you have company?"

"Yes, I do. I'll call you back later, okay?"

"No, it's not okay. I'm the one who should be there with you right now."

"Well, yes you should, but you're not and I have to go."

"You mean what happened yesterday meant nothing to you?"

"You know the answer to that and I know what you're trying to do, so I must go now. I'll try to call you back later."

"You'll try?"

"George, I have to go. Goodbye."

Then I went back and sat down on my beanbag and I put my hand on my forehead. I don't know why I let George get to me. Why did I have to answer the phone? I was doing just fine here with Chris before I heard George's voice. Then Chris asked me something but I didn't hear what he said.

"I'm sorry. Did you just ask me something?"

"Yeah, are you okay?"

"Yes, I'm fine."

"Well, all of a sudden you seem distant. So was that your married friend on the phone?"

"Yes, it was him."

"So is everything okay?"

"Yes, everything is fine."

"Okay, then come back over here and sit on my lap like you started to do before the phone rang."

Then I gave Chris this half of a smile and I went and sat between his legs. Then he pulled my hair to one side and whispered in my ear, "If you give me a chance, I promise I'm gonna make you forget all about George."

Then I turned my head around and told Chris that's one promise I'm going to see to it that he keeps.

"Oh, this should be interesting," he said. Then he kissed me on my neck and we continued to watch the movie. After a few minutes, I told Chris I didn't feel comfortable sitting like that with him. I told him I preferred that the girls didn't see us like this. He thought I was making a big deal out of nothing but he said okay. Then he asked me if I had always been so proper.

"What are you talking about?"

"Will you promise you won't get mad with me if I ask you a question?"

"No, I won't get mad. I may not answer your question, but I won't get mad."

"Well, I want to know if you have always talked so proper?"

"What do you mean? I don't think I speak proper at all."

"Yes you do. In fact, you sound like a white girl. Has anybody ever told you that before?"

"Yes, I've heard it before. But I also have a problem with that. I think that's an insult. Why are you associating being proper with being a white girl? Why can't I sound like an intelligent black girl? But don't answer that because you'll never win this argument with me. I've had this conversation too many times before. So let me ask you a question. Do I speak like Marissa's mom?"

"Hell no. That girl can't even complete a sentence without cussing. Hell no, you don't sound nothing like her."

"So I really don't sound like a white girl after all."

"No. I guess you got a point."

Then Chris reached over and kissed me on my cheek and said he was sorry and I smiled at him and said, "It's okay. Just don't let it happen again."

We continued watching what was left of the first movie and then I decided to go and check on the girls. I couldn't believe what I saw. I went to get my camera and then I took Chris by the hand and brought him to Amelia's door. We stood there and looked at each other because the girls had gotten ready for bed. They each had on a pair of Amelia's pajamas as they lay there looking worn out across the bed. As I took their picture, I agreed with Chris that they must have been trying to tell us something.

Chris said, "Well can we?"

"Well, can we what?"

"Can we spend the night?"

I took another look at the girls and said, "How can I say no?"

So instead of trying to move the girls, I put a blanket on top of them and turned the light off. As we walked away I guess we weren't supposed to hear the two older girls giggle. But we let them think they had gotten away with something again.

Chris and I started watching the second movie when we realized we both were getting tired. Actually I think I fell asleep on Chris's chest a few times but I didn't admit it.

"Are you asleep, Cassandra?"

"No, I'm not asleep."

"Well, I'm getting kind of tired so where do I get to sleep tonight?"

"You get to sleep right here. I'll go and get you a pillow and some blankets right now."

"Now I'm insulted. You mean I don't get to sleep with you?"

"Yes, that's exactly what I mean. So how many blankets would you like?"

"You're serious, huh?"

"Yes, I am. In fact, I'll show you where the blankets are and while I'm taking a shower you can make yourself comfortable."

When I got out of the shower Chris had made himself a nice comfortable looking spot on the floor in my room next to my bed.

"I hope you don't mind. I promise to stay on the floor."

"Yes, I do mind. I'd rather you slept in the living room."

Chris didn't argue. So we moved his comfy pile into the living room and I stayed in there with him a couple more hours. Everything was really nice, that is, until my phone started ringing. It rang about four or five different times but I didn't want to get it. I knew it was either George or Robert. I knew it was about time for Robert to start bugging me again.

Chris asked me a couple of times if I was going to answer my phone and I told him I was sure it wasn't anyone of any importance. So we sat there and held hands and watched another movie. Then I told Chris I was tired and was going to bed. So I kissed him on his cheek and went to bed. Chris behaved himself and stayed in the living room all night. Even though he and I didn't sleep together it felt nice having him and his children in the house with me. It felt like we had a complete family and I knew the girls were happy since they orchestrated this entire scheme.

The next morning no one would let me cook breakfast for them so we went out to eat. Chris and his girls didn't stay long because they didn't have a change of clothes. But the girls really seemed to enjoy each other. I know they were like the sisters Amelia had always wanted but never had.

Chris and I continued to talk on the phone every chance we got and so did the girls. Chris even invited Amelia and me to spend the night at his house the next weekend and I accepted. We planned on taking the girls to Great America. It should be a lot of fun.

THE DILEMMA

During the course of the week I kept getting calls from Robert and from George. It started getting pretty redundant listening to the two of them beg. Although they were so different from each other, they both seemed to be trying to obtain the same goal. Robert would call and say he wanted me back and each time I would tell him it was too late, and then he would end up calling me a name. And not once did he mention seeing his daughter. I know in Robert's own little way he loved Amelia and me but the problem was just that; it's his own way. He didn't know what it was like to really love me the way I deserved to be loved. He didn't know that to love someone it shouldn't hurt and I hurt every time I look at the photos of me that the police took a few months ago. And every time he called me a name I associated him with the word "stupid." So he may as well have given it up because stupid doesn't have a chance. Stupid doesn't live here any more.

On the other hand, I knew George would never hurt me physically and in his own little way he probably loved me too. But again, love shouldn't hurt. And I hurt every time I thought of the word "wife." And every time I thought of the word "liar," I thought of him. And I certainly don't want to be with men who remind me of stupid liars. So I wonder what word Chris is going to make me think of. So far I see him as being a compassionate and loving father. I only hope he stays that way and if there's no hidden agenda, maybe he's the one for me.

That next weekend, just as I promised, Amelia and I packed our things and we drove to Fremont. Even though Chris only had a one-bedroom apartment we all somehow seemed to fit just fine. We stayed up most of the night watching movies and eating popcorn. The next day we got up early and Chris fixed breakfast for everyone. Since he wouldn't let me help with breakfast, the girls and I cleaned the kitchen and then we were off to Great America.

Chris and I held hands a lot and, as usual, the girls snickered and pretended not to see us. We were having so much fun we stayed until closing time. When we got back to Chris's apartment he said he didn't want me driving home so late. I agreed to spend another night but I told Chris that Amelia and I would be leaving early in the morning because I didn't want to get used to staying at his house. But he said he didn't see anything wrong with that.

We both expressed how much fun we had been having around each other and how much the girls seemed to enjoy each other. Then Chris asked me if I would ever consider moving to Fremont and I told him no. I was comfortable living in Fairfield and I didn't want to change Amelia's school. So I asked him if he would ever consider moving to Fairfield and he also said no.

"So, what are we going to do?" he asked.

"I don't know. I guess we'll both stay where we are," I said.

So we left the conversation like that but we agreed we still wanted to get to know each other so we continued talking on the phone and doing things together with the girls. If we weren't skating, we were at some park or at the movies or just hanging out at Chris's apartment playing games or doing puzzles with the girls. One weekend, we even drove the girls up to Tahoe to let them play in the snow.

Spending time with him was like clockwork. The girls knew exactly when they would see each other. They even started planning what they were going to wear so they could be dressed alike. Everything was going okay, that is, until I got sick one Friday. I told Chris I didn't think we would make it that weekend. I was so sick I asked my mom if she could keep Amelia overnight and she agreed.

George happened to call me just after I dropped Amelia off and I told him I didn't want to talk because I wasn't feeling well. Then the next thing I knew he was at my door so I let him in. He had two grocery bags in his hands and I asked what that was. He brought me several cans of soup, juice, 7-up, and some herbal tea. I kissed him on his cheek and thanked him. Then I told him I really didn't feel like being bothered but he insisted on making me a can of soup and a cup of tea and tucked me in before he left. He made it really hard for me not to forgive him. I really hoped I was doing the right thing.

The following morning there was a knock on my door bright and early. It was George again. He said he wanted to come over to see how I was doing. Even though I knew he was only coming over to see if anyone else was here with me, I just let him think I didn't know what he was doing. So I told him I was feeling much better. Then he started back on the conversation about the two of us. He told me he had decided to move out of his house with his wife and if he and I couldn't be together then he was moving out of state. So I asked him which state he was moving to. Then he tried to tell me he was serious and he really wanted to be with me.

"I really want us to be together, so will you give me another chance?"

"You mean will I give you another chance to hurt me? The answer is no."

"Cassandra, I know you love me so stop fighting it."

Then one thing led to another and I ended up in bed with him again but this time he was Mr. Protection again.

"So, why are you using condoms again?" I asked.

"Because I know you've been seeing that other guy so we can't be too careful."

"Just because I've been seeing him doesn't mean I've been sleeping with him."

"I know you've been spending a lot of time with him because I've come by here several times at night and you haven't been home. So are you trying to tell me you haven't been seeing him?"

"No, that's not what I'm trying to tell you at all. In fact, yes I have been spending a lot of time with him. I've even spent the night at his house but I haven't slept with him. And you of all people should know that I don't just hop in the bed as soon as I meet someone."

"I know that sometimes things just happen and sometimes it doesn't take that long," George said.

"You mean if the chemistry is right it doesn't take a long time to jump in the bed with someone. In fact, all it takes is for two people to have one thing in common like a tragic accident, if there really was an accident, and then they're in bed together and the next thing you know they're married. Is that what you mean?"

"Cassandra, that was really cruel. And, yes, our fathers really were in accidents."

"I'm sorry. I really shouldn't have said that."

"No, you shouldn't have."

"So what you're telling me is that you don't trust me much. And if you don't trust me, why did you just sleep with me?" I asked George.

"You say you don't trust me either, so why did you just sleep with me?"

"That's a good question. I guess because I love you but it still doesn't justify what we just did. We were wrong and we can't let it happen again. So if you really meant what you said about moving then I guess you'll just have to move because I'm not going to keep having an affair with a married man. I hope you can respect and understand that."

"Well, I'm going to be honest with you. I respect how you feel but I also know that you love me and I know we'll be back together someday. So you haven't gotten rid of me yet."

"Well, you're entitled to your opinion. We'll just have to see what happens. In the meantime, while you're still at home with your wife, I may or may not be with my other friend."

George finally left and I called Chris to let him know I was feeling better. But again, I didn't tell him I had just slept with George but I was making a promise to myself that I was not going to sleep with George again. Chris and I had so much in common; just maybe he was the man for me. We'll see.

"Cassandra, I know we have been spending a lot of time together with our girls but I really want to spend some time with you alone. Do you think that's possible?" Chris asked.

"That sounds really good."

"But before we do I have a personal question to ask you."

"What is it?"

"Are you on the pill?"

"No, I'm not. I'm not on anything."

"Okay, I just wanted to know."

"That's fine, but I'm feeling sick again. I'm going to have to get off the phone. I'll call you back later, okay?"

"Okay, but can I ask you one more quick question?"

Then, as I grabbed my mouth to keep from throwing up I said, "Hurry up. Make it quick."

"Is there any chance that you could be pregnant?"

"Why would you ask me something like that?"

"Because both of my girls' mothers had so-called morning sickness but they had it in the evening and I wondered if that's what was wrong with you."

I really didn't want to lie to Chris and tell him that I hadn't been sleeping with George so I said, "I guess anything is possible; highly unlikely, but possible I guess. But I have to go now. I'll call you back."

I barely made it but I ran straight to the bathroom where I stayed for the next half-hour barfing and thinking and barfing some more. What if Chris were right? What if I was pregnant? Come to think of it, I hadn't had my period that month. And my period was really regular. I knew exactly when it would start and when it would stop. Then I started crying. Why me? I guess I just didn't even think about my period with all of the other things going on in my life. So now what? Even though I'd told George I wanted more children, I never said I wanted more now. He and I both knew that now was not the right time. Actually, in light of everything that had recently happened, I don't think there would ever be a right time for George and me. But if he loved me like he said he did, then he'd make it the right time. So, I guess I'll call him and give him the news. But things didn't happen the way I planned. I called George's number and a female voice answered.

"Hello. Hello, is anybody there?"

I was so shocked that she answered the phone I just couldn't say anything. What was she doing answering his phone anyway? I hung up and started crying again. About a half-hour later I decided to call again and if she answered this time, I was going to ask for him. Then a female voice answered again.

"Hello. Hello, is anybody there?"

"Um yes, I'm sorry, is George there?"

"Hold on. Let me check." Then she yelled to someone and said, "Honey go and check in the garage to see if your dad is here."

To see if your dad is here, I thought. His son lives with his mother and his daughter is away in school. So who is she talking to? Then she got back on the phone.

"No, I'm sorry, honey. George isn't here right now. Can I take a message?"

"Um, yes you can. Will you tell him Sandy called?"

"Sure. Does he have your number, Sandy?"

"Yes, he knows how to reach me. Thank you." Then I hung up.

So why is she answering his phone and who's there calling him Daddy? How many more lies and secrets does he have? How many more children does he have?

I called back an hour later and she answered again so I hung up. Where is he I wondered. He finally called me back and asked me if I had left a message saying I was Sandy because I had never referred to myself as Sandy before. I told him that, yes it was me, and with an attitude, he asked me what was so important that I had to leave a message.

"What do you mean what's so important? I thought you told her everything. So she shouldn't be surprised when I call there, now should she?"

"Cassandra, I'm not going to argue with you. So what's so important?"

"I'm not feeling well. Can you come back down here?"

"What's wrong?"

Then I started crying again and said, "I don't know. Can you come back though?"

"I'll see what I can do, okay?"

Then I hung up on him. He'll see what he can do. That means she must have been standing right there. I can't believe I'd got myself in this situation. Pregnant by a married man. So I just lay there in my bed and cried. A few minutes later my phone rang and it was my mother. Even though I tried to hide the fact that I had been crying, she knew something was wrong.

"I just don't feel well, Mom, so can you keep Amelia another night?"

"Sure. Amelia is fine but what's wrong with you?"

So I blurted out, "I think I'm pregnant by a married man."

"You're what? And by whom? Now, wait a minute, and let me sit down. When I asked you what was wrong that's not what I was expecting to hear. So now what's going on? Amelia told me that you guys have been spending time with some new guy and his children. But I thought you were still seeing George. So what happened between you and Mr. Wonderful?"

"Mr. Wonderful my butt. The problem is there's a Mrs. Wonderful. That's what happened."

"Now wait a minute. You're telling me you're not pregnant by this new guy? You're pregnant by George and George is the one that's married?"

"Yes, that's exactly what I'm telling you. I found out a couple of months ago that George is married."

"Are you sure it's George's baby?"

"Mom, I can't believe you asked me that. Of course I'm sure."

"Well, I didn't mean to offend you. I know you know what you're doing, so I won't bring it up again. So have you told George? And does your new friend know?"

"No, I haven't told him yet. And Chris, my new friend, knows I've been sick this weekend. In fact he asked me if I were pregnant and I told him I didn't think so."

"You didn't do this hoping George would leave his wife, did you?"

"Mom, you act like I'm stupid or something."

"Honey, I know you're not stupid but this kind of thing happens all the time and I know how crazy you are about George, that's all."

"No, Mom, I didn't do this on purpose and I honestly don't know how he's going to respond. I just talked to him but we didn't say much because he couldn't talk. I can't believe I've been so stupid."

"You're not stupid, honey. I told you this type of thing happens all the time. You're not the first one and you won't be the last one. So how far along are you?"

"I guess I'm a couple of months. I haven't taken a test or anything yet."

"So I guess I'll have to start going to garage sales looking for some baby furniture, huh?"

"I don't know. I don't know what I'm going to do. Mom, I can't afford another baby. I can barely afford to take care of Amelia. Robert isn't helping with Amelia at all and I still have a ton of bills that he and I made together and he's not helping with those either."

"So why didn't you tell me you needed money?"

"Because I haven't had to ask you for money since I was seventeen. And besides, right now George is helping me. But I told him the other day that I was not going to accept anything else from him. He can't buy my love. I told him it's not for sale. But, Mom, I really don't know what to do."

"Well, I don't have much but you can always come back and live here with me. You can stay in your old room and Amelia can stay in the other empty room."

"But Mom."

"In fact, I insist. I want you and Amelia to move back home and that way you can pay off some of your bills so you can get a fresh start."

Then as I started crying I said, "Thanks for the offer but I don't know what I'm going to do yet."

"I just told you what you're going to do. What else is there to think about?"

"I don't know what I'm going to do about this other baby now."

"What do you mean? You don't have any other choice! Now I know you're not thinking about having an abortion and certainly not adoption. Those aren't even options. So from what I see you don't have any problems and nothing to think about. So what are you talking about?"

"I don't know, Mom. You know I don't believe in abortions either and, no, I would never even think about adoption. I don't know what I'm thinking right about now. I still can't believe I'm in this situation. I guess I'll feel better whenever I get a chance to talk to George about it. In fact, someone is at my door right now. I'm sure it's him so kiss Amelia for me and I'll call you back, okay?"

"Okay, sweetheart. Don't worry about Amelia. She's fine. Call me later."

So I went to open the door for George and he took one look at me and said, "Come here sweetheart. You've been crying. What's wrong?"

"I think I'm pregnant," I blurted out.

Then George kind of pushed me away and said, "You're what?"

As I started crying again, I said, "I'm sorry but I think I'm pregnant."

"You're pregnant? So what are you going to do?"

Me? I can't believe he's wondering what *I'm* going to do. He's acting as if I'm the only one in this. He better watch out before my Miss Thang attitude comes out on him. So as calmly as I could, I said, "What do you mean what am *I* going to do? What are *we* going to do? Or better still, what are *you* going to do?"

"Well, you know my situation. And I never made you any promises."

"You never made me any promises. What about telling me you wanted more children. In fact, the one time you didn't use a condom is probably when it happened. So that was a lie too, huh?"

"No, I wasn't lying. But you and I both know a lot has changed between us in the past couple of months. You've been telling me you don't want me to be a part of your life. So I know you're not considering having this baby."

"Just what are you trying to tell me, George? Did you say you wanted a baby because you thought it was what I wanted to hear? Was that your way of getting me back in the bed with you?"

"No, that wasn't it at all. I really do want more children but just not right now."

"Oh, so you thought we could screw now and I get pregnant later. What's that, a fucking plan deferral?"

"Cassandra, I know whenever you use that kind of language you are really upset. I know I've hurt you but I'm sorry."

"You sure are. But I should be the one who's sorry. Sorry for being your little sex kitten. I see now that's all I was to you."

"Cassandra, you know you're more than that. It's just that right now is not a good time."

"Well, whenever it becomes the right time for you, you can look us up."

"So, you're trying to tell me you're going to go ahead with this?"

"You haven't given me a good reason why I shouldn't."

"One reason is because financially I know you have a lot of bills that Robert left you with and I know you can't afford to support another child."

"Well, excuse me, but isn't that where you come in?"

"Cassandra, you just don't know. I stay broke."

"Stay broke my butt. You need to save that lie for someone else. Someone who might be inclined to believe you."

"And, Cassandra, it's not only the financial issue. There are other people who will get hurt if you decide to keep this baby."

"Other people like who?"

"Um, uh, like the children we already have. My daughter will suffer because I won't be able to continue to support her through college and my son will be hurt because I won't be able to do much for him either. I barely see him now. And not to mention Amelia. You two are really getting to know each other now and you're doing a good job of getting your life back together after your divorce. You don't need a baby interfering with that right now."

"Interfering? Is that what you think of this baby, an interference? Well, you know what? You still haven't given me a good reason for not going through with this. But I'm not going to beg you. I didn't beg you to get me pregnant and I'm not going to beg you to stick around. So if you want to abandon this baby just like Robert has abandoned Amelia you go right ahead because somehow we will make it without you."

"Cassandra, that's not fair. How can you even compare me with Robert? If you really loved me like you said you did then you wouldn't go through with this."

"Don't even start. Even though you don't deserve it, my love for you is real. You know how I feel about you and I'm not afraid to say it. But there's one thing that apparently you haven't learned about me and that is the fact that my child or should I say *my children* always come before any man, including you."

"I know Amelia is your heart. And that's the way it should be, but this baby isn't even born yet. You're only about two months pregnant so it's not even a baby yet."

"You know what? You're beginning to remind me more and more of Robert. You're so stupid too. It looks like you can't come up with a good reason for me not to go through with this so unless you have something different to say, I'm getting ready to go lie down. Because it really sounds like you're trying to protect someone else. So who is it, George?"

"I know you want me to mention Gloria."

"No. I wanted you to mention Gloria over a year ago."

"Well, actually it is Gloria. I don't want her to be hurt either."

"You didn't care about her being hurt when you told her you wanted more children. So now all you have to do is tell her I'm pregnant. What's the big fucking deal now? Oh I get it. Like I said before, you were lying about that too. So why don't you just get your lying ass out of my house."

"Cassandra, stop crying and come here. I do love you and I never meant to hurt you. I'm sure our love for each other will get us through this. Okay?"

I know what George is trying to do. He's trying to manipulate me and make me choose him over this baby but it's not going to work. I've let him get away with thinking that he has manipulated me in a lot of other situations but not this time. Even though I love this man so much, I not stupid.

I told George that he could let himself out because I was tired and I was going to lie down. About five minutes after I got in my bed George came and joined me. At first he sat on the side of my bed for a few minutes apologizing. I guess we both calmed down because I apologized to him also. He sat there a while and massaged my back then my legs, then he asked me to turn over and he massaged me some more. Then George and I gently kissed each other and apologize again. Then my phone started ringing but I didn't answer it. And I slept like a baby, excuse the pun, in George's arms all night. But I refused to have sex with him.

A TRUE GENTLEMAN

As soon as George left the next morning I checked my answering machine and called Chris back. I told Chris everything. I told him that maybe he was right and maybe I really was pregnant. I told him that George wants no part of being a new father. Then Chris shocked me by what he said.

"Cassandra, I know we haven't known each other long but I really do care about you and I care about what's important to you. That includes your children, both of them. So if that bastard doesn't want to be in his child's life then I'll be there for the two of you, I mean the three of you. Where is Amelia, anyway?"

"Amelia's still at my mom's and Chris, I think that's really sweet of you."

"Well, I'm not saying it to be sweet. I mean what I say. I'm actually finding myself falling in love with you."

"You're doing what?" I said.

"I said I'm falling in love with you. I don't know what it is about you that makes me feel like this, but it's something."

"I really like you too but we need to know more about each other."

"I know all I need to know about you. I think you're perfect for me and I'm perfect for you. And our girls already think they're sisters."

"Yeah, that's true. But we have other issues; one of them being the distance between us. And even though we're getting off the subject, the other issue is the fact that I think I'm pregnant with another man's baby."

"That's not getting off the subject. That's why I brought

this whole thing up. I would marry you tomorrow and raise this baby as my own if you would let me. So let me ask you this one question."

"No. I don't want you to ask me any questions right now because you sound way too serious and I don't think I'm ready to answer any serious questions. I have too many other issues to think about. But thanks for the offer."

"Oh, do you think I was getting ready to propose to you over the phone because that's not it at all," Chris said laughing.

"Okay now I'm embarrassed. What is it then?"

"Are you in love with George?"

"That's not a fair question either. I wasn't expecting that one."

"Well, let me re-phrase it then. Do you think you could ever love me the way that you love him?"

"Do you really want me to answer that?" I said.

"Yeah, I want to know."

"Well, I know George and I will never be together and I know now that we're not right for each other, but I only wish I had known it before now. So to answer your question, I would really like to fall in love with someone; someone who could make me forget all about George and, yes, I think that someone could be you."

"Would you like that someone to be me?"

Then with a smile on my face and in a little girlish voice I said, "Stop asking me those kinds of questions. We'll have to wait and see what happens."

"You mean wait and see what happens between you and George or between George and his wife?"

"No, that's not what I mean at all. I mean you and I will have to wait and see what our relationship brings. But what I can and will promise you is that whatever George and I did have together is gone."

"You mean everything except for the baby."

"Yes, everything except for this baby. But I DO NOT want to be with George."

"Okay, I believe you. So where do we go from here?"

"I'm not sure. What do you think?" I said.

"I want to continue seeing you every weekend and even more than that if I can. I kind of got used to having you around and so did my girls. But I still want to spend some time with you alone. Just the two of us."

"That sounds good to me. I just don't know when it's going to happen."

"Well, if we both want it badly enough we will find the time. So how badly do you want to see me?"

"I told you about asking me questions like that," I said.

"But I can tell you're smiling though. Right?"

"I guess."

"So how about today?" Chris said.

"How about today for what?"

"Spending some time together. Cassandra, you mean you forgot already?"

"Oh. No, I didn't forget. That sounds good. So are you driving down here?"

"Yeah, I'll be down in a couple hours. Is that okay?"

"That sounds good. I'll see you then."

Okay, so now what do I do? I really don't want to be with George and deep down I know that Chris and I have a lot in common but I'm not sure that is enough. Sure the girls are crazy about each other but that isn't enough either. I can't believe Chris would really raise this baby as his own. There are not too many men who would do that. Hell, I've just experienced two men who don't even want their own children, let alone raise someone else's. But even though Chris seems really nice and we both seem to put our children first, there's got to be something wrong with him. So I'm going to look at him through a microscope before I make any more bad choices.

When Chris came over we decided to start the day by going to the movies. We watched one movie and then Chris wanted to watch another one that was just starting on the next screen so he suggested we go and watch that one too. I told him we couldn't do that because we only paid for the first one. Then Chris took me by the hand and told me to loosen up and he walked me right into the line that was forming to see the other movie. We stood there just like every one else. Well, actually he stood there like every one else while I stood there nervous, thinking I'm going to jail because I didn't pay another $4.75.

I volunteered to go and buy us another ticket but Chris looked at me and smiled as the doors were being opened. Then he told me it was too late because we were already inside. I couldn't believe he had me doing that. He's making me mischievous and I already find myself speaking more and more like he does. Not that there's anything wrong with the way he speaks. I'm just not use to talking that way.

On the way back to my house I told Chris I had a really good time. The movies were great. Then out of the blue he asked me if I had already taken a pregnancy test and I told him that no, I was just late.

"Late. What do you mean?"

Do we have to spell every thing out to guys?

"I haven't had my period for this month, okay?"

"So what if you're not pregnant? Then do the two of us have a chance?"

"I thought we had a chance even if I am pregnant. Was I wrong for thinking that?" I asked.

"No, not at all. I want to be there for you through the good and the bad. I meant what I said and if you want me to prove it to you right here in the car I will." And then with a big smile on his face he said, "Or if you want me to prove it to you when we get back to your place then I'll do that too."

"No thank you. I believe you, Chris. You don't have to prove anything."

"What's wrong? You're scared you're gonna like it or something?"

Then I smiled and said, "Yeah, or something."

"How about if I stop and get you a pregnancy test just so we can be sure?" Chris said.

"Let's do it. But I already know what it's going to say."

I bought the kind of test that had two tests in one box and they sure were expensive. But if I think that's expensive, how am I going to afford the baby? Anyway, I went in the bathroom and did just what the directions told me to do. Then I left the test in there. I told Chris I had taken the test and he could go in there and get the results. He came out of the bathroom smiling.

"What are you smiling for? I know it's positive."

"Come here, honey. Give me a hug," Chris said.

"Stop it. What does it say?"

"It's negative."

"Stop joking with me."

"Okay, if you think I'm joking let's make a deal. If you're pregnant you get to have anything you want from me and if you're not I get to have anything I want from you. Is it a deal?"

"No, it's not a deal. But what would you want from a pregnant woman anyway?"

"Sweetheart, you really aren't pregnant. Look!"

Then I looked at the test and sure enough it was blue. Not pregnant. But how could that be? I know I haven't had my period since I've moved in here and it's been about two months now.

"I see it really is negative. But I feel like I am. Something is definitely going on with my body."

"Why don't you make a doctor's appointment for tomorrow and I'll come down and go with you if you want me to."

"That sounds good but you don't have to drive all the way back out here. Thanks for the offer though. And why are you being so nice to me anyway?"

Then Chris took my hand and kissed it and said, "I know you're used to men being assholes but I promise you that I don't have any skeletons in my closet or any wives in there either. What you see is what you get. It may not be much but it's me. And if it does turn out that you really are pregnant then I still want to be there for you guys. All three of you."

"Chris, that all sounds too good to be true and I'm just afraid of being hurt again. Even though I don't think anyone could ever hurt me the way that I've been hurt in the past. I just don't want to be hurt again period. So I guess I'm not ready to take that chance."

"I don't think you're afraid of being hurt; I think you're afraid of being happy. You need to loosen up and let me show you that we're right for each other. In fact, you know what? I've never even mentioned the word marriage to any other woman before. I don't say that word loosely. And pregnant or not pregnant, I want to marry you some day. So are you going to the doctor's tomorrow?"

"Yes, I'm going and I'll make sure you're the first one I call."

The next day after work I went to take another test. The nurse asked me several questions including when my last period was, so I told her. Then I took the test and she said the doctor would be in to give me the results. When the doctor came in the first thing she did was confirm that I was not pregnant and what big sigh. I wanted to give her a big hug but I didn't. She didn't know what a relief that news was. Then I asked her what was going on with my body if I weren't pregnant.

She asked several more questions as she came to the conclusion that my period was being delayed because of the stress that I've been experiencing lately from the divorce and the move and I'm sure other things that I didn't mention to her. She told me it was quite common to miss a couple months during stressful conditions. She also explained that an increase in exercise could have the same effect and I told her that I had been skating a lot more than usual. She assured me again that I was not pregnant. Then she started to suggest I use another form of birth control, something other than condoms. Before she could get the words out of her mouth, I told her that, yes, I wanted a prescription for birth control pills.

When I left her office I felt like a new woman. I felt as if a huge burden had been lifted. Actually, one had been lifted. A 200 pound one name George. I promised myself then that George was history. I will never get myself in that situation ever again. Boy, if I were the drinking type I would go and get drunk but instead I picked Amelia up early from her after-school program and, even though it was freezing outside, we went to have an ice cream.

When I got home I called Chris and gave him the good news. I also thanked him again for volunteering to help me through this had the outcome been different. As soon as I hung up the phone George called.

"Hi honey. How are you doing?"

Then with an attitude I said, "I'm fine. What do you want?"

"I wanted to know if you've thought any more about your situation."

And before I could tell him the news he made me mad. "What do you mean *my* situation? You keep acting like I'm in a situation all by myself."

"No, but since you don't want to listen to me and since you don't care about how I feel, then you've made this your situation. You're the one acting like I don't exist."

"George, do you have something else to say? I'm really busy."

"Will you at least give it some thought?"

"Sure will. Goodbye George." And I hung up the phone. I probably should have told him that there is no situation but since he's been such a jerk I think I'll play one of his games. I think I'll keep that little secret all to myself. What goes around comes around, asshole.

Now, even though I don't have the pregnancy problem anymore, I still have other problems. Like the fact that Robert is still living in the house and it's not sold yet. Not to mention the mortgage company has been calling me because he hasn't made any payments since I left. Maybe it wasn't a good idea after all for me to keep the same telephone number when I moved out; but then again I don't want to dodge people either. I know I'm equally responsible for the mortgage but I also know that Robert has a roommate and he's collecting that guy's money and pocketing it. Not only that, since all the bills were in my name, guess where they're coming now and guess who's responsible for paying them.

When I asked Robert to help me with the bills he told me to get my new man to pay them. And when I asked him to give me some money to help with Amelia he told me to get it from her real father. So I see it's going to be another fight with him just to get him to help take care of his daughter. It's a good thing I had the child support issue included in our divorce papers. Now it's only a matter of having it enforced.

I scheduled an appointment which the District Attorney's office and they informed me that it could take anywhere from six months to a year for them to start the procedures to have child support come directly out of Robert's check. They told me in the mean time to try to work something out with him directly and to make sure to let their office know of anything he gives me. Yeah right. Like I can really work something out with Robert directly. So I guess my only alternative at this point is to take Mom up on her offer and move back into my old bedroom. So I did.

Before I moved back, I had one last conversation with George and of course he pleaded with me to have an abortion. He told me that he and Gloria were selling their house and he was moving out of state. He basically left here thinking I was pregnant with his child. That dirty dog. But I still didn't tell him any differently.

WHO'S MOVING?

Moving back in with Mom wasn't as bad as I thought it was going to be. I was anticipating Mom telling me that everything that had happened was my fault but she didn't. She was back to being the mother that I knew before I had gotten pregnant with Amelia, but I wasn't going to get used to it because she was likely to change at any given moment. But I really appreciated her letting me move back in so I could get some of my bills paid off and get back on my feet.

I put all my things in storage but the hardest part was transferring Amelia to a new school in her sixth grade year but I promised her it was only temporary. This brought back a lot of memories because I was in the sixth grade when my parents got a divorce and I had to switch schools also. So I know what Amelia's going through even though she doesn't say much. In fact, the only thing she ever mentions is the fact that she doesn't see her dad anymore and she says she knows he never loved her. But each time she says this I try to make excuses for him. I don't want her to ever feel unloved. I try to tell her that he and I divorced each other. We didn't divorce her. But it's kind of hard for her to believe it when she doesn't see him anymore. I don't ever want her to feel unloved. In Robert's absence I try to give her enough love for the two of us. And Chris has been spending a lot of time with her too.

Speaking of Chris, he has been an angel. During the eleven months after I moved Amelia and I spent even more time with him and his girls. I also got a chance to meet both of his daughters' mothers and Marissa's baby-sitter. Eboni's mother seemed really nice. We seemed to get along from the first day

I met her. She told me that at first she was a little jealous because the only people Eboni ever talked about were Amelia and me. Then she laughed and said she soon got over her jealousy because the more time we spent with Chris the more free time she had to herself.

Then there was Marissa's mom and the baby-sitter. I didn't hit it off well with either one of them. First of all, I had no respect for Marissa's mom because supposedly she was off drugs but yet she hardly spent any time with her daughter. She wasn't working and therefore I thought she should have been keeping her own daughter during the day instead of Chris having to pay a baby-sitter.

Speaking of the sitter, she and I didn't seem to like each other from day one either. I had a funny feeling about her but she and Chris lived in the same apartment building so it was really convenient for her to keep Marissa. Whenever she would see us coming she would make it a point to come and pick up Marissa and give her a kiss or some candy or something. I told Chris on several occasions that I thought she was trying to make me jealous of her relationship with Marissa. I told him it was like a competition, only I wasn't going to play her little game. My love for Marissa was genuine. There was no hidden agenda.

Chris assured me that my feelings about her were wrong. He said he had absolutely no interest in her and she had no interest in him. In fact, he described her as being "a trampy looking white woman who was on welfare but loved to baby-sit all of the neighborhood kids so she could make some extra money." He said she treated all the kids in the neighborhood the same way. He said I was trying to create problems where none existed. So I told him maybe he was right but I still didn't trust her.

During that same year Amelia and I were rarely at Mom's house on the weekends and whenever there was a break at school we spent the night at Chris'. I would even go to work from there sometimes and Amelia and Eboni would stay home and watch Marissa which saved Chris on a baby-sitter. A few times when I had a day off during the middle of the week, I would drive to Fremont to pick Marissa up from the sitter's and spend the day with her, just the two of us. Chris and Eboni would on occasion come and pick up Amelia and take her places with them, without me.

Chris and I never argued about anything. We were the perfect family except we lived in separate residences, in cities about fifty miles apart. Chris would often tell me he loved me but it seemed I could never allow myself to tell him I loved him too, even though I did. I guess I was still afraid of being hurt.

Robert and I finally sold the house and not a day too soon. It sold only two days before the foreclosure was final. We basically took the first offer we got. The people that bought it got a steal. We didn't get any money out of the house and, in fact, there wasn't even enough to pay off the second mortgage we had taken out to get the pool. So there's another twenty-five grand that they're going to come after us for. But at least now I don't have the worry of that house anymore.

Amelia and I lived with Mom for nearly a year and then it was time to move on. I couldn't thank my mom enough for what she allowed me to do. I was now able to move out with just a few bills instead of a whole ton of them. And the month we moved was the same month the District Attorney's office started collecting child support straight from Robert's check. Even though it wasn't much it was more than he was doing on his own. In fact, during that year he picked Amelia up only three times. But as I promised Amelia, we moved back to our old neighborhood. I rented a three-bedroom house only a few blocks from where we lived before. I thought everything was going very well.

New Year's was coming up and since Chris and I had just met right before last New Year's he wanted to do something really special for this one. Mom agreed to keep Amelia so I went to spend the weekend with Chris. He told me again that he wanted this New Year's to be special. I wondered what he had planned. I was really surprised he wanted to spend it with me because he knows I don't like to party. I would be perfectly happy staying at his place and just enjoying each other's company.

When I got to Chris' apartment I was really shocked. He had cooked steak and lobster and said he wanted to stay in for the night and I told him that sounded great to me. Then I saw his bottle of champagne and asked him where my apple cider was and he admitted he forgot to buy me some. So before we ate dinner we drove to the corner liquor store where they had no apple cider. Then we drove to probably every supermarket in town and there was no apple cider to be found. Chris felt really bad but I told him not to worry about it. It really wasn't that important. Chris kept apologizing and saying he wanted the night to be special. I told him it was already special because things were finally beginning to calm down in my life and I was practically stress-free. Then he reminded me of our perfect relationship except for the distance between our homes. I agreed with him but told him I didn't know how we were going to resolve the issue.

We finally got back to his house and ate our cold dinner but it was still romantic. I kept teasing Chris by reminding him that I had nothing to drink while he had his champagne. In fact, I saw that he had several bottles of champagne and some other liquor. We sat and listened to music and talked about the two of us while he held me in his arms. Then he started getting really serious and right at midnight he said he had something to ask me.

"What is it, Chris?"

"Cassandra, you and I have known each other a little over a year now and you know that I'm in love with you, right?"

"Come on, Chris, don't start getting serious on me now."

"Cassandra, there is something I need to tell you."

"Okay, what is it? I feel like you have some bad news to tell me. So go ahead and spit it out."

"Oh, did I say I had something to tell you? I mean I have something to ask you."

"What?"

Then Chris got on his knees and although he was slurring

his words he managed to say, "I'm totally fuckin' in love with you. Will you marry me and make me the happiest man alive?"

"Chris, please. Don't ask me that."

"What do you mean, don't ask you that? Woman, I have never loved someone as much as I love you. What do you fuckin' mean, don't ask you that?"

"Chris, I think you've had a lot to drink tonight and I don't think you know what you're saying."

"I know exactly what I'm saying. Oh, but I know why you haven't answered me. I forgot to give you your ring but I have it in my room somewhere so just hold on."

Then, as Chris was stumbling to his bedroom, there was a knock on his door.

"Who the fuck can that be at this time of night?" Chris said.

"I don't know but I would sure like to find out."

Chris opened the door and it was his baby-sitter, Stephanie. What is she doing here I thought. Then Chris asked her, "What the fuck are you doing here?" and I could have sworn she asked him if he had asked me yet and he said yeah and closed the door.

"What was that about, Chris?"

"Who, Stephanie? She just came to bum a cigarette, that's all."

"Am I supposed to be crazy or something? She came over here for more than a cigarette. So what's going on?"

"Nothin'. Nothin' baby. I promise you, nothin'."

"Did you tell her what you were going to ask me tonight?"

"Yeah, I told her I was gonna ask you to marry me but I didn't tell her when."

"Chris, you really don't see it, do you?"

"See what?"

"She didn't come over here for a cigarette. She came over here because it's New Year's and what better time to ask someone to marry you. She came over here to stop you from asking me."

"You're crazy. She would never do that. I have no feelings for her. She keeps my daughter, that's all."

"Chris, that may be all she is to you but, believe me, she wants to be more than your baby-sitter. And she can't say she didn't know I was here tonight because she saw me when I pulled into your parking lot earlier."

"Cassandra, you're wrong. You're dead wrong."

"Okay, whatever. We'll see. But in the meantime I think you need to lay down and go to sleep."

So Chris did just that. I stayed up and watched television for a few more minutes and, of course, the only thing on was Dick Clark, so I joined Chris in bed. He was knocked out from all the alcohol he had to drink but I gave him a body massage anyway. Although I'm sure he won't remember it in the morning.

I know Chris wants to marry me but I can't accept his proposal right now because of the one thing that we can't seem to agree on. Where are we going to live? I feel that Chris should be the one to move because Marissa's only five years old and it would be easier for her to adjust than Amelia. And I live just a couple of blocks from the elementary school and Amelia's old baby-sitter is only a couple of blocks away too. Actually, Amelia and I have already discussed the possibility of Chris and Marissa moving in with us and she has already agreed to watch Marissa after school. Amelia is really looking forward to it.

I also told Chris that his moving to Fairfield wouldn't interfere with him seeing Eboni because she could spend every weekend with us just like she spends with him now. None of his plans with his girls would have to change, except getting rid of the baby-sitter. Chris and I decided to drop the issue about either one of us moving right now and suggested we go out to breakfast. Before we walked out the door I kissed Chris and told him we would figure out something.

"Hey, you know what they say; the person you spend New Year's with is the person you'll be with the rest of the year. And don't think I forgot that you didn't answer my question last night," Chris said.

"Well I might have until we were so rudely interrupted. But let's not start the year out with a disagreement. Let's begin on a happy note, okay?"

"You know that's one of the reasons I love you. You are so independent and you don't get jealous over some stupid stuff. You say what you have to say and that's it. Do you ever let other women bother you?"

"No, I don't. But don't mistake my kindness for weakness."

"Come on, baby. You know I love you so much. Let's go."

Then I kissed Chris again and held his hand as we walked down the hallway to the parking lot. But when we got to the parking lot something was missing.

"WHERE'S MY CAR?" I yelled.

"Where *is* your car?"

"I parked it right behind yours last night like I always do. Where's my car?"

Then at the same time we noticed a ticket on his car. The ticket stated that my car had been towed away because it was illegally parked. But I had always parked my car in the same spot, time after time, and it was never towed away before. Then I turned around and saw Stephanie peeking from her window.

"I know it was her, Chris. I can't stand her. Maybe you'll believe me now. She wants to be more than your baby-sitter. She wants you."

"Cassandra, you're just mad right now. The sign does say any unauthorized cars will be towed away."

"I know that but it hasn't been towed away before. So why now? Just take me to pick it up so I can go home."

"You really think she did it, don't you?"

"I know she did. And if you don't think so, you have a lot to learn about women and the games they will play."

"So do you play games too?"

"I know *how* to play games and she definitely doesn't want to get me started. She's messed with the wrong woman because I'll get her back when she's least expecting it. Just take me to get my car."

I was fuming but I didn't really let Chris see it. When we got to the towing yard they told me it was going to be one hundred and fifty dollars to get my car back. I asked Chris if he had any money and, of course, he said no. Why did I even bother to ask? Then before I knew it my Miss Thang attitude was beginning to surface. Then Chris asked me what was I going to do. So I pulled out my checkbook and wrote them a check. I told Chris I was going home and he said he would call me later. "Yeah, whatever," I said. Well, that will be the last time I spend the night over there. If he wants to see me he'll have to do all of the driving.

Chris brought his girls over the following weekend so they could see Amelia's new room. It was almost as big as her room in our old house. We were even able to fit all of her furniture in it. Actually we had a house full of furniture, even though I had to buy it back from Robert.

When Robert finally moved out of the old house, or should I say got kicked out, he told me he was moving back in with his mother and he was going to sell all of our furniture. I told him not to sell it because I would take it back. Then he told me it wasn't going to be that easy. He said that I could have it back if I took him back or if I bought it back from him. So I ended up giving him back his child support money for one month just so his daughter would have something to sit on if she watched television in the living room. Like I said many times before, he's so stupid. Even though it wasn't that much money, it was the point of it all. But you watch, one of these days that bastard is going to get just what he deserves.

After the New Year's Day incident with my car, Chris and I didn't talk to each other as often as before. In fact, we would go days without calling one another. One reason we didn't talk as much was because Chris' hours got changed at work and he was now working the swing shift. So when he got off work I would be asleep and when I got off he would be asleep. So now we had this scheduling problem on top of the fact that Chris refused to move and so did I. When we did get a chance to talk to each other we agreed we wanted to be together but we couldn't agree on where we would live. So one day I think we both got tired and said just forget it. So we agreed to stop seeing each other for a while. But I think we both had hopes that we would somehow work this out. That is, until we started having this other problem.

One evening Chris called me when he got home and I overheard a female's voice telling him good night.

"Who was that, Chris?"

"Oh, that was Stephanie."

"What is she doing over there at this time?"

"She agreed to keep watching Marissa for me even though I get off work late now."

"So why was she at your apartment? Doesn't she keep Marissa at her own apartment?"

"Yeah, but she had her apartment exterminated today so I told her she could watch her here."

"What did she do with the other children she watches during the day?"

"I don't know. That's a good question."

"Chris, you still don't see it, do you?"

"What? You still think Stephanie has the hots for me, don't you?"

"Yes, I know she does."

"Well, she knows you're the love of my heart and can't nobody change that."

"You don't know women like I do. So what if she can't have your heart, she'll go after something else."

"I can't believe it. Are you getting jealous?"

"Not jealous, just wise and cautious." Then I told Chris I was going to sleep and I would call him tomorrow. But I didn't call him for about a week and when I did it was basically the same thing.

"Hello, Chris. Did you just get in?"

"Yeah, I just walked in the door."

"So how is Marissa?"

"She's fine. She's asleep."

"Oh, you picked her up already?"

"No, actually I didn't. Stephanie kept her here today because Stephanie's teenage son is giving a party and I didn't want Marissa over there."

"So where is Stephanie now?"

"She's here on the couch sleep."

"So wake her up and send her home."

"Come on Cassandra, she's already sleep and as nice as she's been to me for keeping Marissa during these hours, I owe her."

"Well, then pay her and send her home."

"Cassandra, you're acting like you're jealous. Are you?"

"Chris, I can't believe you. I know you would do just about anything for Marissa, but this. And don't even try to tell me it's for her because Stephanie has done her job for this evening and now it's time for her to go home. And she probably isn't even asleep. She's probably right there smiling listening to you because things are happening just the way she planned them."

"You're taking this all wrong. She didn't plan any of this."

"Okay, Chris how would you feel if I let my landlord spend the night because he worked on something here in my house until it was dark?"

"Cassandra, that's not the same thing and you know it."

"I knew this was coming. Remember when I warned you about her last year? Remember I told you she didn't like me and she wanted to be more than your baby-sitter? I knew I was right. And you still can't see it. It's just like when you first met Marissa's mom. You felt sorry for her, took her in and then you had Marissa. Do you feel sorry for every white girl you meet? Or maybe if I acted helpless and moved in with you then things would be different. I see the pattern now. You say you love me because I'm strong and independent but in reality you want some one that's weak and someone you can control."

"Cassandra, you're way off base. But I don't want to talk about it now just in case she really is listening."

"That's all the more reason to send her home. So now you and I can't even talk on the phone because of her. Well, you don't have to worry about that anymore. Goodbye, Chris."

A couple of weeks passed and I hadn't heard from Chris. I

decided to call him one afternoon before he went to work and this is what happened.

"Hello," a female voice answered. I was shocked at first but I knew it had to be Stephanie.

"Stephanie, this is Cassandra. Where's Chris?"

"He just went to the store to get something for us for dinner."

"For us? What do you mean, for us?"

"Oh, Chris didn't tell you? I'm moving in with him."

"Yeah right."

"Actually, I'm not moving in with him, we're moving to a bigger place together so I can be here for Marissa all the time."

"Yeah, sure it's Marissa you're thinking about. You know you don't care about her. You're only using her to get to Chris. I saw right through your scheme a long time ago."

"Bitch, all I know is that Chris asked you to move in with him and you turned him down. So why are you so fucking worried if I move with him? You had your chance and now it's mine."

"First of all, my name is Cassandra, and don't ever forget it because I'm sure Chris won't. And if you think you have taken Chris away from me you're sadly mistaken. But at least you know where his heart is and if I wanted to be there with him I would."

"Yeah, I know where his heart is. It's with Marissa, and Marissa is here with me. All I know is you should have married him when you had the chance because now I'm here and you're not."

"Just remember it's my choice not to be there and you better hope I don't ever change my mind."

"Oh, one more thing Cassandra. Chris doesn't want to talk to you anymore so don't call back."

"Goodbye, Stephanie, and tell Chris I'll call him at work this evening or I'll call him at home tonight." Then I hung up the phone and you know what, I wasn't even mad with her. And for that matter, I don't know why, but I was not mad with him either. But if she thinks she's heard the last of me she's wrong.

Because it could be next week or next month or even next year, but if and when I decide that I want Chris back there wont' be anything she can do to stop me from having him.

I'm so glad I had not given this man my heart. I knew I was holding on to it for something. Somehow, I just knew things were not going to work out. It seems like it never does. I know Chris really loves me, he's just not used to the games that women will play to get what they want but he'll learn some day even if I have to be the one to teach him. I promise you that. However, I still couldn't let it end without hearing from Chris so later on that evening I called him at work and of course he didn't know about the little conversation his baby-sitter and I had.

She told him that I had called and nothing more. I told him she called me a bitch and at first he didn't believe it but he said he would make sure it never happened again and I told him not to worry, it wouldn't. Then I asked him if it were true that they were moving together and he hesitated before answering my question so I answered it for him. Then I reminded him of how she had been planning this for some time but he insisted they had not slept together and that he was considering moving to a bigger place in Fremont. I asked him how all of that came about. He said she was getting evicted and he felt sorry for her so he let her move some of her things in with him while her son moved in with some of his friends.

He tried to tell me that she was a single mother and she couldn't afford to live there because they had just gone up on the rent and she had been kicked off welfare because they found out she was running a day care and not reporting her income. *I was sooo surprised to hear that. I wonder how they found that out?* So I asked him, what about me? I'm a single mom, living from payday to payday, but he said he knew I could make it because I had a good job and a nice car but Stephanie just wasn't able to support herself right now.

So I asked about her baby-sitting all of the children in the neighborhood. What happened to her money from that? Then he had an answer for that too. He said most of the parents took their kids from her when she had the extermination problem.

And I said, "You mean when she had the roach problem because she's nasty and now you're going to have them too."

"No, that's not what happened. She just let the other kids go when the welfare department started investigating her because she didn't have her day care license either. So now she just keeps Marissa."

I told Chris it was just like I'd said all along. She didn't like those other children anyway. She was after him from day one. Then he told me he didn't want to talk about it because it wasn't what I thought it was. He's only trying to help her out and she's doing him a big favor. Actually she's doing me a favor too. She let me know how naïve Chris was before he and I really got together.

I called Chris' telephone number about two weeks later and it was disconnected. I guess they've found themselves a place together. I wish them good luck and I think I'll even leave him alone for now. But if and when I get ready to play Stephanie's little game, they both better watch out.

THE YEARBOOK

I decided to go on with my life; just me and Amelia. Everything was fine until Amelia started junior high school and she didn't want to do the weekend things with me anymore. She had real friends now and even though I was glad for her, I started getting lonely. Then one weekend when she was spending the night at her friend's house, I pulled out some old photos and started reminiscing and crying.

I looked at photos of the three of us. Amelia, her dad, and me, and then I started crying even more. Why did I let him screw up my life? I started thinking about how I felt after the initial shock of being pregnant and having Amelia. I truly wanted my marriage to last. Even though the odds were against us for being so young, I still tried and tried. Why did he have to mess everything up? I hate him.

Then I found some old letters from Marcus that he had written me from jail. I'm sure he's still in there for one reason or another. Then I found some cards and some love letters from George but I hate him too. As far as he knows, I could be right here rocking our baby to sleep and he never called back to check.

Next I found my yearbook or what I thought was my high school yearbook until I realized it was really Aaron's. Remember him? He was the butt hole that slept with my best friend in high school, at least those were the rumors. I wonder what he's doing now. I wonder if he and Beverly ever got together. I wonder if his telephone number is listed in the phone book. So I looked it up and there it was. I couldn't believe it. I must be bored or something.

Actually I know what it is. This is the first time that I've truly been alone. I mean this is the first time I've been without a man since I was seventeen when Robert and I moved in together. Because when I was going through my divorce, George was there; and when I was going though my break up with George, Chris was there. I have never been with out a male friend in my life so I guess I'm either bored or lonely or a combination of the two.

So now that I have Aaron's number, should I call it? I think I will. I just want to see what he's been up to. He's probably married and has a house full of babies. Let's see.

"Hello, may I speak to Aaron?"

"This is Aaron. Who's this?"

"It's a blast from your past."

"Who is this?"

"So what have you been up to? Are you married?" I asked.

"No, I'm not married but your voice sounds very familiar. Who is this?"

"You have to guess, but don't guess wrong."

Then Aaron starting laughing and said, "I think I know who this is but I don't want to say your name."

"Why not? Is your girlfriend there?"

"I don't have a girlfriend."

"Why not?"

"Is this Cassandra?"

"Yep. It's me all right. So what have you been up to?"

"I can't believe it's you. What made you call me after twelve years? The last I heard from you, you told me not to call you anymore and that you were marrying that guy from out of town. What was his name, Robert?"

"Yes, that's his name but that's not what I remember. The last I heard from you or about you was that you had slept with my best friend, Beverly. You remember her?"

"Yeah, I remember her."

"So what happened? Never mind. I really don't want to know. So what have you been up to? Did you ever get married? Do you have any children?"

"No, I never got married but I have a son, Jamar. He's two years old. What about you? I heard you were pregnant in high school."

"Yes, I had a daughter. Amelia's twelve now. She's a big girl."

"So is she by Robert?"

"Yes, we got married and divorced."

"So what happened?"

"It's a long story. What about you and Jamar's mother? What happened to you guys?"

"That's another long story."

"I have time. What happened?"

Then Aaron laughed and said, "I can't believe you called me after all these years. What's really going on? What made you call me and how did you get my number?"

"Oh, actually I was sitting here going through some old pictures, kind of reminiscing on the past and I noticed I had your year book. So I looked your number up in the phone book and there it was. So I called."

"So, that's where my year book is. I didn't know what happened to it."

"Actually, I forgot I had it until now."

"So, you decided out of the blue to give me a call? You must want something more than to just tell me you have my yearbook."

"No, really that's what happened. I just found it. So I decided to call you but I was really expecting you to be married with a house full of children."

"Not me. Every since you broke my heart I haven't been able to get serious about anyone else."

"Oh, stop lying. Flattery will get you no where."

"I'm not lying. You can ask my mother. You know you were my first love and there's something about that first love that you can't quite shake off. You just don't know. You really broke my heart when you told me that you were getting married."

"Well, it broke my heart too when I heard that you were sleeping with Beverly."

"But that didn't happen until after I found out you were pregnant, not before."

"So who told you I was pregnant?"

Then Aaron laughed and said, "Beverly."

"Oh, so now after twelve years I can finally put the story together. Beverly started spreading rumors that you two were sleeping together and then when you and I stopped seeing each other she made it a point to tell you I was pregnant and *then* you two slept together."

"You know you're really good at figuring out puzzles. I guess that is what happened. We both tried to get back at the other one for cheating but neither one of us had cheated at the time."

"Nope, we hadn't. In fact we were both still virgins. And I use to think you didn't like me because you never tried to come on to me."

"And in reality, I was in love with you and I wanted everything to be perfect. I wanted us to finish high school, then college, and then get married and have lots of babies but I never told you that. I was scared to tell you a lot of things because I was afraid I was going to lose you. And then I lost you anyway."

"Well, now you found me, or I found you. So what are you going to do now?"

"You're crazy, Cassandra. That's one thing I like about you. You get straight to the point."

"So now what?" I said.

"I don't know. I'm still in shock that you called me. So where do you live now? Are you still in Vallejo?"

"No, I moved to Fairfield a long time ago. I like it up here."

"You do? I work in Fairfield."

"Where do you work?"

"I'm a children's counselor down at the Juvenile Hall."

"Oh, really. Did you go to school for that?"

"Yeah, I got my degree in children's psychology and I minored in criminal justice. So this is the perfect job for me. The kids wear me out sometimes, well most of the time, but it's okay. What about you?"

"I work for the phone company and I've been there every since my daughter was born."

"So, you didn't go to law school?"

"No, instead I had Amelia and went to work."

"Oh, that's a shock because I remember how you used to talk about going right to college."

"Well yeah, I took a slight detour from those plans, but I'm happy about it."

"So, when am I going to get to see you, Cassandra?

"You don't want to see me. I'm all fat and ugly now."

"I'm sure you're not and even if you are I still love you."

"Yeah right."

Aaron went on to tell me that he lives with his grandmother, where he's been ever since we graduated. He also said he has always wanted to get out of Vallejo but has never made that move. I told Aaron he could stop by and see me one day after work. So he did.

I learned a lot more about him. I pressured him into telling me what happened with his baby's mother, Annie. He said he met her in college where he played basketball. He described her as a being a groupie that followed him to all of his games and everywhere else he went. She kept coming on to him all the time so he finally gave in and took her out on a date. He really began to like her so they made plans to get married but he wanted to join the Army reserves first. When he returned home a few months later from basic training, Annie was nowhere to be found. He called her old number but it was disconnected. He went to the church were her father preached and still couldn't find her. Then one day she showed up at his grandmother's house and told him that she had been out of town. She then insisted on Aaron moving out of his grandmother's house and getting his own apartment so she could join him.

During the two months that Aaron stayed in the apartment she spent the night with him only twice. He said she kept being very mysterious. She wouldn't tell him where she lived, whom she lived with or what she was doing. The only way he could reach her was by pager. He said he didn't like living alone so he moved back in with his grandmother. For the next seven months or so, he didn't see her at all. They communicated via pager and a call back. When he did finally get a call letting him know where she was it was from her husband. Yes, husband. She had gone and gotten married while he was in basic training. And not only that, her husband was calling to tell Aaron that Aaron was the father of a two-month-old baby boy. Shocking huh? No, I say trampy.

Anyway, the husband had a feeling she had been messing around because of all the pager calls she would get and then she would leave. So as soon as the baby was born he was smart enough to get a blood test and it wasn't his. Aaron was extremely hurt so he told her he didn't want to have anything to do with her but he started doing things for his son. He would also pick him up every chance he got. But his chances were pretty slim because Annie made it clear to him that they came as a package. If he wouldn't take her back he couldn't see his son. So unfortunately, he doesn't see him too often. Annie brings the baby to see Aaron's grandmother but only when she knows Aaron is at work. So that's his story and I told him mine.

We seemed to get along great, just as we did in high school. He still seems like he's pretty quiet and shy. He hasn't changed at all. We started doing things together just like we did back then. He's very athletic so he would take Amelia on Mare Island and Travis Air Force base to play tennis, racquetball, basketball and anything else athletic she wanted to do. They got along great too. Even better than she got along with Chris and I was glad. He even started referring to her as his daughter. Aaron kept telling me that it was fate that brought us back together. He said every since he got hurt by Annie he hasn't felt comfortable enough to put his trust in another woman. Not until now, that is.

Aaron kept reminding me that I was his first love and he would never stop loving me. I told him I loved him too. We started spending a lot of time together and my feelings for him got stronger and stronger and then problems with Annie started creeping up. She noticed Aaron hadn't been home too often so she figured out that he was seeing someone then she started playing more games with their son. She started telling him that if he didn't drop whomever he was seeing she would move his son out of state. I told him that I would never come between a man and his child so I suggested we stop seeing each other but he refused to stop seeing me. So we carried on.

Then one day he asked me to meet him at my mom's house but he wouldn't tell me why. When Amelia and I got there he called my mom in the room, got on his knees, handed me a ring and this is what he said.

"Miss Grant, I'm getting on my knees here in front of you and Amelia to ask for your daughter's hand in marriage. Cassandra, I lost you thirteen years ago and I'm not going to lose you again. I have been doing a lot of praying lately. Praying to the Lord to send me a good woman and then you popped back in my life. Say what you will, but this is no accident. Will you marry me?"

I was bewildered. I was shocked. I was speechless. But you would have thought Amelia and my mom were his cheerleaders. They were yelling, "Say yes. Say yes. Say yes." For a moment I couldn't say anything. Then Aaron said, "Are you just going to sit there or are you going to answer me?"

"Aaron, I would love to marry you but I really think you need to work out your problems with Annie first. I told you I don't want to come between you and your son."

Then my mother said, "Cassandra, don't be ridiculous. I'm sure you two can work those problems out together. So don't be a fool and let someone stand in your way of you finally being happy."

"But you guys don't understand," I said.

"Say yes, Mom," Amelia said.

"Okay. Yes, Aaron, I will marry you under one condition."

"What?"

"That we agree to have a long engagement to make sure you get the issues worked out between you, Annie, and your son, first."

"That's fair enough. You had me scared there for a minute." Then he hugged me and said, "You will never regret this. I promise to make you the happiest woman alive because you've just made me the happiest man. So Amelia, what do you say; how about going to get some ice cream to celebrate?" So they did.

During the next few weeks Aaron and I talked about us living together. We agreed that he would move into my place and we would save our money and try to buy a house together in about a year. We joked about being engaged without us ever having slept together. We also talked about having more children. We both wanted more children and we decided that now was a good time. So from the very first time we had sex we tried to get pregnant.

I asked Aaron over and over if trying to get pregnant was a good idea right now because I still didn't want to come between him and his son but he insisted that all was okay. He said he didn't see his son too much anyway and of course I had to tell him how I felt about a man not spending time with his children. I told him that Annie didn't make Jamar all by herself so he should be there for him whenever possible. So he kept trying to make arrangements with Annie but when she found out he and I were living together she told him that if he didn't take her back he would never see his son again.

I asked him what he wanted to do about the situation. I told him that since we weren't married yet and since I hadn't gotten pregnant yet that he could move back in with his grandmother until he got his business taken care of. I also told him that it wasn't too late to take her back and then he asked me if I were crazy. He told me Annie was only calling his bluff and he said he wasn't going to let Annie or Jamar stand in the way of his happiness. He said that if Annie wouldn't let him see his son he wasn't going to push the issue right now.

So I told him that I still thought he should do something about the situation, like going to the District Attorney's office, start paying child support on a regular basis and getting visitation established all in one effort. Then, he wouldn't have to worry about her saying, "yes, you can see your son, or no you can't." But for whatever reason, Aaron didn't want to do it. So I agreed to stay in the background on that issue for a while.

THE PLANNED PREGNANCY

Aaron and I made it a point to buy a pregnancy test every week.
Those tests can sure get expensive. Then after about five weeks,
the test came back positive.

"Aaron, come look. It's positive this time."

"Are you sure? Let me see."

We were both happy. I immediately got on the phone and
called to make myself a real appointment and that one came
back positive also. We were so excited I completely forgot
we had not set a date to get married. I told Aaron I thought
we did that a little backwards. So Aaron's solution was to go
to Reno that weekend and get married before anyone knew I
was pregnant but I told him I didn't want to do that. So we
compromised. We set a date, which was four months away and
agreed we would go to Reno then.

I told Aaron that having a big fancy wedding wasn't a
priority to me anymore. In fact, I told him that we could renew
our vows, say in five years, and then have a big wedding if he
wanted to. I told him I would just have to wear a maternity
wedding gown but I refused to hide my situation from anyone.
Actually I did quite the opposite. I immediately got on the
phone and told everyone I was pregnant. No one in my family
had a problem with it because everyone knew I was happy.
And Amelia, she was so excited because she would finally have
something she always wanted. She would finally get to be a big
sister.

When Aaron told his mother and grandmother, they were
both so happy for him, you would have thought he had just told
them he won the lottery or something. The only thing Aaron's

mother was slightly disappointed about was the fact that she always wanted Aaron, her only child, to have this big elaborate outside wedding with horses, carriages and doves. She had it all planned. So I told her the same thing. We could have a big fancy wedding when we renewed our vows and she seemed pleased.

So, the plan was for Aaron and I to coast along for four months and then do it. Aaron doesn't know it but I chose four months to see if anything would change with his situation with Annie and his son, and boy did it.

When the word got around that I was pregnant and we were getting married, Annie went to the extreme with her little plan to get Aaron back. First, when Aaron went to meet her at his grandmother's house one day to pick his son up, Annie pulled a gun on him. Yes, a gun. She told Aaron if he didn't take her back she would kill him and Jamar. He coaxed her into going inside to talk about it. He said he had to reassure her that she was still beautiful and that they would always be friends. Then she went on to tell him that he could only see Jamar at his grandmother's house and he could never bring him home. So he agreed to that, at least for the time being.

When he got home and told me about the situation I asked him if he had called the police and he said no because he didn't want to hurt her and he didn't want her to lose Jamar. He and I completely disagreed on this issue. I told him that if she threatened to kill her own son then he didn't need to be around her in the first place. But he insisted that she was just upset.

Then her next move within those four months was to say that very soon she would be moving out of state. So again, Aaron could not see his son. Aaron spent a lot of time going to Vallejo, meeting her at his grandmother's to spend as much time with Jamar as he could. Then the day came when she was supposed to leave and she again wanted Aaron to come to Vallejo and see Jamar this one last time and Aaron agreed. But this time I was going to make it a little different. I told Aaron I was going with him.

When she walked in she was very surprised and so was I but for a different reason. She got mad and told Jamar that she changed her mind and they couldn't stay and visit with Daddy. She told him to give everyone a kiss, everyone but me that is, so they could go and catch their plane. Then she told Aaron she had something she needed to tell him in private so he went with her in the garage for a few minutes. When they came back she said she had changed her mind again and she would let Jamar stay for a couple of hours.

When she left I started laughing as I told Aaron I was really surprised over the way she looked. He had told me she was very pretty and how she was trying to pursue a modeling career and I guess at first I was a little insecure, but after I saw her I could only laugh. Then I asked Aaron what kind of modeling career was she trying to pursue? What was she going to be, a mascot model? I couldn't believe it and I'm not just talking about her because she's his ex-girlfriend, but she's down right ugly. First of all, not only was she wearing a wig but she also had on some big old dirty looking cotton sweat pants and she didn't even have a nice shape. So if she were going to do any modeling, she would need her entire body covered up.

Aaron sat there and played with his son for a couple of hours and when she came back she wouldn't even come in. She just blew her horn for him to come outside. And of course I had to make her more upset. I walked to the door with Aaron and I gave Jamar a big kiss and waved to him as they left.

On our way home, I asked Aaron what Annie had to tell him in the garage and he said that she was upset because I was with him and she tried to make him feel bad by telling him he had chosen me over his son. Then in a stern voice I told Aaron that he had his chance to be with his son without me, but now that I'm pregnant, my own child is my top priority. Aaron agreed with me and said he wasn't going to let her come between us and if she took his son away from him he wasn't going to put up a fight. He would just wait for her to come back and come to her senses. So we dropped the subject, at least for the time being.

Well, Annie fooled everyone. She actually moved. She called our house the day after she left and gave me a telephone number to give to Aaron so he could reach his son. For about two weeks Aaron would talk to Jamar nearly ever other day. Either Aaron would call him or Annie would call. Then Aaron told me they were moving back.

"So soon?" I said. Then he told me that Annie said she couldn't take it anymore because Jamar kept asking for Aaron every single day. So she apologized and said she didn't want to keep them apart. I told Aaron I still didn't trust her. I told him she probably just went away for a vacation and had no intentions of really moving. He said he wanted to give her the benefit of the doubt. But when she got back nothing had changed. Again she told Aaron he couldn't bring his son home with him. He could only visit him at his grandmother's house and only when the day and time was convenient for her and, oh yeah, only if I didn't come with him.

That's when I told Aaron she wasn't going to run my household. I told him it was time he did things the legal way. Start paying child support through the District Attorney's office and get visitation established, but Aaron refused. He said I was only trying to take Jamar away from Annie but I assured him that even though I loved children I would never try to take a child away from his mother.

So I told Aaron again that she wasn't going to run my household and tell me where I could and couldn't go. I told Aaron we needed to postpone our wedding and we did. For the next several months Aaron continued going along with Annie's schedule. And then two weeks before our baby was due, it was a nice beautiful day outside and Aaron told me he had something to tell me. We dropped Amelia off at one of her friend's house and we went to the park. And that's when he became jerk number five.

"Cassandra, I have something that I really need to tell you."

"What is it?"

"There's no easy way to say this so I'll just spit it out like you always say."

"What? You haven't looked this serious since the day you

asked me to marry you, remember?" I said as I kissed him on his cheek.

"Cassandra, don't do that. You're making this harder."

"You've never complained before when I kissed you. What's wrong?"

"Well, I've been doing a lot of thinking and I don't want to lose contact with my son. I really need to be a part of his life. I don't want him to grow up like I did, not knowing who my father was until I was grown."

"We both already know that Annie's stupid. That's why I've told you how you could take care of it."

"Well, I'm NOT going to the District Attorney's office. You think that's the answer to everything. Just because you went to them for Robert you think that's the answer but it's not. Robert has visitation too but he still doesn't see Amelia, now does he?"

"But you're missing the point. This is a completely different situation. I'm not stopping Robert from seeing Amelia and if I tried to I would be in contempt of court. Robert doesn't see Amelia because he chooses not to. So if you took Annie to court you could establish visitation and if she refused to let you see Jamar then she would be in contempt. So why don't you want to handle it the right way?"

"You just want them to take my son away from her."

"I don't. And I don't know why you are always saying that. Why are you protecting her?"

"That's what I've been trying to tell you. I'm not protecting her but I'm not going to lie to you either. I still love Annie."

"You still what?"

"Cassandra, before you say anything let me explain. I have never lied to you and I'm not going to start now. Yes, I still love her and I'm not sure why. I know she's done a lot of things to me."

"She sure has. Like threatening to kill you and your son."

"Cassandra, let me finish. Yes, I know she's done those things but I still love her. I'm not sure if I love her because she's the mother of my first child or if I want to be with her just so I can see my son. I'm really not sure what it is."

"Wait a minute. So you're telling me you want to be with her but you don't know why?"

"No, I'm not saying that I do want to be with her but I do know that I can't continue living with you because I certainly don't want to have an affair on you."

Then I started crying. Just call me Miss Cry Baby. "What do you mean, an affair? So you've been sleeping with her?"

"No, of course not. But like I said, I don't want to end up having an affair either."

"So you think that's the answer to all of your problems? Leave me and be with her?"

"No, that's not what I'm saying at all. I'm not leaving you for her. I'm not even leaving you to be with her. I'm leaving and moving back in with my grandmother until I get things sorted out. But I really do miss being with my son. He needs me right now."

"Oh, so what about your son that I'm carrying? The son that you and I planned. It wasn't like he was an accident. You know what, I HATE YOU. You're not even going to give our son a chance to know what it's like to be raised by his mother and father under the same roof. I can't believe you're taking that away from him. I knew I shouldn't have gotten pregnant. I should have followed my first mind when you asked me to marry you. I should have waited until you got your business taken care of with Annie. I knew I should have. I can't believe you're doing this to him."

"Cassandra, I'm really sorry. And I didn't say I was leaving forever. Once I move back with my grandmother I might change my mind."

"Change your mind? No, you better make sure you know what you're doing before you do it. I can't believe this. And you waited until I was nine months pregnant before you said anything. You know what? You don't care about me or this baby, just admit it."

"Cassandra, how can you say that? I love you and I love Junior."

"And don't call my baby Junior. Why should I name him

after you? Why don't you go and change Jamar's name to Junior? Oh, I forgot, he doesn't even have your last name. He has Annie's ex-husband's last name. You don't even have a blood test. You have no rights to him at all."

"Yeah, you're right. But I don't want him named after me anyway. I want his name to be left alone." Then he touched my stomach and said, "Junior right here is going to have my name just as we planned."

"Don't touch me. Why don't you just take me home so you can get your things and move back to Vallejo."

"Well, I don't want to move right away. I figure I'll stay there with you until Junior is born and then I'll leave."

"Do you hear what you're saying? You have it all figured out, huh? You're going to abandon your son as soon as he's born. Why wait until then when you can abandon him right now?"

"Cassandra, I know you're upset."

"You're damn right I'm upset. You're going to wait until I'm nine months pregnant, about to give birth to your son, then tell me as soon as I do you're leaving us?"

"I know that sounds bad but I really do want to stay with you to make sure you get to your doctor's appointments and make sure you have a ride to the hospital when the time comes."

"Oh, so now you're just going to be my chauffeur for the next few weeks. I don't need you. We don't need you. So why don't you just leave us now."

"I don't care what you say. I'm not going to leave you now. I already told you what I'm going to do."

"But I don't understand what difference it makes whether it's now or then." Then I got a sharp pain and I grabbed my stomach, "OUCH!"

"What's wrong, Cassandra?"

"I don't know."

"Is it Junior? Is something wrong with Junior?"

"I don't know, but OUCH, there it goes again."

"Come on, I'm going to take you to the hospital. Give me your hand so I can help you get up."

On our way to the hospital Aaron smiled and said, "Do you think this is it? Are you in labor?"

"I don't think so. It didn't feel like this with Amelia." Then in a sarcastic voice I said, "How was it with Annie? Oh I forgot. You weren't there. Her husband was there with her."

"Cassandra, don't start."

"This is all your fault, Aaron. If something happens to my baby I'll blame you one hundred percent and I don't let anyone hurt my children and get away with it. So if something is wrong then, yes, you better move and not to your grandmother's. You better move some place where I'll never find you."

"Cassandra, stop talking like that. Everything is going to be okay."

When we got to the hospital I was admitted on the maternity ward where they checked my baby first and told me he was okay and that I was not in labor. Then they took my blood pressure and told me it was sky high. They told me it was common for an expectant mother's blood pressure to rise near the end of her pregnancy but not nearly as high as mine was. Then the doctor came in and asked me if I had been under any stress lately and I looked at Aaron and said, "Yes, quite a bit." Then he told me that whatever it was, I was going to have to try to let it go because although my baby was okay now, high blood pressure could have a bad effect on him. He told me that he was going to turn the lights off in the room and he wanted me to lie there and relax for about thirty minutes and then someone would come and take my pressure again.

Thirty minutes later the nurse came and took it again but it was the same as before. Then she told me she would take it again in another fifteen minutes and if it wasn't coming down they were going to have to admit me and do some non-stress-test on my baby. So I tried as best as I could to lie there and relax but when she came back it was still high so she told me I would probably have to stay over night. I then called over to Amelia's friend's house and asked if she could spend the night and that was fine. Then I reminded Aaron this was his fault but he wouldn't respond. He just sat there in my hospital room in a chair in the corner.

"Why don't you just leave and go home to Annie and your other son? Or better still, why don't you go home and pack your clothes now so they won't be there when I leave here."

"Cassandra, I don't care what you say. I'm not leaving you like this."

"Oh yeah, you want to wait 'til my baby is born and then you'll leave us both."

"Will you stop talking about that? That's why your blood pressure is high. You know that?"

"Dah, you're so smart to have figured that one out."

"I can't take this. I'm going to the cafeteria. Do you want something?"

"Yeah, I want you to come to your senses and be here for your son."

"I'll be right back."

Then Aaron left and I started crying. When the nurse came back I tried to hide my tears but I couldn't hide from the blood pressure machine. She took my pressure again and told me it was higher than before so she called the doctor in. The doctor examined me again to make sure I wasn't in labor. Then he explained that they were going to hook me up to a monitor to do some tests on my baby. I asked him if it was going to hurt and he said neither one of us would feel a thing. Aaron came back into the room and asked me what was going on and I sarcastically said, "Don't worry about us. We'll be fine."

About an hour later the nurse removed the monitor from around my stomach and took my pressure again but she got the same results. Then she told me I was going to have to stay over night and Aaron stayed right there with me. Throughout the night different nurses came in and took my blood pressure.

By the following morning my pressure was down but just slightly from the day before. Then another doctor came in and examined me and told me I wouldn't be going home until my pressure was normal. So I ended up staying in the hospital another night and was released the following morning. But even though I was released I had to come back to the hospital every morning to have them check my pressure. I did that for one week and then I was told that it was creeping back up so my doctor made an appointment for me to have a cesarean section the following Monday because he didn't want to take any chances on this affecting my baby.

But to our surprise, a couple of days later, early that Sunday morning and as Aaron was getting ready to meet with his Army Reserve unit, I went into labor.

"Aaron, this is it. I need you to take me to the hospital."

"You're in labor?"

"Yes. I was having slight contractions all night but now I really need to go."

"But this is my weekend for my reserve duty."

"So can't you tell them I'm having a baby? Won't they excuse you for that?"

"I don't know. I'm not sure."

"You do want to be there when he's born, don't you?"

"Of course I do."

"Well, how about if you take me to the hospital and drop me off and then you can go to your unit and tell you sergeant what's going on and then you can come back to the hospital because I'm sure it won't be anytime soon."

"Okay, I'll do that. Do you need anything? I know you already have your bag packed. What about Amelia?"

"I'll go and wake her up and tell her we're leaving. She's thirteen, she's old enough to stay here by herself for a little while."

"Are you sure?"

"Yes. She'll be fine," I said.

On our way to the hospital the contractions started getting a little more intense but when we got there the nurses didn't seem to think so. They made me walk around the hospital in hopes that my water bag would break. So Aaron walked with me for a few minutes and then it was time for him to go.

When he left I called everyone and told them where I was. The first person to show up was my sister Sharon, so she had the job of walking around the hospital with me but she didn't mind at all. In fact, now I wish she would go back home because she's starting to be more of a pain than these contractions. Although she has two children of her own they were both born early and by a planned cesarean section so she doesn't know what it's like to actually go through labor.

As I stopped walking at each contraction and held on to my stomach with one hand and on to the wall with the other hand, Sharon would say, "Oooh, Cassandra, does it really hurt? You look like you're in a lot of pain."

"No, it doesn't hurt. It just tickles a little bit."

"For real, does it hurt?"

""NO! For real it doesn't hurt! It just feels like every thirty seconds I've swallowed a lit fire cracker, that's all."

"Oooh, Sandy that sounds painful. You know I didn't have to go through this with my girls."

"Yes, I know. That's only about the tenth time you've told me since you've been here today."

"So, do you want to go back to your room? Do you think it's time?"

"No. The nurse told me to stay gone for at least an hour. So I know it's not time yet."

"But you look so bad and your hair is all messed up."

"Thank you, Sharon. I love you too."

Sharon and I walked around the hospital for about thirty minutes, which was about all I could take. When we got back to my room, my dad, my other two sisters and Aaron's mom were there waiting for me. I don't know what happened to my mother. Then Aaron's mom asked me where Aaron was and I told her. She immediately called his reserve unit and the sergeant was surprised to hear that I was in labor so he said he would send Aaron to the hospital right away.

Just as Aaron was arriving I was being wheeled into the delivery room. After about the hundredth time of my sister Sharon asking if she could come into the delivery room with me, I finally told her that, yes, she could watch. So it was the two of us and Aaron and his mom but the doctor didn't seem to mind. Actually, I wasn't in there too long because after about ten minutes, I gave birth to a healthy baby boy. What a surprise.

They cleaned him up and I held him and kissed him and then handed him to Aaron. He seemed so happy. I wonder if seeing his son being born will change his mind about leaving us. I sure hope so. Then Aaron's mom held him and she called him Aaron Jr.

"Don't call him that," I said.

"What do you mean, don't call him that? You guys have been saying he was going to be a Jr. every since you found out you were having a boy."

Then I gave Aaron this dirty look and said, "We've kind of changed or minds about naming him Junior."

"You mean you've changed your mind," Aaron said.

"Well, let's just say you've changed my mind for me," I replied.

Then Aaron's mom and my sister looked at each other and they both said they were staying out of whatever it was that we were talking about. Then my mom walked into the delivery room.

"How did you get in here?" I asked.

"What's wrong? You don't want your mom here?"

"No, that's not what I mean. Of course I want you here. I was just curious as to how you got in."

"Well, it helps to work here, you know. And by the way, I've arranged for you and Junior to have a private room."

"My baby's name is NOT Junior and I wish everyone would stop calling him that!"

"What do you mean? That's all we've ever called him. Amelia told me how she would call his name and read to him while you were still pregnant."

"I know, but I've changed my mind."

"So what are you going to name him?"

"I don't know yet."

"You can't fool your mom. I know something is wrong but whatever it is you don't need to be worried about it here. You need to concentrate on yours and my grandson's health, whatever his name might be."

"I know, Mom. I will."

I was soon wheeled into my private room, thanks to Mom, and everyone was there waiting for me with balloons, flowers and cards. Everyone stayed for a while and then they left; everyone but Aaron, that is. I told him I was really tired so he held my hand until I fell asleep. Then he went home, changed his clothes and brought Amelia back. Amelia was happy to see me but she was even happier to see her baby brother. She kept telling me, "Junior is so handsome, isn't he, Mom?"

Then I looked at Aaron and said, "Yes, honey, both of my children are beautiful. It's a good thing you two take after your mother."

Then Amelia and Aaron looked at each other and they both laughed. They both sat there in my room about an hour and I told Aaron they could leave and he said he would be back bright and early tomorrow morning.

The next morning the doctor examined me and told me my blood pressure was on the borderline. He said he would release me that day but I must have my blood pressure monitored every week for the next month. When the doctor left the room, one of the volunteers came in and brought two forms for me to fill out. One was a form to have my son's picture taken and the other was for his birth certificate. What am I going to do? What should I name him? Then all of a sudden something hit me. I told Aaron, "I think I *will* name him Aaron Jr. That is if you still want me to."

"Of course I want you to. I would be so proud if you did. I've always wanted a son named after me."

"Okay, I'll do it. Aaron Jr. it is."

"Cassandra, that was too easy. I thought you were going to put up a fight. What's really going on?"

"Nothing, honey."

"Now you have me scared. What are you thinking? What are you plotting?"

I told Aaron that I wasn't thinking about anything but I lied. The reason I named him Junior is because I know Annie has been talking about changing her son's name to Aaron but leaving his middle name as is. So even though he wouldn't be a

Jr., she'll have to either leave her son named after her ex-husband or think of another name. So there. My son is the first and only Aaron Jr. Aaron's attitude seemed to have changed after we signed the papers for Junior's birth certificate. I wonder if he'll change his mind about leaving us. I hope so, for my son's sake.

As soon as we got home I fed A.J. I think that's what I'll call him. Then he went to sleep. I sat up and talked with Amelia for a few minutes and then I got in the bed. I called Aaron in the room and asked him if we could talk and he said sure. I asked him if he was still leaving us and with tears in his eyes he said yes. He told me nothing had changed. I asked him how could he say that after I had just given birth to his son, the son that we had planned.

"Cassandra, I'm really sorry."

"Aaron, can I ask you a question?"

"Yeah, what is it?"

"Are you leaving because I'm fat now? Because I know I can lose weight."

"No, it's not that."

"Well, are you leaving because we haven't made love in a couple of months because I promise you our sex life will be back to normal soon. I just have to wait six weeks."

"No, it's not that either."

"So, you don't love me anymore?"

"Cassandra, please. Yes, I love you and I love Amelia like she was my own but you know I have to deal with the situation with Annie and my son."

"But what about A.J. and how come we can't deal with your other situation together? If you stay here with us I know we can work it out and you'll soon be able to have both of your sons here together. Because no matter what I think about Annie or what she thinks about me, neither one of us can change the fact that our children are brothers and that their father can't be in two places at once. So do you want to be with me or do you want to be with her?"

"I've told you over and over I'm not leaving you for her. I don't know where I want to be right now."

"What is it that I can do to make you change your mind?"

"You can't do nothing. It's not you."

"Why don't you come and get in the bed with me. Let me give you a massage. I'll make it an extra special one. I promise. Okay?"

Later on when Aaron came to bed I did just that. Even though I was still in discomfort myself, for the first time I did whatever Aaron wanted. Hey, maybe that's the problem. Maybe Annie has already been doing whatever Aaron wanted. I don't know why he's ruining our life. And as for her, she's a slut. There is absolutely no comparison between Annie and me. We're as different as night and day. But maybe that's it. Maybe he likes nighttime. Well, if he does, he has a lot of doom and gloom in store for him.

The next morning when Aaron went to work I called and had a dozen roses delivered to our house for him. Inside of his card I wrote, "Please reconsider. We love you." Then I took the twelfth rose and put it on a pillow on his side of the bed. When he came home he asked me what the roses were for and I told him "just because" and when he looked at his card he said, "Cassandra, I'm still leaving." When he saw the rose on the pillow he said, "Stop doing this, okay?" Then he just sat the rose on top of the dresser.

"Why? Is it working? Am I making your decision any harder for you?"

"Yes, you are, but I'm still leaving."

"Aaron, I love you. I'm begging you. Please don't leave us. You're making the wrong decision. Let's work this out together."

"It doesn't matter what you say or do, I still have to leave."

The following day I had a gift basket delivered to Aaron's job with a note that simply said, "Please!" But he didn't even call me when he got it. And again when he got home I had taken another one of his roses and put it on his pillow. But again when he got in the bed he moved the rose and sat it on the dresser.

The next day I cooked a big dinner for Aaron. And even though I couldn't stand on my feet too long, I managed to cook all of his favorites. When he walked in he ate his dinner like it was no big deal. He didn't even acknowledge my efforts. And again I had put another rose on his pillow but he did the same thing.

"Cassandra, I'm moving out this weekend and there's nothing you can do to stop me so stop trying."

Then I guess I somewhat snapped out of whatever it was that I was going through because I said, "All I can say is before you leave make sure she's worth it because you have a beautiful son here. You have Amelia, the daughter you've always wanted. And you have me. So if you think you can do better, go for it. But don't expect either of one of us to want you back when you come crawling."

"I won't. I expect you to go on with your life. You don't need me anyway. You've done a really good job of raising Amelia and I'm sure you'll do the same for A.J."

"So are you saying you don't plan on being a part of his life at all?"

"I'm not sure what I'm saying, Cassandra."

THE BLOOD TEST

Aaron is really starting to scare me. He doesn't seem like himself.
Actually he hasn't seemed like himself every since he first told
me he was leaving. But I can't worry about him or his motives
right now. All I know is that I have two beautiful children and
I'm going to do everything within my power to be the best
mother that I can be.

Later on that night, something woke me up and I noticed
Aaron wasn't in the bed. When I got up I went straight to A.J.'s
crib but he wasn't in it either. Then I glanced in Amelia's room
and she was asleep. Then I noticed the kitchen light was on.
When I walked in the kitchen I was startled. Aaron had A.J.
on the kitchen counter lying naked in his baby bathtub with
shampoo in his hair. And he was just about to pour a bowl of
water over A.J.'s face when I screamed, "WHAT ARE YOU
DOING?" But Aaron turned around like there was nothing
wrong and said, "I'm giving A.J. a bath."

"A bath! It's one o'clock in the morning. Give me my baby!"
Then I took A.J. out of his tub.

"Wait. I need to wash his hair," Aaron said.

"What are you talking about? His hair doesn't need
washing. What's wrong with you? You were just about to pour
that big bowl of water on my baby's face. You could have
drowned him."

"You can finish. I'm going back to bed now," Aaron said
very calmly.

"And besides, it's freezing in here. What were you trying to
do?"

Then Aaron just walked away and went back to bed. I

washed the shampoo out of A.J.'s head, got him dressed, and turned the heater on.

I don't know what that was all about. Aaron really doesn't seem like himself. I really believe that if I had not walked in the kitchen when I did, things would have turned out a lot differently. What was he trying to do and why was he up at one o'clock? All kinds of thoughts went through my head. I kept thinking that maybe Aaron was trying to drown A.J. so he wouldn't have his so-called dilemma. That way he would only have his one son to worry about. So needless to say, I was shaking and I was a nervous wreck and I didn't get any sleep the rest of the night. A.J. and I lay in the living room so I could keep my eye on Amelia's room too. That was a night I will never forget.

The following morning Aaron was off from work so he started packing all of his things, which really wasn't much, but I didn't stop him. Little does he know that when you mess with one of my children, I lose all sense of anything else, especially a man. So he couldn't get his things out fast enough. As he went out the door for the last time he wouldn't even look me in the face but he did walk over to A.J. and kissed him and said, "I'm sorry, man." And as he walked out the door I didn't even cry.

I really wanted things to work out with us. But sometimes things just don't work out the way in which we plan them. But just like I try to teach Amelia, it's better to have a plan that fails than to fail because you don't have a plan. So now that Aaron has completely ruined plan A, it's time for me to move on to plan B.

One thing that I have learned over the years is not to plan anything around a man because I have lost too much doing that. With Marcus, I lost my friend, with Robert, I lost my virginity, with George, I lost my heart, with Chris, I lost my hope and with Aaron, I lost my family. So if you thought I had an attitude before, then you won't be surprised by anything else I say or do. So thanks to those five stupid jerks, I'm making sure that from this day on my plans will be based around me and my two children and that's all. I refuse to let another man take anything from me and I refuse to give away anything that's worth keeping. So even though I was extremely disappointed by Aaron losing his family, it was just that. It's his loss and I'm sure he'll try to come back just like the others will.

So I carried out plan B, which was to continue renting the house for a year and save money by doing whatever it took. I started working overtime and saved every penny I could and it paid off. At the end of the year, I was able to find a home lending program, which enabled me to buy a three-bedroom, two-bath home which was perfect for the three of us. I told Amelia that I hadn't forgotten about the promise I made to get her a house with a pool in the back yard but right now I couldn't afford it. It would happen some day I told her.

Just as we were moving in, Aaron started calling again but this time the shoe was on the other foot. This time he was doing the begging. He wanted to come back home.

"Cassandra, I'm really sorry that I left you guys and I know you have moved on without me but home is where I want to be," he said.

"You have no home here. Your home is in Vallejo with Annie and your other son, remember?"

"It was all a mistake. I never should have left my family in Fairfield."

"You're right. But you did and life goes on."

"Cassandra, I'm begging you. I want to come home. I miss all three of you."

"Well, I missed you too for a while but I soon got over it. Like about two hours after you left I went on with my routine. I didn't skip a beat. And Amelia, I guess she never got her hopes up that you would be sticking around either. And as far as A.J. goes, he doesn't even know you. So why should I take you back? None of us has missed out on anything."

"You should take me back because we love each other and we have a child together."

"No, I think you have that backwards. Those are the reasons you never should have left us."

"Cassandra, you just don't know. It's been miserable without you. And as far as the problems with Annie, I don't have them anymore. I get to see my son every weekend and she said it doesn't matter whom I'm with. She'll let me bring him home."

"Well, that's fine and dandy but you need to listen to yourself. You're still letting her make the decisions. She's only saying that because you're not with anyone at the moment. But as soon as you're with someone she'll change her mind, and like I told you before, she's not going to run her household and mine too. And wait a minute. You've been seeing your other son every weekend and for this past year you haven't even picked up the phone to call and see how A.J. was doing. And you expect me to take you back because Annie says it's okay? You've got to be crazy. Why don't you just take Annie back and the three of you can go on living happily ever after."

"Oh, I get it. You think I've been with Annie this past year but I haven't. The only time I've seen her was when she dropped my son off or whenever I would pick him up. And when I did pick him up I would never go inside of her house. So if you think I've been intimate with her in any way, you're wrong. I haven't. In fact, she and her ex-husband are getting back together."

"You know what? You talk too much. So now what you're really saying is you want me back because Annie doesn't want you. She wants her ex. But you were the fool. You played right into her hands when you left me. And now she's going back to him. Well, no thank you. Again, I'm not going to be with you because Annie says it's okay. You should really feel like a fool."

"Cassandra, that's not what's going on. You act like I left you to be with her but I didn't."

"Well, you left me *because* of her. So to me, it's the same thing."

"Okay, Cassandra. What if I go to the District Attorney's office and get a blood test like you've asked me to and then let them set up visitation so she won't be able to change her mind about the arrangements?"

"That's all I asked you to do a year ago but you refused. So why do you want to do it now?"

"Because I know now that's the right thing to do. Back

then I was so confused I didn't know what to do about anything. And I see now that you were only telling me what was right."

"Yeah, but back then you kept saying I was trying to take her son away from her which wasn't the case at all."

"I know that now and I'm really sorry. I should never have left you guys. So can I please come back home?"

"Aaron, I don't know what to say. You left us once. How do I know you won't leave us again?"

"I won't. I promise."

"OH HELL NO. I don't even want to hear the word *promise* again. Your promises aren't worth anything to me. You need to do a lot better than that."

"What if I go and get the blood test and take care of all that stuff first? Then, when it's all set up can I come back home?"

"Why don't you take care of your business first. Then we'll see."

"Okay, that's fair enough for now. You've given me some encouragement. Even if it's only a little bit."

"Well, that's not my intent. You need to take care of your business for you and not for me. Because if you and I don't get back together you'll have the same problem with Annie and whomever else you decide to be with. So don't do anything for me."

"Okay, I'll do it for me and A.J. Not for you."

"Don't do it for A.J. either because he's doing fine without you too."

"You just won't give me any encouragement, will you?"

"No, I will not. I tried to give lots of encouragement for you to stay with us a year ago but those days are over. I'm not living for a man anymore, not even you."

"Okay, but can I ask you one more question?"

"Go for it."

"Well, if we do get back together can we get married soon because once I get you back I don't want to ever lose you again."

"You need to take one step at a time and make sure you

know what you're doing before you do it this time."

"Okay. I understand your point."

Aaron and I ended that conversation but for the next couple of months we talked occasionally on the phone. However, the more we talked, the more he talked too much. He made several statements that led me to believe that he was mad with Annie because she had gone back to her ex-husband. He told me that Annie and her ex had gone over to his grandmother's house, close to midnight, all dressed up, and left his son with him. I know he felt like he should have been home with me but like I told him, that was his decision.

He also told me that Annie and her ex wanted to change Jamar's last name to Aaron's last name but he said he feels she only wants to do it so she can hit him up for more child support. Then he made me even more upset because he's been giving Annie money every month for Jamar. When I asked him why hadn't he given me anything for A.J. he said it was because he knew I could take care of A.J. on my own and Annie couldn't because she was on welfare.

I tried to explain that it doesn't matter if I hit the lottery and won a million dollars. It's still his responsibility to support his child. Then he went on to tell me that he could only afford to support one child so he chose Jamar because of that same reason. So like I said, the more he told me, the more it made me even happier that we weren't together. So when he does set up his visitation with his son he'll be doing himself a favor, not me. I'm not taking him back, not now or not ever. And I guess I was supposed to have forgotten about his little episode when he was giving A.J. a bath in the middle of the night. HELL NO, I'm not taking him back. And little does he know I've already gone to the District Attorney's office on him anyway. So they should start garnishing his wages sometime soon. So he'll be supporting both of his sons whether he likes it or not.

About a month later, I got another phone call from Aaron. He was crying hysterically and I could hardly make out what he was trying to tell me. I told him to come over. When he got to my house he looked awful. His eyes were red and swollen as if he had been crying for hours. In fact, I told him that his face looked like mine did a year ago when he first told me he was leaving me. I had no sympathy.

"What's wrong with you, Aaron?"

"Cassandra, come here. Please hold me and tell me you love me."

Then I walked over to him and put my arms around him and said, "I never said I didn't love you, Aaron. But what's wrong?"

"I want you back. I want to come back home. Can I please come back?"

"Aaron, I already told you how I felt about that issue."

"But Cassandra, you've been right all along. I can't stand that black bitch. I hate her. I don't ever want to see her again. She made me lose my family."

"Who? What are you talking about?"

"Annie. I hate her. I don't ever want to see her face again."

"Aaron, what's wrong? Is Jamar okay?"

"Here. Look at this. That fuckin' bitch."

Then Aaron handed me an envelope from the District Attorney's office and inside were the results of his paternity test. And guess what? He isn't even the father of Annie's son. Jamar is not even his by a long shot. Not even by a fraction."

"Aaron, is this saying what I think it's saying?"

"Yeah, that bitch lied to me. He isn't even my son. And I gave up my real family for nothing. Cassandra, will you please forgive me? I am so sorry I put you through all of this. If I had listened to you in the first place this never would have happened. I would have found out a long time ago and you and I could have gone on with our life. We would have been married by now. Cassandra, I am so sorry. Will you ever forgive me? That bitch. I hate her."

"Wait a minute. Let me get this straight. You mean you left me for a child who isn't even yours? And you've been paying child support for a child that isn't yours. You left your own flesh and blood for a child that's not yours. You have even been over there baby-sitting every weekend so she can go out and party.

Do you realize you've been paying her to go out? And what have you done for your real son? The son that you know is yours. You didn't even call him on his first birthday. You were not there to see him take his first steps. You weren't there for me, for him, or for Amelia. And all of this for a woman who has been lying to you from day one."

"Cassandra, believe me. You can't make me feel any worse than I do now. I've thought about all of those things plus some. I admit it. I was stupid. But now all I want is my real family back. Please, if you don't let me come back I don't know what I'll do."

"I can't believe her. Do you realize that she got pregnant while she was married and if her husband wasn't the father and you're not the father then she was sleeping with at least three of you around the same time? She's not a bitch. She's a nasty tramp."

"Cassandra, please can I come back?"

"Aaron, I don't know. I feel like you should have listened to me a long time ago. I told you back then that we could work this issue out together and you really hurt me. And you could have hurt *A.J. and me* by telling me that mess when I was nine months pregnant. You jeopardized both of us, and for what? I'm sorry but I was really hurt then and I'm happy to say that now I'm over it and I have moved on. My life now consists of my two children and me and we're happy this way. So I'm really sorry things didn't work out. I really am."

"Cassandra, please don't do this to me."

"That's just it, Aaron. I didn't do anything. You did. You did it all by yourself."

"Cassandra, I can't believe you're being so cruel. That's not like you."

"Cruel? What do you call what you've done to us?"

"I know. I'm sorry. It was a big mistake."

"You're damn right it was a mistake, but I've learned from it and I'm not going to make the same mistake twice."

"Well, I'm not leaving here until you say you're going to take me back."

"Then I guess you'll be sitting there a long time."

So Aaron sat there crying and shaking his head while I tried to ignore him as I washed my dishes and cleaned the kitchen. He sat there probably a half an hour talking to himself and shaking his head. I kept trying to answer him or ask him whom he was talking to but he didn't respond. I know he's really distraught but I keep remembering that I was too, a year ago. He'll get over it.

A few minutes later I heard A.J. crying so I went and changed his diaper and brought him in the living room. Aaron took one look at him and cried even more.

"He's so handsome. What have I done? I've lost my son. I've lost my daughter. I've lost my wife. I've lost everything."

He was crying so much he was frightening A.J. so I asked Aaron to leave.

"I'm not leaving you, Cassandra. I'm not leaving you ever again. I'm not going to make the same mistake twice, either."

"Aaron, you need to go. You're scaring A.J."

"I'm not walking out on my family ever again."

"Aaron, we are not your family anymore. You have to go," I said.

But it was as if Aaron couldn't hear a word I was saying. He just sat there shaking his head and mumbling, "No. No."

Aaron was starting to scare me too so I went in the back and called the police. When they arrived, Aaron looked as if he was in a daze. The officer tried to talk to him but all he could do was shake his head. The officer got on his knees and leaned over on the chair to try to talk to him but Aaron was only mumbling things. The officer kept calmly talking to him for what seems to have been about thirty minutes and then, very peacefully, Aaron got up and slowly walked out to his car and drove off.

When he left I called Aaron's mother and grandmother to tell them something was definitely wrong with him. They asked me what it was but since Aaron had not yet showed them the results of his paternity test, I didn't tell them exactly what it was. I did tell them, however, that he was very upset with Annie about something.

Then I couldn't believe it. His grandmother said that no matter what it was, he needed to get over it. I tried to explain to her that it was really serious but she didn't want to hear it. In her own words, she told me I was just saying that because I was the jealous ex-girlfriend. So she didn't want to hear that something was really wrong with Aaron so I asked her to just have him call me when he got home and she hesitantly said okay. But that evening I didn't get a phone call. However, the next morning, bright and early, I got a collect call from Aaron.

"Aaron, where are you and why didn't you call me back last night?"

"Because I haven't been home."

"Where are you?"

"I'm in Washington. Can you give me your brother's phone number?"

"What are you doing in Washington?"

"I drove here to talk to your brother."

"Well, haven't you heard of a long distance phone call?"

"Cassandra, will you stop being smart and give me his phone number?"

"No, I will not. Why do you need to talk to my brother?"

"Well, if you really want to know the truth, it's because I want him to tell me how I can get you back."

"Well, you're a little late. You should have talked to him last year and asked him that question before you left me. He would have told you then that you should have kept your ass at home."

"Cassandra. Please. I'm desperate. What's his number?"

"Sorry, Aaron. What's the difference between you being desperate now and me being desperate last year? Sorry, but I'm not going to give it to you and don't bother looking him up in the phone book because he's not listed. Why don't you call one of Annie's brothers and see how you can get her back from her ex-husband?"

"I didn't think you were going to give it to me but it was worth a try. So how are A.J. and Amelia doing?"

"They're both doing fine but in the meantime you're

running up my phone bill. So if you want to, you can call me back when you get home."

"Okay, I'm on my way back now. I'll call you when I get there."

When I hung up I called Aaron's mother and told her that he's been on the road all night long trying to get to my brother. Then she asked me what was going on so I told her. I also told her that I was really afraid that Aaron had not been himself lately. But she did as his grandmother and said, "That's something he's gonna have to deal with." I couldn't believe she wasn't more sympathetic towards her own son.

Well, I didn't hear from Aaron when he got home. In fact, the next time I heard from him was about a month later when he called me collect again.

"Aaron, where are you?"

"I'm in the hospital."

"Why! What's wrong?"

"I'm in the hospital on the Air Force Base. I had a nervous breakdown a couple weeks ago."

"Are you serious?"

"Yeah, I'm not doing so well."

"So can you have any visitors?"

"Yeah, I think so. Are you going to come visit me today?"

"Yes, I'll come."

"Will you bring Amelia and A.J. with you?"

"Amelia is in school but I'll bring A.J."

"Cassandra, I'm really not doing too good but do you love me anyway?"

"Aaron, don't ask me questions like that, okay?"

"You know I'm in love with you, right?"

"Aaron, are you sure it's a good idea for me to visit you?"

"Yeah, my doctor said it would help me if you came up here. Do you love me?"

"Aaron, I'm not going to come if you're going to ask me those types of questions."

"Okay, I won't ask you anymore. So can you come up here around one o'clock when visiting hours start?"

"I'll be there."

A.J. and I went to the hospital. It was only about five minutes from my house. When we got there I was in a state of shock. It was nothing like I expected. Even though it was the middle of the afternoon, Aaron was wearing hospital pajamas, a hospital robe and some slippers. When A.J. and I first walked through the double doors to get to the psychiatric ward I saw Aaron walking towards us. He was walking very slowly as if he were in slow motion. Then he hugged and kissed us both. He turned around and reached for my hand so he could show me where to go to sit down. We went into this large room that had lots of tables and chairs, a television, some games and some puzzles in it. It looked as if it was home to a lot of people.

Aaron looked really bad. His skin had gotten darker and he was even drooling from his mouth a little bit. All he talked about were the good times that we had together, only he didn't associate them with the past. He talked as if we had just done things the day before. But even with that, I could barely understand most of what he was saying because his speech was slurred. At one point he reached over to pick up A.J. but all he could do was smile as he said that he was too weak to do it. I wanted to cry but instead I told him we had to go and that we would see him tomorrow evening. He seemed to be satisfied with that.

When I got home I called his grandmother to see why no one had told me he was in the hospital.

"No one told you because you don't need to see him."

"Why not?"

"Because you're bad for him. If it weren't for you he wouldn't be there."

"How can you say that? I want what's best for Aaron."

"If you did you would have taken him back."

"What do you mean? If you're going to be mad and blame someone then you need to look in Annie's direction because I haven't done anything to Aaron."

"Why would I be mad with Annie?"

"Didn't Aaron tell you what she did?"

"You mean about the blood test?"

"Yes, I mean about the blood test."

"Well, I haven't seen no blood test. He wouldn't show them to me and quite frankly I believe you had something to do with those tests."

"What are you talking about? I don't even know when Aaron went and took that test. So how could I have something to do with them?"

"Don't act like you're innocent. You've been trying to get my grandson to take blood tests ever since you've been with him. We all know that baby is his. I know it, Annie knows it, and you know it too. I just don't know how you did it."

"Mrs. Jones, honestly I didn't have anything to do with it."

"You've been sneaky from day one and now look what you've done. Maybe we should have a blood test taken on A.J."

I couldn't believe that witch said that but since I always respect my elders I responded as nicely as I could.

"Well, maybe you should have one taken on A.J. Be my guest. That way you guys will get to see what a positive blood test looks like. Goodbye, Mrs. Jones."

I cannot believe that they are blaming this on me. It is not my fault and I am not going to accept the blame. I told them last month when Aaron was at my house that something was wrong. But no one wanted to believe me because I was just the jealous ex-girlfriend.

The next evening, I went to visit Aaron but this time I left A.J. at home with Amelia. Aaron was really glad to see me. He talked quite a bit about being in the hospital. He says he knows he's really ill and that he's not sure when they're going to release him. He said he was diagnosed as having paranoid schizophrenia. I told him that although I didn't know what the symptoms or cure for that were, he needs to make sure he followed his doctor's orders and he promised me he would. He asked me if I would come and visit him again tomorrow evening and when I told him yes then he looked at me and gave me a slight smile. Then I reached for his hand and told him that everything was going to be okay. It was so sad seeing him in that condition. Again, I cried as I was leaving the hospital.

I know he needs me there for him because, from the sound of things, he doesn't have too much support from his family. When I talked to his mother she basically blamed me for the whole thing too, but she was a littler nicer than his grandmother. I also called his father to see what he thought and he was in denial also. He said he couldn't believe that a child of his would get himself into that situation. His solution for Aaron was for him to get off of his medication and "snap out of it."

I went to see Aaron the following evening just as I promised, but this time when I got there, the hospital staff wouldn't let me in. They told me that Aaron's mother had gotten power of attorney over Aaron and she stated that she didn't want anyone visiting him that wasn't a blood relative. Then I got smart with the staff and asked them what I was supposed to do with his son. "Should I just drop him off at the hospital door because you can't get any closer in blood than that?" Then, the administrator told me she was sorry but that was the rule. I started crying and apologized to her for what I had said.

When I got home I called the hospital and asked for Aaron's room and, to my surprise, I was put through to him. I asked him how he was doing and he asked me why wasn't I there so I told him. Then he said he guessed his mother was trying to do what was best for him and he admitted that he was in no position to fight her on the issue. So we agreed we would talk on the phone every day. At least, until the wicked witch found out.

Aaron and I talked almost every day for the next two months and he was really starting to make some improvements. He told me he really enjoyed talking to me because I was the only one he said that understood how he felt. I didn't mind being there for Aaron but at the same time I didn't want to give him any false hope. Aaron was soon released from the hospital and he went home to his grandmother. He looked and felt much better but he was given medication to take daily that he wasn't too fond of but I was able to convince him that he needed it in order to stay out of the hospital.

I also called Aaron's doctor to see if his condition was hereditary. I wanted to know if A.J. was going to be affected by it, but as I suspected, Aaron's doctor wouldn't give me too much information for fear of breaching patient-doctor confidentiality. So I called A.J.'s doctor and he gave me general information as well. They both told me that paranoid schizophrenia can afflict anyone, but children of someone who has been diagnosed with it are at a greater risk. And both doctors confirmed that Aaron probably had this condition long before the Annie incident but they said that when someone suffers from a mental trauma the condition is likely to surface. So as I think back, I believe Aaron's condition was starting to surface the night that he woke A.J. up to give him a bath. I feel so blessed that I caught him in time that night because he probably really didn't know what he was doing.

For the next few months I continued talking to Aaron on the phone but I made it clear that there was not going to be a reunion between us. He eventually accepted that and we agreed to be friends for A.J.'s sake.

PAY BACK

Just as I was beginning to be truly happy, except for the fact that I would probably be single the rest of my life, I received a strange phone call.

"Hello."

And this deep sexy voice said, "Hello Cassandra, guess who's thinking about you?"

"Chris, I know this is you. Who could forget that voice?"

"Hi baby. How are you?"

"I'm doing great. How are you?"

"I'm okay. I was just sitting here thinking about you. Well, actually I've been thinking about you a hell of a lot lately so I decided to see if you had the same number."

"Well, you've found me. So how are your girls?"

"They're both doing fine. Marissa's still with me and Eboni is still with her mom but we're all in Sacramento now."

"Sacramento? What are you doing up there?"

"It's kind of a long story but I've been here for a couple of years now. Hey, I heard that you have a son now."

"Yes, I do. How did you hear that?"

"I've been doing my research."

"So what else have you been researching?"

"Well, I also know that you're not married. So does that mean there's still a chance for us?"

"For us? You mean as in you and me?"

"Yeah. I told you I have been thinking about you a lot lately. I just can't seem to get you off my mind. So are you seeing anyone right now?"

"No, I'm not, but I'm happy the way I am."

"What? You don't love me anymore? Because I'm still as much in love with you now as I was years ago."

"Chris, love didn't keep us together then, so what does it matter how I feel about you now? And where's your baby-sitter anyway?"

"My baby-sitter? Oh Stephanie, she's here but she's not who I want. I'm in love with you and only you and she knows that."

"Wait a minute. You're telling me you two are still together?"

"We're under the same roof, that's all."

"Yeah, well I've heard that story before."

"Yeah, I know but you've never heard it from me. I've never lied to you. Cassandra, you know that."

"You may not have lied but you sure were naïve about your baby-sitter."

"Well, now I see that you were right and I'm ready to correct my mistake."

"I've heard that before too. So let me hear your story. Why me and why now?"

"Remember I told you a long time ago that you were the only woman that I would ever ask to marry me?"

"Yes, I remember."

"Well, that's still true. I would never marry her. I'm not in love with her and I never will be and she knows that. You're the only woman for me."

"Okay. So why now?"

"Like I said, I've been thinking about you for a long time, I just didn't have the guts to call you. Then I thought if I didn't go after you now that one day it would be too late."

"I still don't understand. Why now? So what's really going on with you and Stephanie? There must be trouble in paradise."

"To be honest with you, there's a lot going on. First of all, I have stopped smoking and she still smokes and that drives me crazy. She also drinks quite a bit and when she gets drunk she starts talking crazy. And I think you were right about her just wanting to take me away from you because I don't like the way she treats Marissa now either. She's not working but she hardly ever does anything with Marissa because she's always drinking."

"Wait, let's get one thing straight. She didn't take you away from me. I chose to let you go. And as far as Marissa goes, she certainly doesn't need to be around a drunk."

"No, she doesn't, and I'm not gonna put up with that shit much longer."

"See Chris, you should have listened to me a long time ago."

"I know and now I regret it every day."

"Yeah, sure you do."

"Come on, Cassandra, I'm serious. Will you at least agree to go out with me?"

"What do you mean?"

"I mean I want us to go out together."

"I mean, what do you expect from me going out with you? You know I don't go out. So what do you really want? Is it that she can't satisfy you the way I can? Is it that you no longer have jungle fever? Just what is it that you want?"

Then Chris chuckled and said, "You sure don't beat around the bush, do you? That's one of the reasons I love you so much."

"So, what is it that you're really asking me for, Chris?"

"I want everything from you. You're a complete package."

"I was a complete package years ago but that wasn't good enough."

"I'm not talking about then, I'm talking about now. I'm a changed man. I've learned my lesson. Now I know all the little games that women play to get what they want."

"You couldn't possibly know them all because we invent new ones every day."

"Cassandra, you're so crazy."

"No, I'm just being honest. The more ways you men hurt us, the more ways we invent to pay you back."

"Well, I know you don't play games like that. You're different."

"Don't be so sure of yourself. I've been hurt just like every other woman."

"So, did I ever hurt you?"

""Why? Are you getting scared?"

"No, I just want to know."

"I can't believe you had to ask me that. Yes, you hurt me. Just look at where you are and whom you're with. Our biggest problem was distance. You couldn't move to Fairfield but you packed up and moved all the way to Sacramento. You moved right past Fairfield and kept on going another hour. I thought you didn't want to move from the Bay Area."

"But I moved here because Eboni and her mother moved here and I didn't want to be that far away from Eboni."

"So you'll move wherever Eboni moves and you'll move your baby-sitter right along with you?"

"No, what I'm saying is that I would do anything for my girls; you know that. Just like I know you would do anything for your kids."

"I guess that's where I've grown over the years. I've learned that if I'm happy my children will be happy and if I'm in a messed up relationship they will suffer too. I guess what I'm trying to say is that, in your situation, I'm sure Eboni would rather you live in a different city if she knew you were happier and I'm sure she wouldn't want her sister in the atmosphere that you have her in now."

"I see your point."

"You need to learn how to make Chris happy, then your happiness will spread to your children."

"So who's the lucky guy that's making you happy?"

"My son, A.J. You see, that's the whole point. I am very content being single. I no longer have to depend on a man for anything and it feels good. No more head aches or high blood pressure."

"Come on, you can't just shut men out of your life."

"I'm not. If and when the right man comes along that will be great. But until then, it's still great."

"So can we go out and do something? Maybe go to the movies or something?"

"When?"

"If you don't have to work this weekend, then how about tomorrow evening?"

"What about Marissa? Where is she going to be?"

"She's staying with her mother this weekend."

"Actually, my children are going to be gone too. They'll be with my sister this entire weekend because her children were with me last weekend. So what about Stephanie? What would you tell your baby-sitter?"

"Let me worry about her."

"So that means you're going to lie to her."

"She doesn't need to know my business. Our relationship is just about over anyway. So do you like roses?"

Chris really doesn't know me well anymore. He doesn't know just how much I have changed. I have no intentions of going out with him. I've learned that lesson before with George and I'm too smart to do it again.

"Yes, I like roses. Why?"

"Just because. So do you like champagne?"

"Chris, you know I don't drink. That hasn't changed."

"So, how about if I bring over some champagne for me and some apple cider for you."

"Wait. I haven't said I was okay with all of this."

"I know, but that's how sure I am. So I'll see you tomorrow evening about seven, okay?"

"If you say so."

Chris must be kidding. He hasn't learned anything about women and, even worse, he hasn't learned about me. Especially now that I know that I don't need another person to survive, it's time for me to show a few people something. Three people to be exact, that once and for all they can't take me for granted and use me. They need to know they shouldn't mistake my kindness for weakness.

Let's see. Since I'm off tomorrow I'll start with Annie. I haven't forgotten about what she did to my family. I'll call the talk shows and let them know that I have a great topic for a show. How about '*I slept with so many men I don't know who my baby's daddy is*' or what about '*Are you my baby's daddy?*' or '*I'm on paternity test number three.*' I would give them a topic like '*I lost my family over a child that's not even mine*,' but I won't say that because I don't want Aaron to have to be put through that. He wouldn't be able to handle it.

So I did just that. I called the talk shows and gave them Annie's phone number and told them all about her. Then the next thing I knew she was ringing my phone.

"Hello."

"Hello, is this Cassandra?"

"Yes it is. Who is this?"

"This is Annie. Did you just call the talk shows and give them my number?"

"No, I did not."

"Well, they said you gave them my name and number and told them something about me not knowing who my son's daddy is."

"Well, you don't, do you?"

"That's none of you fuckin' business, bitch."

"I'm sorry, Annie, but I don't understand that kind of language. Do you have a point?"

"I said it's none of your fuckin' business."

"I know. It's none of my business. It's also none of your ex-husband's business and it's none of Aaron's business either. So whose business is it?"

"Bitch, you're just mad 'cause Aaron don't want your black ass. He says you're fuckin' stupid and he says he don't know what he ever saw in your ugly ass anyway."

"That's funny because even though I don't understand your kind of language, those were the exact words he used to describe you to me. So again, do you have a point to this phone call?"

"Bitch, you're stupid. Just keep my fuckin' name out of your mouth."

Then Annie hung up and I laughed but she called back a few minutes later.

"Hello."

"Yeah bitch, my point is that I'm kickin' your ass."

"Oh, that's pretty good, Annie. Now you're down to three letter words and it only took you about five minutes to come up with that one. Do you have any other points you would like to share with me?" Then Annie hung up and that was the last I heard from her.

Okay, so now I have two more people to show that hell knows no furry like a woman's scorn. But just how will I pay Chris and his baby-sitter back? Let's see. I have a few hours to think of something. Then my phone rang again and I just knew it was Annie but I was wrong.

"Hello."

"Hello, may I speak with Cassandra?"

"This is Cassandra speaking. Who's calling?"

"This is Daniel."

"Daniel?"

"Yes, Daniel from work?"

"Oh hi, Daniel. How are you?"

"I'm fine."

"So what's on your mind, Daniel?"

"Cassandra, when you gave me your phone number the other day, I didn't think I would ever have the courage to use it."

"Why not? I told you I know what it's like being in a new town and in a new job and I would love to show you around, introduce you to some people, and make you feel more comfortable."

"I know. You've been really nice showing me around at work but you don't have to do this after hours."

"Don't be silly. In fact, are you busy this evening?"

"No. That's actually what I was calling to ask you. Do you feel like going out to eat?"

"Sure. What type of food do you have a taste for?"

"I kind of feel like steak and lobster. What about yourself?"

"That sounds good and I know the perfect place. So I'll give you directions to my house. Can you be here by 6:30?"

"Yes, that's perfect."

Okay, here we go. Poor Chris is going to be here at seven with roses and champagne. And after driving over an hour he's going to think that he's going to get me in the bed but Miss Innocent Cassandra won't be here. But that still isn't good enough. I'm going to kill two birds with one stone. So at 6:15, when I knew he was on his way, I called his house.

"Hello."

"Hello, may I speak with Chris?"

"Chris ain't here, who's this?"

"This is Cassandra."

"Cassandra who? His old girlfriend Cassandra?"

"Yes it's me. I'm back."

"What do you want? Why are you calling here?"

"Stephanie, I remember you told me a few years ago not to call your house again but you knew then that Chris' heart was with me. Well, I'm ready to give it back. So the roses, the champagne and the sparkling cider that Chris is going to bring home tonight, well let's just say they were intended for me but I'm giving them to you, so enjoy. And as far as his heart, I'm returning that too but you'll have to get that from him, I can't help you there. And, oh yeah, one more thing. Tell Chris to not ever call my house again and I promise I will never call yours again. Have a good evening, Stephanie. Goodbye."

There, now I'm done and not a minute too soon because I see Daniel has just arrived. Boy, that was perfect timing because as we were driving down my street I saw Chris turning the corner, so I waved at him. I guess one day he'll learn, just like Robert, George and Aaron learned, that you can't hurt a woman, especially a black woman with an attitude, and expect to get away with it. And, oh yeah, not that it matters, but did I mention that Daniel is white?

ABOUT THE AUTHOR

Cornelia Gibson was born in Richmond, California and has lived in the Fairfield/ Suisun area for the past fifteen years. She is a Computer Systems Manager and currently studying to be a Psychologist. Cornelia's passion involves mentoring adolescent girls. Surviving Broken Promises is her first novel. She has big plans for this novel and has already written the lyrics for a soundtrack to go along with it.

ABOUT GREATUNPUBLISHED.COM

Made in the USA
San Bernardino, CA
21 November 2019